"Kuligin's book on salvation is a thoroughly biblical, balanced, and very practical study of the subject. I warmly recommend it as an introduction for those who are new to the faith and a powerful reminder for those who have been Christians for some time."

Douglas Moo, Wessner Chair of Biblical Studies,
Wheaton College, Illinois; Chair, Committee on Bible Translation

"This is one of those books every student of the Bible wishes they had read at the beginning of their walk with the Master. Thirteen massive theological truths skillfully unpacked in a language every reader can understand and enjoy. The priceless diamond of God's salvation is made to shine in splendor as the full light of truth sparkles in every facet. Kuligin is one of my favorite expositors, and it is an honor for me to endorse a book I only wish had been around when I started proclaiming the message of God's great salvation fifty years ago."

John Broom, Pastor, United Evangelical Fellowship,
Fish Hoek, South Africa

"Like a new homeowner who is unaware that a priceless diamond lies hidden under the floorboards, most believers have little awareness of the magnitude or the consequence of all that they have inherited in Christ. In these pages Kuligin deftly unwraps that treasure, revealing facet by brilliant facet the richness of the biblical concept of salvation. Prepare to be inspired and strengthened as this book leads you on a life-changing spiritual journey!"

Steve Richardson, President, Pioneers-USA

"Kuligin's book is an excellent introduction to a key Christian doctrine. Kuligin manages to demonstrate the depths of the Christian view of salvation. *The Language of Salvation* is thoroughly biblical, easy to read, extremely practical, and a personal book. It is a must-read for all Christians who look for a clearer understanding of what it means to be saved."

Thorsten Prill, Senior Lecturer,
Namibia Evangelical Theological Seminary, Africa

"Jonathan Edwards once said, 'Of all the knowledge that we can ever obtain, the knowledge of God, and the knowledge of ourselves, are the most important.' Kuligin brings both forms of this precious knowledge together in his latest book, *The Language of Salvation*. He shows what it means to be saved, carefully digging into the language and concepts of Scripture, enabling us to grasp the riches we have in Christ, and equipping us to share the multifaceted diamond of the gospel with those around us. This book is ideal for pastors, teachers, small groups, students, and ordinary Christians who desire a deeper, more satisfying understanding of all that the triune God has done for us."

Stan Guthrie, Editor at Large, *Christianity Today*

"While Kuligin has chosen the imperfect number thirteen to explain the riches of our salvation, he has written the perfect book for evangelicals who have forgotten the Bible's multifaceted portrayal of what God has done for us in Christ. And like a perfectly cut diamond, all thirteen facets—from the often-discussed justification and redemption to the often-neglected fruitfulness and participation—reflect the brilliance of our glorious God. This Christ-centered, Bible-saturated, and theologically deep study will enrich all who read it!"

Douglas Sean O'Donnell, Senior Lecturer in Biblical Studies and Practical Theology, Queensland Theological College, Brisbane, Australia

"This book is exactly as Kuligin describes it: a multifaceted look at the priceless gem of salvation. Describing each feature in terms that are clearly biblical and eminently accessible, this wonderfully illustrative work heightens one's appreciation for the riches that are in Christ while deepening faith in his saving work. The questions at the end of each chapter make this book especially valuable for student discussions or family devotions."

Randall J. Gruendyke, Campus Pastor, Taylor University, Upland, Indiana

"When J. I. Packer was asked what theological issues he would recommend Christians study in order to prepare themselves for the next half century, number one on his list was regeneration—what it means to be saved. In *The Language of Salvation* Kuligin takes us through thirteen biblical pictures of salvation. Like a diamond, he argues, salvation is multifaceted, with each picture portraying a different aspect of the beauty of the jewel. As Kuligin draws on his experiences as a missionary, pastor, and Bible college lecturer, we are treated to a wonderfully rounded portrait of how the Bible pictures salvation. I trust this book will aid in remedying the mass confusion so prevalent even in the church over the nature of God's saving activity. Furthermore, I hope it will lead us again to worship the God who conceived and carried out 'such a great salvation.'"

Bradley Trout, Pastor, Mountain View Baptist Church, Lakeside, South Africa

"Kuligin is a rock-solid theologian and master illustrator. In *The Language of Salvation* he brings theology to life with clarity and color. I heartily recommend this helpful treatment of biblical salvation to clergy and congregants alike. Pastors will preach better. Churches will understand better. Hopefully, we'll all better appreciate what God has done for us in Christ. Without question it is an important book for the modern church."

Kenneth Carr, Elder and Senior Pastor,
Christ the King Church, Batavia, Illinois

"I commend Kuligin's book to anyone who wants to have a deeper understanding of salvation for four reasons. First, the book is a product of years of Christian ministry and teaching students. Second, the book is crystal clear and Christ centered. Third, the book brings out the richness of salvation by looking at the different facets of the doctrine such as regeneration and justification, adoption and redemption, citizenship and participation. Fourth, the book is practical. After discussing each facet of salvation he gives some practical application, and each chapter concludes with questions for further discussion. Seminarians, pastors, Christian workers, college students and seminary teachers, and other interested persons will benefit from this book because it provides a clearer understanding of what salvation means in Christian theology, either as an apologetics or evangelistic tool in Christian ministry."

Daniel Simango, Principal, Bible Institute of South Africa;
Elder, Kalk Bay Community Church, Cape Town, South Africa

"The high calling of the church is to see and celebrate the unrivaled, radiant glory of God, especially the glory of his grace. Sadly, in our day, much of the church is being distracted with other glories, lesser glories, which do not exalt God or save souls. With this book Kuligin turns our heads back in the right direction—up, by showing how our Trinitarian God rescued us from the grip and destruction of sin in every realm of life. This book will force you into Scripture, deepen your knowledge, and fan the flame of your worship as you read about your rich salvation in God's language!"

Mark Reed, Teaching Pastor, Rosemont Baptist Church,
Winston-Salem, North Carolina

"Even mature Christians tend to have an impoverished understanding of the significance and implications of the salvation that they enjoy in Christ. Kuligin skillfully unfolds the richness and comprehensiveness of this salvation by examining the many metaphors the New Testament authors use to present the gospel. Using contemporary analogies to enable even new believers to understand complex concepts, he retells the story of the gospel—both plight and solution—in each chapter of the book. There may be no greater need in the life of a child of God than to consistently meditate upon the gospel, and *The Language of Salvation* is an ideal book to facilitate this. Reading its pages inevitably fills the heart with gratitude and worship."

Jamie Viands, Lecturer and Dean of the School of Theology,
Scott Christian University, Machakos, Kenya

In this book Kuligin significantly broadens common evangelical understandings of salvation by exploring the rich and varied biblical terminology treating this topic. The book reveals insights into thirteen biblical words used for salvation, exploring their uses both in Scripture and in extrabiblical sources. Kuligin argues that all these terms are necessary for a comprehensive understanding of salvation, that each facet must be considered in light of the others. *The Language of Salvation* challenges both complacency and a lack of curiosity about biblical salvation through its rich and multifaceted perspective. The book is clear and well written, and is enlivened by Kuligin's personal experiences as a missionary in Namibia and South Africa."

Mark Peters, Chair, Arts and Languages,
Trinity Christian College, Palos Heights, Illinois

"This book fills a gap in the market of Christian literature for all serious Christians. In fact, I believe it should be compulsory reading for all Bible students—indeed for every Christian who desires to deepen their knowledge of God's wonderful offer of salvation. God has given Kuligin the gift of being able to explain deep spiritual truths simply and easily understood by all. He has written this book in a very personal way, which is a pleasure to read, making it difficult to put down. If you are looking for a book focused on you and how to make you feel good, this book is not for you. But if you are looking for a book to challenge you and help you grow—you've found it!"

Syd Eaby, Pastor, Villiersdorp Community Church,
Cape Town, South Africa

"Kuligin has hit his mark by explaining to laypeople theological terms for salvation that can only be properly understood given the secular context that the authors of Scriptures employed. His writing style is very engaging and logical, which leaves the reader wanting to go to the next chapter. The book is a rich resource tool that Christian leaders will want to read themselves and recommend to their laypeople."

Brian Medaglia, Director, Office of Christian Outreach,
Wheaton College, Illinois

"The deeper roots go into soil, the taller and stronger an oak becomes. Here is a book that is both deep and wide for believers seeking to go beyond the surface. The author explores the diamond of salvation from every angle in chapters filled with doxological doctrine and arresting application. Drawing from his own experience as a seasoned missionary, Kuligin uses gripping illustrations to elicit our worship at the wonder of what God has done in Jesus. It is like fresh air to the soul in a politically correct culture that is often tempted to dumb down the message of the cross. The questions for application and sidebars on worshipping and witnessing make this a great tool for small groups and Sunday school classes. Read it, put it on your church book table, and give a copy away!"

Roland Eskinazi, Pastor,
The International Baptist Church of Brussels, Belgium

"This engaging, enlightening book will warm the hearts and capture the imaginations of Christians old and new. Kuligin brings down-to-earth insights to central truths of Scripture, and he will challenge readers to live more passionately and authentically for God."

Paul Carden, Executive Director,
The Centers for Apologetics Research (CFAR), San Juan Capistrano, California

"Kuligin provides us with a much-needed critique of our often simplistic understanding of God's redemptive work through His Son, Jesus Christ. The soteriological realities in Scripture are much more nuanced than we might think and provide us with a firm foundation for a robust understanding of this important doctrine, which leads to fully orbed praxis. Every Christian needs to have a clear understanding of the Savior's saving work, whether a seminary professor, an auto mechanic, a stay-at-home mom, a hedge-fund manager, or a line cook. This book will help you walk in faith until Jesus returns to take us home."

Geoff Dennis, Vice President of Business and Strategy,
The Southern Baptist Theological Seminary, Louisville, Kentucky

The
LANGUAGE
of
SALVATION

VICTOR KULIGIN

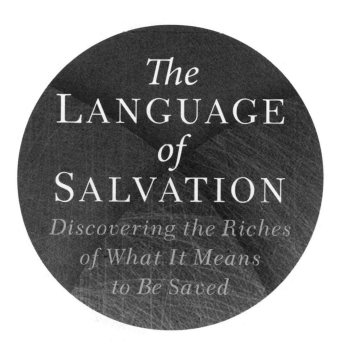

The
LANGUAGE
of
SALVATION

Discovering the Riches
of What It Means
to Be Saved

Foreword by

Robert W. Yarbrough

WEAVER BOOK
COMPANY
WOOSTER, OHIO

First edition published by
Weaver Book Company
1190 Summerset Dr.
Wooster, OH 44691
Visit us at weaverbookcompany.com

Cover: LUCAS Art & Design
Interior design and typesetting: Frank Gutbrod
Editing: Paul J. Brinkerhoff

ISBN: 978-1-941337-09-7
ISBN (e-book): 978-1-941337-27-1

Library of Congress Cataloging-in-Publication Data
Kuligin, Victor, 1964-
    The language of salvation : discovering the riches of what it means to be saved /
    Victor Kuligin ; foreword by Robert W. Yarbrough. -- First edition.
        pages cm
    Includes bibliographical references and index.
    ISBN 978-1-941337-09-7 (pbk.) -- ISBN 978-1-941337-27-1 (e-book)
    1. Salvation--Christianity. 2. Salvation--Christianity--Terminology. 3. Salvation.
    I. Title.
BT751.3.K85 2014
234.01'4--dc23

                                                      2014043901

Printed in the United States of America
15 16 17 18 19 / 5 4 3 2 1

I dedicate this book to my grandfather, Rev. Philip R. LiCalzi,
Baptist minister and itinerant evangelist for over fifty years,
who taught me what it means to be a tireless disciple of Jesus.

Contents

Foreword

Who doesn't want to be rich? Lotteries are popular in much of the world. Sports figures with their huge incomes are idolized. In religion, a "health and wealth" approach to God is common on TV broadcasts. For over a decade, in nations worldwide, *Who Wants to Be a Millionaire?* traded on that question's simple answer: everybody!

Victor Kuligin wants you, the reader of this book, to gain riches . . . but not in the form of dollars, euros, or the rand (currency in South Africa where Kuligin lives). Rather, he wants you to tap into resources that God pours out in those who seek him.

This is a book of *urgency*. The author knows that people everywhere are looking for something more. This includes Christians, who are often frustrated that they don't see more of God in the world and in their lives. This book warns in chapter 14:

> Countless Christians run here or there looking for a word from the Lord while their Bibles sit on the shelf collecting dust. The reason why we have so many scrawny, malnourished Christians is because they are not being properly fed on God's Word.

This book aims to connect readers with "a word from the Lord" that will feed and guide them rather than provide a sugar high of syrupy thoughts and false promises.

This is a book of *global experience*. In addition to his Western and U.S. background, the author has lived for a generation in various locations in the south of Africa. This gives him perspective, the ability to see Christian teaching (and its distortions) from multiple angles. It lends a freshness to his explanations of what Scripture says and how readers may best understand and live it, not just in some protected enclave, but in all the world.

This is a book of *balance*. As the title indicates, it's about one thing: salvation. But this simple and clear biblical priority, the author shows, is a jewel of over a dozen facets. The author avoids boiling Scripture's rich complexity down into a mush of baby food. There is here rather a full-course meal.

In basketball, sometimes a defense will mount a full-court press— players try to stop the offense not just at one end of the court but wherever they try to advance the ball. In Scripture, God mounts a full-court press against human confusion, error, weakness, and . . . *sin* (a word that Kuligin thinks needs more attention than people want to grant it). In over a dozen explicit ways, God is at work seeking to rescue the fallen, the lost, the errant—in a word, people like me and you, inside and outside the church. And this is God's full-court message: he wants to put a broken world back together. He wants to bring a wandering world back to its Creator and highest Hope.

The Bible puts it this way: "in Christ God was reconciling the world to himself, not counting their trespasses against them" (2 Cor. 5:19). Further, that same verse says God has long been "entrusting to us," that is, to Jesus' followers, "the message of reconciliation" (see chapter 7 of this book!). The reader will encounter here the breadth and strength of God's appeal to people to consider their ways and come to terms with God in life-changing, indeed world-changing, ways.

This is a book of *engagement*. The writer interacts with ideas and convictions of people in the church, people in society at large, Catholic teaching, Eastern Orthodox views, Hindu belief, and more. This book is not about theory but about actual beliefs that determine people's lives and, in Christian teaching, affect their final destiny (see comment on *urgency* above).

This is a book of *interpretation*. While the author has marshaled a creative and convincing presentation, his ideas spring not from his theories, imagination, or some secret vision but from God's Book, Holy Scripture, the Bible. There is great power in that Word wherever it is reverently handled. A strength of this book is the deep meditations it will spawn over the many Bible passages it cites and explains.

If you have read the Bible all your life, you are still likely to see many things from fresh angles thanks to this book. If you have only nibbled around Scripture's edges, these pages will lure you to take a bigger and deeper bite. If you see yourself as just a seeker, this book will open up vistas that can help you glimpse God: Father, Son, and Holy Spirit.

God's wisdom says this in Scripture: "Riches and honor are with me, enduring wealth and righteousness" (Prov. 8:18). *The Language of Salvation* opens to readers wealth that stock markets cannot erode, age cannot tarnish, and even death cannot threaten. Here is language and light leading to abundance and life.

Robert W. Yarbrough
Professor of New Testament
Covenant Theological Seminary, St. Louis, Missouri

Preface

*And there is **salvation** in no one else, for there is no other name under heaven given among men by which we must be saved.*

Acts 4:12

An unfortunate confusion exists in Christian circles today, centered on the misunderstanding of what it means to be saved. Part of the uncertainty rests in the common slogans or catchphrases that have made the rounds, phrases like "Jesus died for my sins" or "I asked Jesus into my heart." I am amazed how many Christians, when asked to explain what "Jesus died for my sins" actually means, are unable to verbalize it.

Consider this simple question: What did Jesus save you from? Most will answer, "My sins," but that answer lacks theological precision. It is not as though your sins are running after you, as if they have a separate being from your own. Normally, when we speak about being saved, that something we are saved from is a "thing" or "being" that aims to harm us. It is this lack of exactness in our understanding of Christian salvation that is the cause of much confusion. If we do not properly know the answer to this question, how can we say we truly understand the gospel?

Our misunderstanding of Christian salvation stems from our inability to see its manifold aspects. We look at salvation rather one-dimensionally, as if salvation merely deals with the removal of guilt, or the granting of eternal life. However, the language of biblical salvation is far more varied than most Christians realize. I hope this book will shed some light on this critical issue.

A further problem accentuates the misunderstanding, and that is the relegation of Christian doctrine and theology to that esoteric realm where college professors and theologians (what I call "eggheads and academics") reside. Theology is not for the layperson, only the academician. This is certainly our own fault, we who spend our time in academia. We throw around words like propitiation, justification, and atonement, arguing among ourselves as to their precise connotations, without spending the necessary time training people in our churches as to their meaning. What happens is that an unnatural gap is created between those who study theology for a living, and "average, everyday believers."

Given this disparity, we tend to do one of two things. Either we ignore the topics altogether when teaching the laypeople in our congregations, or we attempt to water down the terminology in an effort to make it more understandable. The first error is inexcusable, but even the second has pitfalls. By ignoring the classic terms of Christian doctrine and replacing them with a diluted lingo, we have cut off laypeople from access to the vast wealth of material from the theological world. It is as if theology is a playground for the intrepid, while the other 99 percent of the Christian world looks to shun it.

Language has a wonderful way of unifying people, but it can also provide a formidable barrier to interaction and relationship. When pastors and professors use theological jargon, while feeding a baby-language to their parishioners, they unconsciously set up a wall between the two groups.

For example, if you stumble upon people who are talking about a pitch, bowling, innings, and wickets, you will likely stand there silently, wondering what is going on. For Americans, confusion results because some of the items are familiar from baseball, while others do not fit. However, if you are familiar with the sport of cricket, you immediately join the conversation. Vocabulary, when it is unrecognizable, becomes an obstacle to informed interaction and learning. Poke your head into an operating room and listen as the doctors and nurses employ terminology unknown to the vast majority of humanity. Only the "elite" will understand it, while the rest of us stand outside the operating room gawking.[1]

---

1. Another factor that accentuates the problem is the increasingly popular post-modern inclination away from doctrinal conversation. In the beliefs of this emerging segment of Christendom, doctrine and theology alienate and segregate us, whereas we are supposed to simply love each other and not get bogged down in divisive issues. This attitude undercuts any solid discussion about Christian salvation, alienating the people of Christ's body further from what is meant to be transformative in the lives of believers.

Spending time overseas as a missionary has made this evident to me. Countless times I stood as an outsider, listening to a foreign tongue I could not understand, feeling entirely left out, unimportant, and uninformed. Many believers feel the same way when it comes to Christian doctrine.

The confusion is intensified by the fact that theologians favor vocabulary that, while scriptural in its content, is rarely used by the biblical writers. Regeneration and illumination are two such concepts that, while summarizing solid biblical teaching, are not themselves used in the Bible as major terms to describe salvation. When theologians utilize extrabiblical language, many Christians are baffled.

Then there are words that are pregnant with meaning in the Greek, but have virtually disappeared in English translations. The classic example involves propitiation, which has all but dropped from common usage in English, but is a magnificent theological term for the doctrine of salvation.

My approach will be to avoid both errors. Obviously, I intend to broach the topic of salvation, but I will not avoid complicated theological terminology. Rather, that terminology will be made understandable by viewing it through the lens of the secular world in which the biblical material originated.

The biblical authors employed commonplace language to convey their understanding of Christian doctrine. In some instances, ideas from Judaism and the Hebrew Scriptures were borrowed but refined, such as atonement and propitiation. In other instances, language from the marketplace or the business world was co-opted by the biblical authors and given new meaning.

Origins

The idea for this book came from a weekly Bible study I led in a suburb of Windhoek, the capital of Namibia, southwestern Africa. For over a year, we worked through Paul's epistle to the Romans. As we studied chapter 3, I was struck by the different ways salvation is portrayed. Consider verses, 23–25a:

> For all have sinned and fall short of the glory of God, and are justified by his grace as a gift, through the redemption that is

in Christ Jesus, whom God put forward as a propitiation by
his blood, to be received by faith.[2]

Justification, redemption, and propitiation are all used by Paul to
describe Christian salvation. Whereas justification is language from
the courtroom, redemption comes from the Roman marketplace, and
propitiation has strong Old Testament connotations. Each has its value
in describing what it means to be saved. I eventually settled on thirteen
valid yet different ways we can speak of Christian salvation.

I often think about Christian doctrine from the standpoint of how
to share it with unbelievers, or how to defend it against attacks from
skeptics and critics of the Christian faith. Evangelicals have concentrated
on one description of salvation at the expense of other valid models. In
particular circumstances, we may find that people are more receptive to
another explanation.

For example, evangelicals tend to focus on the forgiveness of sins
paradigm understood in the word "justification." This is a biblical
portrayal of what it means to be saved, but it is not the only biblical
picture. Redemption—the purchasing of freedom for a captive—may
be more appropriate to share with a drug addict or someone captive
to pornographic addiction. Christian salvation is certainly portrayed in
Scripture as the release of someone bound by sin. Therefore, we need
not speak solely about guilt and forgiveness, at least not initially.

There is great value in recognizing the multifaceted portrayal
of salvation in the Bible. At times, we evangelicals can be rather one-
dimensional in our explanation of what it means to be saved. Instead
of exclusively speaking about roses, perhaps we can talk about other
flowers in the garden as well.

A contextualization of our understanding and proclamation of
Christian salvation is needed. Instead of pretending that one size fits
all, we need to approach individuals in their specific context and share
the gospel in light of their particular struggle. Given this evangelistic
emphasis, each chapter has a sidebar or breakout that highlights that
model's usefulness in witnessing to unbelievers.

---

2. All biblical references are from the English Standard Version unless otherwise
indicated. The ESV is one of the few modern translations to use "propitiation." Most
speak here of "atonement."

Historical Differences

There has been much debate about the Christian understanding of salvation, with some churches accentuating one feature to the minimization of others. For example, whereas Protestants have tended to concentrate on the legal aspect of salvation—having our sins forgiven and being declared innocent before God—Eastern Orthodox Christians have emphasized a salvation where we actually become like God. Where Protestantism's concept of salvation is more forensic and takes place outside the believer, Orthodoxy's understanding is more participatory and internal.

The stress given to one model of salvation can also be conditioned by culture and era. Christians in the early centuries stressed a salvation whereby sinners were ransomed from the clutches of Satan, while medieval theologians laid greater emphasis on satisfying the violated honor of God, much like a feudalistic lord.

My aim is to show that a proper understanding of salvation recognizes the validity of numerous explanations, each with its own biblical point to make. It is my conviction that the Christian formulation of salvation is encompassed by *all* thirteen of the models we will discuss. Although several of the terms are used more frequently by the biblical authors than others, none of the concepts is excluded from the biblical portrayal. While we can expect occasional overlap in meaning, they are distinctive enough to deal with separately.

Some scholars view salvation as a chain of events (e.g., adoption follows justification), what is called the "order of salvation." But instead of viewing salvation as a chain of links, perhaps it is more appropriate to view it as a diamond with many facets, each portraying the beauty of the jewel in its own right. Adoption *is* salvation, not simply something that comes after justification. Redemption *is* a proper elucidation of biblical salvation, not an inferior explanation that should be shunned in preference to forgiveness of sins. What does it mean to be saved? It certainly does mean that your sins are forgiven, but it equally means that you are adopted into the family of God, or you are made a citizen of a new kingdom. All of these explain the *same* salvation, just from a different angle.

Lastly, there is no particular order in the way the terms will be tackled. However, I placed regeneration first because that is fundamental to understanding everything else.

A Key Ingredient

Suppose we want to describe an automobile. We could do so in contrast to an airplane, in which case we would talk about how an automobile travels on land and not in the air. Or we could describe its disparity with a bicycle, at which point we may note that an automobile has four and not two wheels. In each definition of what constitutes an automobile, all descriptions are correct but do not provide the entire picture.

Now consider that this is an *automobile*. It is a self-powered (auto) vehicle that moves (mobile). We can enumerate the various parts—a steering wheel, four tires, seats, and a stick shift—but to really speak of the essence of an automobile, we would have to mention an internal combustion engine. Even though the other components are important, it is here that the core of an automobile is found. Furthermore, an internal combustion engine is only as good as its fuel.

Concerning Christian salvation, any analysis that does not speak about sin is missing the fuel that runs the internal combustion engine. In every category covered in this book, sin is vital to the discussion. For example, the reason why we need reconciliation is because our sin puts us at enmity with God. Justification is the removal of the guilt of sin, illumination becomes necessary when sinful human minds are darkened, and so on.

Any attempt to describe Christian salvation that excludes reference to sin is not a fair portrayal of what it means to be saved. We must elaborate on the problem of sin. If we do not, we cannot say we have accurately described biblical salvation.

In each chapter some practical application is presented that flows from the proper understanding of that particular model of salvation. A list of key terms is provided for each, as well as discussion questions for further clarification. Similar to the sidebars for witnessing, a sidebar is included in each chapter to highlight the implications of that particular portrayal of salvation for worship.

Lastly, a word about methodology. It is my conviction that we can only say correct things about God and his plan of salvation that have first been revealed by God himself in his Word. Anything I write in this book that does not agree with Scripture or does not find its source in the Holy Word is nothing more than my personal opinion, which, on an issue involving matters of eternal consequence, is pretty much worthless.

In the Bible we have the self-revelation of God. We would be foolish to ignore what God says about God's plans. As such, each chapter is bathed in Scripture. However, I have often placed biblical references in footnotes so the text reads more smoothly. Note that the bibliography includes most works cited in the footnotes, so shortened citations are used even at first citation of a particular work; full citations are used for any works not cited in the bibliography. Consult the bibliography for publication details and other information. An index is included at the end of the book cataloging all the biblical passages referenced.

I hope this book will assist those looking for a clearer understanding of what salvation means in Christian theology, either as an apologetics or evangelistic tool, or simply to help in their own walk with Christ. By the end of each chapter, the reader should be able to clearly verbalize why theologians use these terms to describe the mechanism of Christian salvation.

Acknowledgments

Thank you to Bob Yarbrough (whom I've known since he was a prof of mine at Wheaton Graduate School in the late 1980s) for reading through the manuscript and writing an eloquent foreword for the book.

I want to thank my friend of over twenty-five years, Wayne Harbuziuk, who gave me constructive criticism for each chapter, helping me see things I missed, and making this book better than it initially was.

Fellow author Stan Guthrie was an encouragement on this project for several years and urged me to keep at it.

Thanks to Jim Weaver for catching a vision along with me for this book, and for giving me some creative suggestions on making the book better, especially as they relate to its focus on witnessing and worship. I appreciate his willingness to publish it.

Several friends and colleagues read through the initial manuscript and provided encouragement and correction, including Thorsten Prill and Bradley Trout.

Paul Brinkerhoff of Grace and Truth Communications worked on the final editing and provided substantial improvements. I enjoyed the back-and-forth on the project with him. I would also like to thank Robert Ludkey for his attention to the tedious details of proofreading the final proofs.

Lastly, I want to thank my wife, Rachel, and my children who gave me the time and space to complete this project.

1

The Language of Biology
From Death to Life

REGENERATION

Therefore, if anyone is in Christ, he is a ***new creation***.
The old has passed away; behold, the new has come.

2 Corinthians 5:17

In theology, a term may become a catchword for biblical teaching even though it is not regularly used in Scripture. We have such a term with "regeneration." Some readers may find it surprising I begin here. Would it not be wiser to initiate a discussion about biblical salvation by sticking to common biblical terminology?

The Greek word *palingenesia* (*palin*: "again," and *genesia*: "to bear") means "new genesis" or "return to existence."[1] Before the Greek word *genesia* was employed by the biblical authors to signify a spiritual rebirth, it was used in everyday Greek to refer to birthdays.

Palingenesia is found two times in the New Testament to signify regeneration (Matt. 19:28, Titus 3:5). Yet, in Matthew the word refers to all things in general and not the matter of personal salvation, so we have

---

1. Kittel, *Theological Dictionary of the New Testament*, 1:686–89. Consult the bibliography for full publication and other details.

just one reference in which *palingenesia* is used precisely for individual salvation. Despite this fact, it is an appropriate word to use when speaking of Christian salvation. The beauty of "regeneration" is that it is an umbrella term for several biblical concepts. New creation, rebirth, and born again are all encompassed in the idea of regeneration, and repentance and conversion only make sense in the context of regeneration.

You are either spiritually dead or you are alive. Those who are regenerated have moved from death to life. This is the fundamental way to articulate biblical salvation.

Reborn Misunderstanding

The quintessential passage for regeneration is found in the conversation Jesus had with Nicodemus.

> Jesus answered him, "Truly, truly, I say to you, unless one is born again he cannot see the kingdom of God." Nicodemus said to him, "How can a man be born when he is old? Can he enter a second time into his mother's womb and be born?" Jesus answered, "Truly, truly, I say to you, unless one is born of water and the Spirit, he cannot enter the kingdom of God. That which is born of the flesh is flesh, and that which is born of the Spirit is spirit. Do not marvel that I said to you, 'You must be born again.'" (John 3:3–7)

Nicodemus misunderstood Jesus and was limited to thinking in fleshly categories. The same may be true in particular Christian circles today. I am fearful that we have thrown around the term "born again" in such a sloppy manner that we have lost the power of the phrase.

An example can be seen in the definitions used by the religious pollster George Barna: "'Born again Christians' are defined as people who said they have made a personal commitment to Jesus Christ that is still important in their life today and who also indicated they believe that when they die they will go to Heaven because they had confessed their sins and had accepted Jesus Christ as their savior. Respondents are not asked to describe themselves as 'born again.'"[2]

---

2. George Barna, "Survey Explores Who Qualifies as an Evangelical," The Barna Group, accessed July 23, 2014, https://www.barna.org/barna-update/article/13-culture/111-survey-explores-who-qualifies-as-an-evangelical.

There is something unsatisfactory about this broad definition.[3] I fear that once the understanding of born again is watered down to this level, any measurement of who constitutes this group becomes of little use. Those who believe they are born again according to this definition may find the actual requirements of Jesus to be far more stringent, and they may be fooling themselves into believing they are genuinely among the regenerated.[4]

In Namibia, the African country in which I served as a missionary and seminary professor for fourteen years, a strange development has taken place in its Christianity. To be "born again" is tied to certain groups or denominations, normally those of a charismatic or Pentecostal flavor. I would ask Christians from mainline denominations if they were born again and I frequently received utter shock or outright laughter. "What, me, born again? No way!"

A young lady who wanted to learn more about the Bible came to our seminary and I suggested she take Old and New Testament Survey. When she told her Christian mother and siblings what she planned to do, they were aghast. "You aren't going to become one of those 'born agains' are you?" they asked. The simple desire to know more about God's Word was met with opposition.

I fear that evangelicals around the world have begun to similarly misunderstand the dramatic nature of what it means to be born again. That misunderstanding finds its root in the misapprehension of another key Christian concept: sin and its effect.

Spiritual Cancer

Every person has a sickness, a disease that results in spiritual death, thus making regeneration necessary. If no such illness existed, we would have no need to speak of regeneration or rebirth or being born again.

During the presidential race that took place in the early 1990s between George H. W. Bush and Bill Clinton, there was a famous line

---

3. Barna's definition of evangelicals is much more specific, defined as those who "meet the born again criteria (described above) *plus* seven other conditions" (ibid.). Whereas evangelicals are defined as a subset of born again believers, I prefer that the categories be reversed.

4. I deal with this topic in more depth in Victor Kuligin, *Ten Things I Wish Jesus Never Said* (Wheaton, IL: Crossway, 2006).

from Clinton's side that bluntly summed up the reason why, according to Democrats, Bush didn't get it. "It's the economy, stupid." Theologically speaking, the same could be applied to any system of salvation that does not take into account the problem of sin. "It's sin, stupid."

It is not uncommon to find Christians who shun discussions about sin. Theirs is a desire to be positive. The "power of positive thinking" preachers actively eliminate all talk they deem damaging to a person's self-esteem or that could cause people to think lowly of themselves. However, it does little good to tell a man standing on the rails oblivious to the oncoming train that he should ignore the existence of trains and instead concentrate on positive things, so as to not damage his tender ego. When the train eventually arrives, it will be more than his ego that is ruined in the collision.

Why do so many people want to avoid the topic of sin? Perhaps it is because a proper, biblical recognition of the plight of humanity yields a realization that there is not one spiritually acceptable thing about us. This perspective is loathsome to those who prefer a loftier view of humanity.

In Paul's discourse in Romans 3:10–18, this is the verdict when it comes to the evaluation of sin and its effects on humanity:

> "None is righteous, no, not one;
>> no one understands;
>> no one seeks for God.
> All have turned aside; together they have become worthless;
>> no one does good,
>> not even one."
> "Their throat is an open grave;
>> they use their tongues to deceive."
> "The venom of asps is under their lips."
>> "Their mouth is full of curses and bitterness."
> "Their feet are swift to shed blood;
>> in their paths are ruin and misery,
> and the way of peace they have not known."
>> "There is no fear of God before their eyes."

Incredibly, the majority of Paul's quotations in this passage come from the Psalms, that book in the Old Testament most liked by Christians for its feel-good messages and power to lift us up when we are down. Paul gathers these Old Testament quotations to make a comprehensive point that serves as the crowning argument begun in the first chapter of this epistle.

That argument follows a straightforward path. The wickedness of humanity has caused sinners to suppress the truth of God's existence as found in his creation. We have a hypocritical propensity to judge the sins of others while ignoring our own failings. Despite knowing the truth, humanity under the power of sin is unrepentant and unwilling to turn from its evil. Jesus concurs:

> And this is the judgment: the light has come into the world, and people loved the darkness rather than the light because their works were evil. For everyone who does wicked things hates the light and does not come to the light, lest his works should be exposed. (John 3:19–20)

Paul continues the argument in Romans by saying that the Jews disobeyed the law of Moses while the Gentiles violated their own consciences. In every measurable way, the conclusion comes up the same. Everyone is under sin and its power. The problem is universal, and no one escapes it.

In the Romans passage above, we see sin's damning effect. Sin has destroyed the ability of sinners to perform acts that are righteous and good. Both their character and their conduct are corrupt. In turning from God, "their feet are swift to shed blood." The absence of the fear of the Lord results in creatures who are "worthless."

However, no matter how much we read the Bible, virtually none of us is willing to admit that we are this bad. Self-righteousness is the common ailment of all humanity. When we read this indictment of sinners, our natural tendency is to think that Paul is referring to somebody else.

We ignore in our own lives the list of atrocities enumerated by Paul earlier in Romans 1. Because we have never committed murder, we think it fair to overlook the hatred in our hearts. Because we have never stolen, we think it reasonable to ignore our motives driven by greed. We may not slander, but we often gossip. We may not boast, yet we still harbor pride in our souls. We have become so adept concentrating on the sins of others that we ignore our own. The really nasty sins are the ones performed by "those people." We have placed price tags on iniquity, and our sins receive the bargain values. Is it any wonder why self-deception is a real possibility when a sinner is under the deadening power of an unregenerate soul?

The realization of humanity's utter corruption smacks human pride to the core. It is why wicked sinners can suppress the truth readily evident in God's creation (Rom. 1:18–20). Spiritual destitution is not pretty, but instead of sugarcoating our plight, God gives us the straight talk. We are corrupt to the core and nothing but a new beginning can cure us. It is not as if all we have is a gangrenous appendage that must be removed. The entire carcass is riddled with the cancer of sin. The whole body needs to be discarded in order for a new one to be raised up.

A spirit of humanism is still alive and well today, but unfortunately it is also flourishing in many of our churches. This is why secular concepts of self-esteem and self-reliance have so easily infiltrated Christian circles. As surely as Adam and Eve were inclined to recast the words of God to their own liking, sinful human beings are similarly inclined today. We hear talk of the "spark within" or some phrase that implies humanity has the ability to reinvigorate and revive itself. In certain Christian circles there is an implied "pull yourself up by your spiritual bootstraps" attitude. Humankind is spiritually dead, but we will have none of that talk. The fruit does not kill but rather gives genuine life. And the serpent still lisps the same lie today: We are not spiritually dead, and if we sincerely try harder, God will approve of our efforts.

When I was growing up, I had the distinct impression that regeneration came *after* conversion. After I had repented of my sins and converted, then I would become born again. I had a faulty impression that a dead person could first repent and turn to God and then enjoy regeneration. How wrong I was.

It Is Not a Cooperative Effort

Virtually every religion is based upon human effort. In Islam, for example, one's salvation is determined by "five pillars" upon which the Islamic faith is built.

1. The confession of faith (*kalima*): "There is no god but Allah and Mohammed is his prophet."
2. Prayer five times a day

3. Fasting in the holy month of *Ramadan*
4. Charitable giving
5. A pilgrimage (*hajj*) to Mecca, if possible, once in a person's lifetime.[5]

Devout Muslims believe that in religiously following these pillars they will have the hope of attaining eternal life. In many respects, salvation is quite simple in this system. A confession of faith and a few good deeds is all it takes.

In Roman Catholicism, there is a similar reliance on human effort, albeit more nuanced. This system of salvation can be summarized in five steps:

1. Salvation involves becoming righteous like God. The basic assumption is that God cannot accept you unless you are righteous.
2. This righteousness can be obtained through works of merit given by God.
3. Individuals want to have these merits count towards their salvation.
4. Christ earned this merit, which the priest can access through the sacraments.
5. By partaking of the sacraments, individuals become more righteous and able to perform good works that increase their righteousness.

There is a mutual effort in Catholic salvation, a "God helps those who help themselves" approach. God does his gracious part through the sacraments, while sinners via their own good works cooperate in the process. There can be no question that at the end people can say they have contributed to their salvation.

All the religions of the world have spiritually dead people trying to save themselves. Even some self-professed evangelicals believe they are going to be saved because of their good works. This was driven home to me a few years ago during a Bible study at an evangelical church in Windhoek. About

---

5. Some Muslims add a sixth pillar, *jihad*, the notion of holy war against infidels who reject the Islamic faith.

twenty-five young people were there. The simple question was asked, "Why do you think you will go to heaven when you die?" One after the other spoke about the good things they had done, or the bad things they had avoided. Just one spoke about faith in Jesus and his own inability to get to heaven any other way. Yet every person was a professed evangelical Christian.

Worship and the Language of Regeneration

Some believers operate under the principle that as long as they pray, read their Bible, and tithe, God is obligated to give them what they want. Many Christians approach worship this way as well, seeing their two hours spent every Sunday morning as worthy of divine remuneration. However, once we realize that we are dead and bring nothing to God that he does not already have—"Who has first given to me, that I should repay him? Whatever is under the whole heaven is mine" (Job 41:11; also Rom. 11:35)—we recognize that even in worship, we are the ones who must receive from God.

Jesus announces an incredible truth, one that even the chosen people of God, the Jews, had failed to grasp. Salvation can never come about by human effort, because salvation involves something that transcends fleshly ability. This is why it can only be by grace. Salvation via human effort must inevitably be by merit, an earned salvation. But as we will see in the next chapter on justification, no such possibility exists.

Dead Flesh

We are not dealing with whole or healthy humans who then attempt to save themselves through their works of righteousness. As unbelievers, we are "dead in [our] trespasses and sins" (Eph. 2:1). There would be no demand for rebirth or regeneration if we were still spiritually animated. Jesus' words would be nonsensical. Why the need to be born again if you are already alive? The formulation *birth—still alive—rebirth* makes no sense. But *birth—death—rebirth* does. Only that which is already dead must be born *again*.

What spiritual deadness implies is the inability to positively respond to God's call. A person must be "born of the Spirit" to make spiritual choices. Paul writes in Romans 8:7–8,

> For the mind that is set on the flesh is hostile to God, for it does not submit to God's law; indeed, it cannot. Those who are in the flesh cannot please God.

There is both an inability and an active hostility toward the will of God in unregenerate humanity. The corpse cannot do anything pleasing to God. Its power solely exists in the ability to do evil and as such, it can never please God. Paul communicates much the same thing in his letter to Titus, where he says that unbelievers are "unfit for any good work" (Titus 1:16).

In Romans 8, Paul envisions two kinds of people, those who have been given life by God's Spirit, and those who still remain dead in their sins. There is no third option. Either a person is dead or regenerated, controlled by the sinful mind or controlled by the Spirit. Paul uses the word "flesh" ten times in the span of seven verses (3–9), plus three more instances in verses 12–13. When he speaks of those who live "according to the flesh," we see the intimate connection between Paul's teaching and that of Jesus to Nicodemus. Sinful flesh continues to produce sinful flesh; it can never please God. God is exclusively pleased by works performed through the power of his Spirit.

This is why salvation can never come about by human effort. Salvation must be 100 percent the work of God. Even a 1 percent cooperative effort on the part of humankind is not a correct formulation of biblical salvation, as if spiritually dead men and women can participate in anything.

It All Began with Adam

The problem began with our first parents in the garden of Eden. Adam and Eve rebelled against the will of God and brought both physical and spiritual death to the entire human race. As the book of Genesis shows, despite faithful examples like Abel, Enoch, and Noah, the downward spiral of humanity was steady after the transgression of Adam. Every human bears the stain of sin, what is theologically referred to as *original* or *inherited sin*.

Frequently the objection is made that it is not fair that Adam's sin counts against us. This is especially true in democratic societies that have a "one person, one vote" mentality that balks at any idea that infringes upon our individual rights. "I wasn't in the garden. I didn't have a chance to decide for myself whether or not to eat that piece of fruit. How can this be fair?" Paul touches upon this point in his analysis of the two Adams in Romans 5:12–21.

> Therefore, just as sin came into the world through one man, and death through sin, and so death spread to all men because all sinned. (v. 12)

A common misreading of this verse is as if Paul were saying, "Adam sinned and with his sin came death. Now death spreads to all people because all people sin." But that is an errant understanding. Paul is not saying that we die because we sin. He is saying that we are dead because *Adam* sinned. The Greek "because all sinned" is in a tense that speaks of a completed act in the past, not of an ongoing activity in the present. In this sense, then, Adam does not merely represent humanity; Adam *is* humanity. The blunt reality is that the penalty of Adam's sin is experienced by every human being, even before there was a law given that prohibited sin. Adam's fall resulted in death for the entire human race. The only remedy can be new life, regeneration, rebirth.

Adam did not murder someone, or commit rape or adultery, or any of the other sins we tend to categorize as "major." Rather, Adam's infraction was simple disobedience, the essence of sin. He ate a prohibited piece of fruit, something many of us would find minor. Yet, this one sin was enough to alienate Adam from God, have him banished from the garden, and result in physical and spiritual death. When compared to Adam's situation, we who have sinned countless times can hardly claim a morally superior position. In fact, we have voluntarily eaten the fruit until our bellies were gorged.

A proper diagnosis of the disease is necessary in order to prescribe the appropriate medicine for the cure. If humanity's illness is a scratch on the arm, a Band-Aid and a little time will do the trick. But if it is a gaping gunshot wound to the head, more drastic measures are needed. This is precisely the case with sin, and the required cure is as dramatic as God himself becoming a man.

The Sovereign Will of God's Spirit

Looking back at John's third chapter, we see that rebirth is the work of God's Spirit.

> The wind blows where it wishes, and you hear its sound, but
> you do not know where it comes from or where it goes. So it
> is with everyone who is born of the Spirit. (John 3:8)

Some modern Bibles note that the phrase "born again" can also be translated "born from above."[6] Regeneration must be initiated from above, separate from the flesh, because the flesh is dead. It requires the sovereign activity of the Holy Spirit. This is why Jesus can say, "It is the Spirit who gives life; the flesh is no help at all" (John 6:63).

Jesus establishes an eternal truth about God's Spirit that is often lost today. He is sovereign in his activities. God's Spirit is not an *it* that is subject to the whims of mere mortals. Rather, the personality of the Spirit is seen in his unilateral activity in the hearts of sinners.

Witnessing and the Language of Regeneration

The only people who can communicate life to dead people are those who have been given life by the one who has life in himself, Jesus Christ. If more Christians understood that apart from the gospel and the regenerating work of God's Spirit, no one can ever become spiritually alive, perhaps more Christians would take evangelism seriously.

This understanding of the will of the Holy Spirit should have dramatic effect on our view of evangelism. Some Christians errantly believe they are responsible for converting people, emphasizing means by which conversion becomes more of a human- than Spirit-driven endeavor.

For example, the evangelist Charles Finney (1792–1875) redesigned revivalism in America, packaging it as a marketing enterprise. Finney introduced "new measures" that were designed to "perfect" revivalism. These techniques were thought to break down a person's resistance to

---

6. Jesus is not the only one to utilize "born again" language. Peter speaks of believers as "born again" in the opening of his first epistle (1 Peter 1:3, which the KJV translates as "begotten"; Peter uses the term again in 1:23). James similarly employs birth language when he says that believers are "brought . . . forth" (1:18; the Greek is literally "given birth") by the will of God.

revival and to convict him of sin. In Finney's mind, the revivalist became a master persuader.

"Seeker-oriented" churches take much the same approach today. Revealing their misunderstanding of the sovereign activity of God's Spirit in the preaching of his Scripture, they look for ways to make the gospel more palatable and attractive. They excise the parts of the biblical message they find repellent, or make the "worship" event more entertainment focused than Word centered. Such activities disclose a belief in conversion that is human-driven, not Spirit-enabled.

As Jesus teaches, the Spirit is like the wind, blowing wherever he pleases. Regeneration is wholly a sovereign act of God's Spirit on spiritually dead sinners.

Regeneration Implies Something New

The terms "rebirth" and "born again" imply a dramatic change from one's prior state to the next. The first birth reveals something drastically wrong with humans, and only a second birth can solve the problem. The term "new creation" (2 Cor. 5:17) likewise implies that the old is entirely scrapped and a new project initiated. In *The Parables of Grace*, Robert Farrar Capon says it like this:

> When God pardons, therefore, he does not say he understands our weakness or makes allowances for our errors; rather he disposes of, he finishes with, the whole of our dead life and raises us up with a new one.[7]

The very act of conversion is an act of creation, or more properly, *re-creation*. Paul uses creation language to signify the change that takes place in regenerate sinners: "For God, who said, 'Let light shine out of darkness,' has shone in our hearts to give the light of the knowledge of the glory of God in the face of Jesus Christ" (2 Cor. 4:6).

The parallels are striking. Just as God created "in the beginning," so again he must re-create us. As in Genesis we see God taking an earth that was "formless and void," so too must he take our empty lives and remake us. Just as in the beginning he spoke, "Let there be light," he must make light shine in our hearts. Regeneration is as much an act of creation as the initial creation of heaven and earth.

---

7. Capon, *Parables of Grace*, 9.

Echoing the words of Jesus to Nicodemus, Paul writes that this new creative act of regeneration comes from God's Spirit.

> He saved us, not because of works done by us in righteousness,
> but according to his own mercy, by the washing of regeneration
> and renewal of the Holy Spirit. (Titus 3:5)

Rebirth. Renewal. Regeneration. Terms that describe what the Holy Spirit does to those who have faith in Jesus, making them new creations.

Be Honest with Yourself

The great eighteenth-century British evangelist George Whitefield said, "The reason why congregations have been so dead is because dead men preach to them." Flesh merely produces flesh. However, people who admit they are dead can have the opportunity of life.

Do not fool yourself. Only those who confess that in themselves they can do nothing to please God—those who recognize their spiritual poverty and beg for mercy at the feet of Jesus—can be saved.

All talk of Christian salvation necessarily begins here, because it is fundamentally about life and death. Spiritually dead people cannot save themselves nor can they contribute to that salvation. Through regeneration, a sovereign act by God's Spirit to enliven sinners and give them new life, salvation comes to fallen humanity. Only a cure greater than the illness can treat the patient. When the illness is death, the prescribed remedy must be life.

Sinners require regeneration, and anything short of new life by God's Spirit simply leaves a corpse a corpse. No matter how much makeup we put on a dead man lying in his coffin, no matter the amount of rouge used to make his cheeks appear rosy, the man is still dead.[8]

What does it mean to be saved? It means turning away from an empty life of sin to faith in Jesus, through the enlivening power of the Holy Spirit. It means experiencing the re-creative activity of God. It means moving from death to life.

---

8. Although Vladimir Lenin, the founder of Soviet communism, died in 1924, his body is still on display in a granite and marble mausoleum in Red Square, Moscow. Sealed in a glass sarcophagus, his body is kept at a constant temperature and humidity so that it maintains a lifelike appearance. Each week his skin is carefully examined and treated; a mild bleach is employed to remove any fungus or mold spots. Specially filtered lighting is used to give Lenin's skin a healthy glow. Yet he is still dead.

If the Spirit of him who raised Jesus from the dead dwells in you,
he who raised Christ Jesus from the dead will also give life to your
mortal bodies through his Spirit who dwells in you.

Romans 8:11

Key Terms for Salvation Expressed in the Language of Biology

regeneration, renewal, born again, new creation, new birth,
reborn, rebirth, original sin, inherited sin

Questions for Group Discussion

1. If unregenerate people are spiritually dead, what can we conclude about the plethora of non-Christian religions in the world today? Do they make people alive and spiritually aware? Are they congruent with biblical teaching? If so, how? If not, why not?
2. Apart from Christ and the Holy Spirit, do you believe you are basically a good person, one with whom God is pleased? How does your answer to this question affect your relationship with God?
3. How would your view of missions and evangelism differ if you believed, (a) people are spiritually dead without Christ, or (b) people are essentially good and can spiritually please God, even if they do not know Jesus?
4. Do you consider yourself born again? If yes, what evidence could you present to an unbeliever that would serve as proof?

2

The Language of the Courtroom

From Guilt to Acquittal

For we hold that one is *justified* by faith apart from works of the law.

Romans 3:28

There was a stern king whose word was law and whose edicts were strictly obeyed. Three times a week he heard legal cases. One morning, an old woman guilty of stealing was brought before him. The king had decreed that stealing was subject to the lopping off of the offender's right hand. As the old woman was brought before the king and her crime declared, the king sank in his throne in despair.

"Is this true? Did you commit this crime?" he asked the woman.

"Yes, I did, my lord," she replied.

The king hesitated. He leaned forward and asked, "Mother, how can this be?" She made no reply.

The entire court was watching. If the king were to free his mother, the moral foundation of his rule would disintegrate. However, to put his mother through this terrible penalty was too much for him to bear. Was there no way out of this dilemma?

The king stood up, removed his robe, and walked down to his mother. He looked her in the eyes, and then walked over to where the penalty was to be executed. "I'll take your penalty for you," he declared, placing his hand on the block of wood.

Perhaps the most common model of salvation verbalized among Protestants involves justification language, such as "Jesus died for my sins" or "Jesus saved me from my sins." However, for many people, the problem with Christians is our fixation on sin. The evangelical conviction that we are sinners in need of forgiveness (and deserving punishment) strikes nonbelievers as offensive. In a tolerance-loving society, Christian values are viewed as repressive and backward.

Numerous Christian leaders have succumbed to this pressure, eliminating virtually all talk about the topic. Discussing sin is bad for business. The church should be open and welcoming, but if the pastor preaches about iniquity and the judgment of God, that will turn people away.

However, if we do not talk about sin, we cannot say we have shared the gospel. It is precisely from the effects of sin that we are saved. In this chapter, we will investigate the biblical language of justification, how it should be understood in the context of Christian salvation, and how a holy and just God can allow sinners to be justified without paying for their sins themselves.

Alien Righteousness

In general Greek usage, "justification" was the terminology of the courtroom. It involved a judicial hearing or divine acquittal.

As we saw in the previous chapter, the Roman Catholic Church maintains a righteousness that comes via a cooperation between the individual and God. It is a righteousness that grows over the course of the believer's life, with the hope of attaining enough righteousness to enter heaven.

We call this view of righteousness *infused* righteousness. It posits that a seed of righteousness has been placed within the sinner, who then works with it to make it grow. Infused righteousness appears to have the benefit of encouraging proper behavior, as individuals understand that their future depends on their good deeds.

However, there is a downside. It has the potential of producing arrogance on the part of the individual. "I have done enough to merit eternal life, and you have not." A certain spiritual pride may set in.

Furthermore, it has the potential of producing fear. "Will I find out when I die that I did too little?" The sixteenth-century Catholic monk and priest Martin Luther knew how this fear could wreak havoc on one's faith. A salvation based on human effort produces insecurity and anxiety for those truly honest about their own sins. Only the self-righteous will find comfort in a system that encourages earning salvation. Notably, it was the self-righteous that Jesus particularly chastised.

A righteousness from within also encourages selfishness. Good works are not performed out of gratitude but for personal gain. The focus ultimately becomes self-centered, not others-centered.

The Catholic system of salvation has it right on one score. In order to spend an eternity with God, we must be righteous. In fact, we must be perfectly righteous, as just one stain will banish us from God's presence, as it did Adam and Eve in the garden. However, this righteousness cannot come from sinful humans. When imperfect sinners are expected to attain perfect righteousness, we can expect them to fail every time.

The alternative to infused righteousness is *imputed* righteousness. From the language of commerce and accounting, when we impute something we credit it to someone's account who did not earn the credit himself. This is the evangelical view of righteousness, one that has tremendous biblical support. It recognizes that sinners must be given righteousness, what Martin Luther called "alien righteousness." It is not natural to us. It comes from outside ourselves.

Paul speaks of this when using the example of Abraham in his discussion about justification in Romans 4. Quoting Genesis 15:6, Paul notes that it was Abraham's faith that caused him to be justified before God, not by keeping the law or performing good works. "Abraham believed God, and it was counted to him as righteousness" (Rom. 4:3). Later in the chapter, Paul comes back to the same Genesis account, which the King James Version renders this way, using the idea of imputation:

> And therefore it was imputed to him for righteousness. Now it was not written for his sake alone, that it was imputed to him; but for us also, to whom it shall be imputed, if we believe on him that raised up Jesus our Lord from the dead; who was delivered for our offences, and was raised again for our justification. (Rom. 4:22–25)

Note that Paul expands the application of Abraham's act of faith to all believers who possess a similar faith in Jesus. This is the Protestant understanding of justification, that God imputes righteousness to Christians, who do not possess any righteousness themselves.

Is God Unfair?

Christians frequently ask, "How could God send people to hell when they have never heard about Jesus?" The number of books penned in the past two decades concerning this matter is staggering. This question is particularly vexing for evangelicals who have traditionally believed that faith in Jesus is the only way to heaven. It appears unfair for God to send people to eternal damnation if they never had an opportunity to believe in his Son.

Incredibly, the Bible never addresses the issue. There is nowhere in Scripture where the matter is explicitly dealt with, and some argue it is not implicitly dealt with either. Many find it odd that the Bible is silent on this crucial question. However, perhaps the question we are asking is not addressed in the Bible because there exists a greater dilemma: How can a holy and just God allow any sinner to enter heaven?

Injustice is seen in a corrupt or incompetent judge who sends an innocent person to prison. But injustice is equally seen in a judge who allows a guilty person to go free, knowing that the person is culpable of the charge against him.

If we understand what it means to be a sinner with no excuse, in a creation sovereignly directed by a righteous and holy God, we would not stand dumbfounded when that same God sends a sinner to hell. What should truly shock us is how anyone could ever get to heaven. We are simply asking the wrong question because we have a faulty view of God and his justice.

Countless people believe they deserve to be in heaven, and no doubt they will attempt to swagger through the pearly gates and place their claim on the mansion designed to *their* specifications. What we really need, though, is a healthy dose of humility. Heaven will be populated by people who never deserved to be there yet were graciously granted admission by a merciful God.

Once we begin to think that people deserve to be in heaven, the charge that God is unfair inevitably crops up when we think of him sending individuals to hell. We arrogantly transpose the role of judge and accused. C. S. Lewis reflected on how these roles get reversed: "The ancient man approached God (or even the gods) as the accused approaches his judge. For the modern man the roles are reversed. He is the judge: God is in the dock."[1]

Consequently, we unwittingly reject the biblical teaching about sin and its effects. Romans 3 plainly teaches there is no one who is deserving, "all . . . are under sin" (v. 9). Notions of "noble pagans" or the hypothetical innocent man in the jungle simply do not exist in Scripture. That is why we do not find Scripture asking the same question we ask. Although the question makes for interesting theological debate, it lacks the substance of biblical curiosity.

To those who angrily demand justice from God, watch out what you ask for. If sinners got what they deserved, all would be eternally condemned. The question should not be how can God send someone to hell. Rather, it should be, how could God ever allow a rotten, wretched sinner like me into eternal paradise?

Paul addresses this matter of justice in his discussion about God's righteousness. There we find an enigmatic statement:

> This was to show God's righteousness, because in his divine forbearance he had passed over former sins. It was to show his righteousness at the present time, so that he might be just and the justifier of the one who has faith in Jesus. (Rom. 3:25b–26)

To the Hebrew mind, it appeared unjust that God overlooked the misdeeds of sinners. How can God's justice be maintained in declaring the guilty innocent?

Paul later includes this shocking statement: God "justifies the wicked" (Rom. 4:5 NIV84). That is the sole option available to God other than condemning us eternally. There is no option before God that involves justifying a righteous man. Either he condemns the wicked, or he acquits them.

To prove his point, Paul uses two important Old Testament figures, Abraham and David. Whether it be David, a known murderer and

---

1. Lewis, *God in the Dock*, 244.

adulterer, or Abraham, the father of Israel who had come to be known in certain Jewish traditions as having perfectly obeyed God's law, justification is only by grace through faith. Why? Because "all have sinned and fall short of the glory of God" (Rom. 3:23). Whether your sins number in the tens or tens of thousands, you can only be saved by grace.

Witnessing and the Language of Justification

Paul says that sinners suppress the truth of God's revelation due to their wickedness (Rom. 1:18). This means that deep down inside, all of us are aware that we are sinners before God. Despite the dislike some Christians express with an evangelistic approach that confronts people with their sin, if we do not speak to unbelievers about sin, how can we expect them to repent?

When evangelicals speak of being saved by grace, but then turn on God and call him unfair for justly condemning sinners—even ones who have not heard about Jesus—they display a fundamental ignorance concerning grace. For grace to truly be grace, it must be undeserved. If it is deserved, it ceases to be grace and becomes merit, something earned.

From Grace to Grace

Suppose identical adult triplets break into my home but are apprehended by me. All three men deserve to be handed over to the police, but to illustrate a point, I decide to treat them differently. Recall, they are identical triplets so the way I choose to deal with the men has nothing to do with a difference between them.

I hand over the first man to the police as he appropriately deserves. With the second man, though, I promise that if he works forty hours in my yard I will set him free. With the third man, I release him immediately. Which man has been shown grace?

Interestingly, both the second and third men are shown grace, but it is a different sort of grace for each. For the second man, a Catholic style of grace is shown. In his case, "grace" is being given the opportunity to work off his sentence. In a sense he can say afterward that he paid his own penalty and merited his freedom.

The third man is shown biblical grace. He does absolutely nothing to earn his freedom, yet he goes free anyway, despite being guilty. His freedom is an undeserved gift.

Some might object that it is unfair to treat the men differently, allowing one to go scot-free and another to immediately bear his punishment. But there is no unfairness here. There is only justice and grace. All three merit judgment. The first man gets what he deserves. The last man does not get what he deserves (justice) but rather what he does not deserve (grace).[2]

This is the gospel. We have all sinned and fallen short of God's glory and are rightly deserving condemnation. "The wages of sin is death" (Rom. 6:23). Yet the second half of that verse speaks of a gift from God, eternal life through Jesus Christ. We deserve death but are given life.

We should be dumbfounded that God saves anyone. If as evangelicals we declare that salvation is by grace, how dare we turn around and pretend that it is somehow merited? We did not deserve to hear the message of redemption, let alone to receive salvation. Once we firmly understand how despicable our sin is and what an affront to the holiness of God our rebellion has become, we will stop wondering why God doesn't save this or that person. Rather, we will confess, "My God, my God, why have you *not* forsaken us all?"

I am frequently asked about "eternal security" or the assurance of salvation by Christians who are worried they have done something to threaten their salvation. The fear of losing salvation leads to many a sleepless night for Christians who are legalists when you scratch the surface. Theirs is an implicit belief that God has saved them because they are basically good people, but when they stumble into a sin that calls that premise into question, they begin to doubt their salvation.

I recently had a friend put it this way: "I am sometimes worried that I am not a good enough person, that I don't try hard enough, and that at some point I will cross the invisible line and be lost forever." My response was fairly straightforward. "Of course you aren't good enough! That is the point of a gospel of grace. We fail continually, but God never fails to keep his promises." The moment we begin to think we can merit

---

2. Jesus teaches this same truth in the parable of the workers in the vineyard (Matt. 20:1–16). It is the entitlement of the vineyard owner to generously grant more than the workers deserve, and no one has a right to object to his graciousness.

or demerit the love of God—even if we have walked with Christ for fifty years—we reveal a basic misunderstanding of grace.

Only when we understand the biblical teaching on sin—that one single sin is worthy of eternal condemnation—can we understand the biblical teaching on grace—that despite our sin, God shows us undeserved kindness. A misunderstanding of either of these concepts will result in a misunderstanding of the gospel.

Balancing the Grace and Justice of God

We are all familiar with corruption, especially in the legal setting. A judge who condemns one man for a crime, yet allows another to go free because that criminal is his relative, is rightly labeled an unjust judge. Nepotism and cronyism can undermine an entire judicial system. So how can a righteous judge allow any criminal to go free without having that criminal pay for his crime?

In our opening story about the king who was forced to judge on the crime of his mother, it seemed the king basically had two options if he wanted to maintain the justice of his throne. The first was to exact the punishment on his mother decreed by his law for the crime committed. The second would be to make someone else pay for it. This would be quite unjust had the king found a random guy on the street, even if the man himself was a criminal. But once the king devised a third option, by paying the penalty himself, he produced a wonderful display of both grace (as shown to his mother despite her guilt) and justice (the penalty decreed by the law was indeed met). No one in his kingdom could ever dare question the integrity of the king knowing that he had his own hand lopped off in order to maintain the justice of his court.

Similarly, had God overlooked our sin, he could not be considered holy and just. Further, had God punished someone else for our sins, that would have equally been unjust. It is hardly right for a judge to find someone guilty of a crime, and then sentence an innocent bystander for the infraction.

There is a third option, one that deals with sin as sin, and also preserves God's justice. God *himself* pays the penalty. This is true grace! He does not simply brush our sin aside, nor does he allow the full weight of the burden to fall upon our shoulders. This is how a holy God can remove the guilt from fallen humans while himself remaining just.

What about the Law and Good Works?

God's dealings with humanity after Eden have always been by grace. We must avoid the error of thinking that Old Testament believers were saved by the law, while New Testament believers were saved by grace. This error is based on the premise that there is a radical difference between the nation of Israel and the church, as if there are two distinct people of God. "From law to grace" has been indelibly impressed on the minds of many evangelicals, so that they unwittingly regard the law as a vehicle of salvation.

The apostle Paul strongly rejects this notion. Writing to first-century believers in both Rome and Galatia who were familiar with the Hebrew Scriptures, Paul makes some hard-hitting comments about the law and its inability to justify the sinner. Rather than produce an opportunity for salvation, the law has a negative effect. It awakens the desire to sin that is naturally within us, making us conscious of sin and actually increasing it. Paul argues that sin is your master as long as you are under the law.[3]

This is why Paul speaks of "the curse of the law" (Gal. 3:10–13). Consider the following verses from Galatians:

> Yet we know that a person is not justified by works of the law but through faith in Jesus Christ. (2:16)

> For if justification were through the law, then Christ died to no purpose. (2:21 RSV)

> For if a law had been given that could give life, then righteousness would indeed be by the law. But the Scripture imprisoned everything under sin, so that the promise by faith in Jesus Christ might be given to those who believe. (3:21–22)

If the law kills, then how can Paul conclude that the law is good (Rom. 7:12)? Because a key purpose of the law was precisely that, to kill. Its purpose was to reveal our need for grace, through Christ. "So the law was put in charge to lead us to Christ that we might be justified by faith" (Gal. 3:24 NIV84).

---

3. Rom. 3:20b; 5:20; 6:14.

Christians who look to earn their salvation or imply that their entrance into heaven will be based on their good works, return to being under the curse of the law. Since the requirement is perfection, one sin is enough to expel any notion that a person can stand justified before God via his or her works of righteousness. That is why the author of Hebrews says, "the law made nothing perfect" (7:19).

The Old Testament teaches similarly. Salvation has always been by faith; it has never been by works. To prove this point in his epistle to the Romans, Paul uses examples from the three main portions of the Hebrew Scriptures. In chapter 4, his illustration from the life of Abraham comes from the books of Moses ("the Law"). In the same chapter, his example of David comes from the Wisdom Literature (as a corpus commonly referred to as "the Psalms" or "the Writings"), and his quotation of Habakkuk (in Rom. 1:17) from "the Prophets." This is why Paul can say that a righteousness has been revealed to which "the Law and the Prophets bear witness" (Rom. 3:21).

Despite what Paul says about the law's inability to justify sinners, he can still conclude that the law is good.[4] The law does what it was intended to do, to expose sin in sinners. It was never sent to justify sinners. If it could do that, Jesus died for no good reason.

Lastly, Paul notes that a unity of divinity implies a unity of salvation (Rom. 3:30). Because God is one, there is one mediator and one way. Because the disease is the same for all humanity, the cure must be the same. A salvation that comes via different means for different people is incongruous given Paul's monotheistic logic.

A Legal Transaction

The biblical words for justification and righteousness come from the same Greek root, *dik*, and are intimately linked. Yet, we may think in English they are unrelated. In order for sinners to enjoy eternal fellowship with God, they must be made righteous. What we often call the forgiveness of sins is a common way of speaking about justification, to be made right in the eyes of God.

---

4. The goodness of the law is also seen in its provision for how to live a God-pleasing life, as well as its self-revelation of the character and nature of God. However, this is not the focus of this present chapter.

God placed righteous requirements upon fallen humanity that could not possibly be met. These were given to drive us to cry for mercy. We are broken and unable to save ourselves, yet God did not leave us in this pitiful state. He sent his Son, "born under the law" (Gal. 4:4), placed in our situation. Jesus then did something we could never do. He flawlessly obeyed the righteous requirements of the law. When tempted, he always sided with the Father's will. By living a perfectly sinless life, he maintained a righteousness that you and I could never produce.

This is what Jesus meant in the Sermon on the Mount when he said, "Do not think that I have come to abolish the Law or the Prophets; I have not come to abolish them but to fulfill them" (Matt. 5:17). Jesus not only came to fulfill the law but was himself its fulfillment. Everything in the law looked forward to him, as he showed the disciples on the road to Emmaus: "And beginning with Moses and all the Prophets, he interpreted to them in all the Scriptures the things concerning himself" (Luke 24:27). That was undoubtedly the greatest Old Testament Survey course ever taught!

Hovering above fallen humanity was the righteous law of God. However, because of our sins, all the law could do was slay us. It made no provision for justification of the wicked, but only stood to condemn them.

> And you, who were dead in your trespasses and the uncircumcision of your flesh, God made alive together with him, having forgiven us all our trespasses, by canceling the record of debt that stood against us with its legal demands. This he set aside, nailing it to the cross. (Col. 2:13–14)

We who are guilty have the perfect righteousness of Christ imputed to us. In this sense, we are not simply forgiven, we are also made righteous. Our account that once was in debt is fully paid. A transaction of righteousness takes place, with those who are unrighteous receiving the perfect righteousness of Jesus. It could never occur via the law, since it was this very law that condemned us. It comes exclusively through faith in what Jesus has done on our behalf. In fact, this was the foreseen ministry of the Messiah.

> By his knowledge shall the righteous one, my servant,
>   make many to be accounted righteous,
>   and he shall bear their iniquities. (Isa. 53:11)

Via this transaction, the just character of God is maintained, since it is he who pays the penalty for our iniquity. The punishment we deserve is borne by Jesus, the God-man.

This is why Paul can make a contrast between the "old way of the written code" and the "new way of the Spirit" (Rom. 7:6 NIV). Here we see how regeneration and justification are linked. This transaction of righteousness is effected by God's Spirit. Because the code that kills has been removed, believers experience new life. No longer subject to an external law that cannot justify us, we now have the indwelling of God's Spirit who brings life.

In the Courtroom

The legal language of salvation is further found in the terms "intercessor" and "accuser." Satan is pictured as an adversary who attacks the children of God:

> Be sober-minded; be watchful. Your adversary the devil prowls around like a roaring lion, seeking someone to devour. (1 Peter 5:8)

In the Greek, the word "adversary" was a common word to denote an opponent in a lawsuit, and Jesus uses it this way in the Sermon on the Mount.[5] However, Peter employs the word to refer to Satan, the arch-adversary of Christians.

The word "devil" means "accuser" or "slanderer" in the Greek, so that the verse literally says, "Your adversary the accuser."[6] Thirty-four times this word is used in the New Testament to refer to Satan. Another Greek word, also translated "accuser," is seen in reference to Satan in Revelation 12:10:

> And I heard a loud voice in heaven, saying, "Now the salvation and the power and the kingdom of our God and the authority of his Christ have come, for the accuser of our brothers has been thrown down, who accuses them day and night before our God."

---

5. Twice in Matthew 5:25. Also used similarly in Luke 12:58; 18:3.
6. The Greek *diabalos* is the root from which both Latin and English "devil" derive.

The imagery is striking. Satan stands before God and demands that believers be punished for their wrongdoing.

However, biblical legal language likewise involves intercession. In his comparison between the priests of the old covenant and the high priest of the new covenant, the author of Hebrews comments about Jesus (7:23–25):

> The former priests were many in number, because they were prevented by death from continuing in office, but he holds his priesthood permanently, because he continues forever. Consequently, he is able to save to the uttermost those who draw near to God through him, since he always lives to make intercession for them.

What a wonderful promise! While Satan accuses believers "day and night," Jesus is interceding for them, and he never sleeps in this task. With each accusation Satan hurls our way, Jesus intercepts it. This is why Paul can say,

> Who is to condemn? Christ Jesus is the one who died—more than that, who was raised—who is at the right hand of God, who indeed is interceding for us. (Rom. 8:34)

This ministry of the Messiah was prophesied as the one who "bore the sin of many, and makes intercession for the transgressors" (Isa. 53:12).[7]

Combining all this imagery, we can picture a courtroom where believers are the defendants, God the Father is seated as judge, Jesus Christ serves as the defense attorney, and Satan is the prosecutor. With each accusation against the defendants, Jesus steps in and intervenes. However, in this trial he is not stating that the defendants are innocent of the crimes for which they have been accused. Rather, he intercedes in taking upon himself the punishment they justly deserve.[8]

---

7. The biblical idea of intercession is not limited to Christ, but also involves the Holy Spirit interceding in the prayer life of Christians (Rom. 8:26–27), and believers interceding for others (1 Tim. 2:1). "The children of God have two divine intercessors. Christ is their intercessor in the court of heaven. . . . [T]he Holy Spirit is their intercessor in the theatre of their own hearts" (Murray, *Romans*, 311).

8. Other legal language concerns Jesus as our advocate (1 John 2:1) and the Holy Spirit as counselor (John 14:16).

Problems Eliminated

We noted earlier that a system of salvation that relies on works can produce fear, selfishness, and arrogance on the part of its adherents. Conversely, a salvation that comes by grace eliminates these problems.

Martin Luther knew that God's law placed upon him a weight he could not remove.[9] For a time, this awareness engendered in Luther a hatred of God. Why would God be so cruel as to place upon his shoulders righteous requirements he could not possibly fulfill?

Worship and the Language of Justification

Much worship today is all fluff and no substance. God is more a friend than a holy Lord. The reverence and seriousness that should characterize our worship has been replaced with a nonchalance that banks on the tolerance of an easily appeased, wishy-washy god. But at the heart of justification is a righteous God who hates sin. Let us approach God in worship with the solemnity he is rightly due.

Once Luther realized that God's righteousness is a free gift, his burden was lifted. Fear was no longer operative. Luther did not have to worry that he would learn upon his death that he had not done enough to merit salvation. Since it is a free gift offered by faith, not by works, God's righteousness is received now. Doubt about one's future is unnecessary. The fear produced by a system of works-righteousness is wonderfully eliminated.

The second problem with a deeds-based salvation is that it is self-focused and ultimately selfish. Works are done mainly with one's own salvation in mind. But in order for us to become Christlike, we should perform good works without the primary motivation of gain for ourselves. Is this not what Jesus did?

With justification by faith, good works are a product of saving faith, not a prerequisite for it. This being the case, the believer can do good works as an outflow of a grateful heart. The works are not done with a

---

9. In his address to the Jerusalem Council, Peter made a similar observation (Acts 15:10–11).

selfish motivation; they can be selflessly performed. Note the sequence of salvation and good works in the passage below. The works come as an outflow of saving faith, not a precursor to it.

> For by grace you have been saved through faith. And this is not your own doing; it is the gift of God, not a result of works, so that no one may boast. For we are his workmanship, created in Christ Jesus for good works, which God prepared beforehand, that we should walk in them. (Eph. 2:8–10)

Scripture speaks of salvation as a "gift," something that is freely given and not earned. Salvation comes from the side of God. As a gift, it is the Giver who determines what the gift will be, not the person receiving it. Mankind has no say in how justification will be determined. Only the Judge can make that decision, and he has decided to offer it freely through his Son.

I often ask my students, "Is self-reliance a good trait to have?" Most of them will emphatically say yes. Who wants to be dependent upon others? This is particularly understood by Africans who struggled under foreign occupation. In the area of our salvation, though, self-reliance is a death sentence. It is the surest path to spiritual pride, and the quickest way to eternal destruction.

If salvation could come from our good works, we would have every reason to boast. It is the same opinion the Pharisee in the temple had: "Thank you, God, that you did not make me like this rotten tax collector." Spiritual self-reliance is a sure way to arrogance.

Not even Abraham, the great man of faith, had a reason to boast. In Romans 4, Paul reasons that if Abraham had been saved by his good deeds, "he has something to boast about" (v. 2). But this is not the case. As Paul notes earlier, a salvation by grace precludes boasting, since it never comes from our own effort or achievements (3:27). This means that we should be supremely humble people, recognizing our spiritual poverty and realizing that it is only by grace that we stand justified.

Pardon Me?

This model of salvation in a legal setting covers several biblical aspects:

1. Jesus earning a perfect righteousness through faultless obedience to the law, which he then imputes as a free gift to everyone who has faith in him;
2. Satan pictured as an accuser of believers and Jesus as our intercessor;
3. payment of a ransom we could not pay ourselves (covered in chapter 4 on redemption); and
4. Christ receiving a penalty we could not possibly bear (covered in chapter 6 on atonement).

As we saw in the first chapter, salvation involves moving from death to life. Salvation that relies on human works is like moving the corpse from one room of the morgue to another. Because we are dead in our sins, we need new life. This we refer to as regeneration.

However, our sins also cause us to stand as guilty before a just judge, God. Salvation as justification is a declaration of innocence, a verdict of acquittal. For the sinner, a pardon has been granted.

What does it mean to be saved? It means having your sins forgiven and being made righteous. It means removing the impossible burden of the righteous requirements of the law and replacing them with a life of grace. It means moving from guilt to acquittal.

> There is therefore now no condemnation
> for those who are in Christ Jesus.
>
> *Romans 8:1*

Key Terms for Salvation Expressed in the Language of the Courtroom

justification, pardon, infused/imputed/alien righteousness, justice, condemnation, intercessor, advocate, counselor, accuser, guilt, forgiveness, free gift, judge, law, faith, grace

Questions for Group Discussion

1. Does God only forgive the sins committed up to the time of conversion and repentance, or does he forgive all sins, even future ones not yet committed? In a related way, for which of your sins did Jesus die on the cross two thousand years ago?

2. Are you certain that when you die you will be found approved by God? How does a biblical understanding of justification help to alleviate fear in this area?

3. If Jesus has already paid the penalty for the sins of every human being who has ever lived, why do people who die without faith in Jesus still bear the penalty in hell?

4. Do you think it is unjust or unfair for God to send people to hell who have never heard about Jesus or the gospel?

3

The Language of the Family

From Rejection to Acceptance

ADOPTION

In love he predestined us for *adoption* as sons through Jesus Christ, according to the purpose of his will.

Ephesians 1:4–5

Phil and Trish wanted a boy. They made the three-day trip from the United States to Siberia in the hope of walking away with a cute, little Russian kid. The orphanage supervisor brought the excited couple into a large room where workers led in about two dozen children. Little boys with spiky hair and toothless grins came running in, made to stand in a row as best they could, overwhelmed at the prospect of being adopted.

Off to the side, however, stood a larger boy. He looked dejected as he stared downward, his foot playing with an imaginary object on the floor. Phil asked the supervisor, "Why is that boy standing over there?" The supervisor explained in broken English, "When you get to be that age, you've been passed over so many times you take for granted you won't be chosen."

Trish gently grasped Phil's hand. They looked at each other, and in that moment knew what they needed to do. "We'll take *him*," they said.

We next consider one of the most comforting models of salvation found in Scripture, especially for those who have experienced lives of estrangement and isolation. In some respects, we are moving from the courtroom to the family room, from a model of salvation that emphasizes forensic declaration of guiltlessness, to the warmer, friendlier feeling of a sofa by the fireplace.

In Namibia, this model of salvation is quite powerful. Some studies put the birthrate of children born out of wedlock somewhere around 90 percent, a shocking statistic.[1] Marriage is a relative rarity, and it is an anomaly to find people who were raised their entire childhood by two parents.

In the Bible study that first sparked the idea for this book, I asked who had been raised from infancy through high school by two parents, and not one could answer in the affirmative. Most were raised by just a mother who had gotten pregnant at an early age and had been abandoned by her partner. Others were raised by relatives like uncles or grandmothers. Incredibly, in all three instances that involved a married couple at birth, the parents later divorced.

There are few Namibians who can speak of the warmth and security that come from an intact, nuclear family. Those who *can* have a great blessing that many of their fellow compatriots will never know. It is in this atmosphere of the disintegration of the family that the adoption model of salvation can be quite moving.

With this chapter we will initially establish the first-century context of adoption before we see how the concept is used in the New Testament when portraying the relationship believers have with their heavenly Father. Then we will look at the practical implications of what it means to be part of God's family.

A Cultural Disconnect

When I was growing up, adoption had a stigma attached to it. Often, adoptive parents did not tell their children they were adopted, because this implied a lower status than natural-born children. I can distinctly recall two cases involving adopted classmates who were mistreated by both the parents who adopted them and their natural-

---

1. For comparison, the 2010 figure is around 40 percent in the United States.

born children. Today, in the mind of some, to be adopted regrettably speaks of a lower position.

This unfortunate caricature may cause some to view adoption in a negative manner, but in first-century Rome, adoption was a high honor. Adoption in that ancient culture was not seen as second rate, but rather as a necessary privilege of the first order. With this biblical term for salvation, the original first-century understanding is far more powerful than our modern, English equivalent.

"Adoption" (*huiothesia*) in biblical Greek comes from the conjunction of two words, *huios* for "son" and *thesis* meaning "a placing." Adoption was putting someone in the position of a son. When the apostle Paul used the word, his first-century readers would have immediately understood it in their context.

Roman adoption involved the moving from one family to another. Frequently, affluent but childless couples looked to adopt, as is the case today. Conversely, families with numerous children viewed adoption as a way to make money. Often the childless family paid a considerable sum of money to adopt a child. Living in first-century Rome was quite expensive, and large families were financially disadvantaged. Sending your fit, older sons off via adoption had the dual benefit of immediate income and a decrease in the family's daily expenses.

Roman adoption usually involved teenagers and in many instances, adult males. Perhaps the most famous Roman adoptee was nearly twenty years old when he was adopted by the emperor Julius Caesar. Octavian, later known as Caesar Augustus, became ruler of the Roman Empire. He was the emperor who reigned during the birth of Jesus.[2]

Theologically, being born again and adoption are two different things. One is being born into the family, the other being given the rights and privileges of that family. They are twin concepts of what it means to be saved. Even a natural-born son in Roman times had to be

---

2. Another excellent case from Roman history showing how legally sacrosanct adoption was regarded is from the life of the despot Nero. The emperor Claudius adopted Nero in order to succeed him to the throne. They were in no way blood relatives. To cement the alliance, Nero requested Claudius' daughter Octavia to be his wife. However, in the eyes of the law, due to Nero's adoption by Claudius, Nero and Octavia were considered siblings. The Roman Senate had to pass special legislation to allow Nero to marry his legally recognized sister.

adopted by his father in order to become heir of his possessions. In fact, there was no higher honor for a son, and no greater disgrace than when another male was adopted into the family who took the position from the natural-born son.

The opening story in this chapter has a warm and fuzzy feeling to adoption that was not necessarily the case in the first century. Adoption was more of a practical decision than a sentimental one. However, regardless of the lack of emotional weight, first-century adoption was a privilege without equal. The adoptee gained the right to the name and property of his new family, and this is precisely the emphasis that Paul wants when he uses it to refer to believers, to which we will turn shortly.

Outside the Family

But first, consider what Paul says to the Gentiles who were outside the covenant benefits that the Israelites enjoyed. Paul can speak about his fellow Jews as enjoying "adoption as sons" (Rom. 9:5) as he enumerates numerous blessings Israel received. However, Paul notes in another epistle that the Gentiles were shut out of those blessings, "separate" and "excluded," "without hope and without God in the world" (Eph. 2:12 NIV). Unfortunately, these same things can be said about unbelievers today.

The very word adoption implies someone not naturally a member of that family. The popular mantra that everyone is a child of God does not correspond with God's revelation in Scripture. Although humans can be called God's "offspring" in that they find their existence only in their Creator ("in him we live and move and have our being," Acts 17:28–29), as fallen sinners we are not naturally God's children. This privilege is something that is solely given from above. Consider what John says in his Gospel (1:12–13):

> But to all who did receive him [Jesus], who believed in his name, he gave the right to become children of God, who were born, not of blood nor of the will of the flesh nor of the will of man, but of God.

It is by faith in Jesus that we are "given the right" to enter God's family. This is why it is vitally important we first have a proper understanding of our position apart from Christ and outside the family of God. Only then can we truly grasp the momentous godsend of biblical adoption.

Consider an orphan who endures a meager existence on the streets. In want of proper clothing and shelter, this child does not know if he will have anything to eat on any given day. Forced to beg, or worse, to sell his body to survive, the child has little hope for a normal life. In today's world, this is very much a reality.

Now suppose that a rich and prestigious couple were to take pity on this child. They take him into their home where he is provided a comfortable, warm bed. He is given clothing and shoes, and every day he never wants for food. Greater still, this couple loves the child and cares for him, and he experiences an affection he never had before. In every respect, the child is better off now than when he was homeless and on the streets.

We must begin to understand our adoption by God in similar terms. Spiritually speaking, we were beggars with no hope in the world. As much as we tried to clothe ourselves with good works, that clothing was nothing but filthy rags. We went from day to day hoping for a scrap of food or a piece of bread to fill our bellies, but most days we lived with piercing hunger pangs. Malnourished and emaciated, we were spiritually destitute.

Then one day we were picked up off the streets and given a family, the family of God. Unless we fully grasp our dire state before this adoption, we will not appreciate what God has done for us. Too often we imagine the situation as far better than it was. Instead of a beggar adopted from the gutter, we envision someone taken from one cozy apartment to another. Instead of moving from the slums to a mansion, we visualize ourselves as simply moving across the suburban street. But our adoption by God is a far more dramatic move than relocating down the block.[3]

Paul refers to us in our pre-conversion state as "children of wrath," and Jesus notes that when the Pharisees lie, they speak the native language of their "father the devil."[4] There is no neutral ground. Either you are naturally in the family of Satan, or supernaturally born into the family of God.

---

3. The most direct first-century contrast to adoption was slavery, dealt with in the next chapter on redemption.

4. Eph. 2:3; John 8:44.

Relational Beings

Much of our life is spent looking for a sense of acceptance and belonging. Whether it be a certain clique in school, or from sororities and fraternities in college, to social clubs and gangs, human beings are constantly seeking a place where they can feel at home. This is why peer pressure can be a powerful force, and why a strong nuclear family is so important in God's economy. The weaker the home bond, the more likely the child will seek emotional and relational satisfaction elsewhere, frequently in unseemly ways.

Human contact and the desire for intimacy are built into the human condition. While we like to say in evangelical circles "all you need is God," apparently that was not the case with Adam. God created us in such a way that a need for intimacy and closeness with fellow humans is part of our design. Encompassed in the image of God in humans is that we are relational beings, just like the Trinitarian God who exists in eternal relationship between Father, Son, and Holy Spirit.[5] In fact, people who suffer from extreme antisocial behavior are often deemed psychopathic.

Is it any wonder that one of the key forms of punishment in our correctional system is solitary confinement? Psychobiologists tell us that long-lasting loneliness not only can make you sick, it can kill you. Emotional isolation is as high a risk factor for mortality as smoking. Both the Bible and modern psychology tell us that loneliness is not conducive to human survival.[6]

Witnessing and the Language of Adoption

Many people feel isolated and alone in this cold world, and they often look for a sense of belonging in all the wrong places. To those who feel lonely and friendless, we have genuine fellowship, community, and hope to offer them in Christ. Be bold as you share your faith. Christians have the meaning of true family.

---

5. More will be said concerning the image of God in humans in chapter 11 on transformation.

6. Sometimes an unbeliever will defiantly say he or she cannot wait to get to hell because "all my friends will be there." This cheeky retort to a very real eternal danger misses the mark. I wonder if hell will not be eternal, solitary confinement, with sinners left only with their evil thoughts and feelings of deep regret.

This is why Scripture consistently utilizes the language of family when speaking about those who have faith in Jesus Christ. However, only part of that language centers on the word adoption.

Family Language Old and New

There is rich family language in both Testaments. In the Old Testament, Israel's unique relationship with God is consistently couched in the language of family. God is portrayed as a Ruler and Judge, but he is also a Husband, Shepherd, and Redeemer, and much of this terminology is household language. However, no biblical term better exudes the idea of family than Father.

While the depiction of God as our Father is most often used by Jesus, it is frequently found in the Hebrew Scriptures. God is pictured as the One who gives birth to Israel, who cares for her and raises her, and who wants to bless the nation, while Israel is his children or sons.[7]

This is wonderfully expressed in Deuteronomy where Moses is recounting to the people of Israel how God cared for them both in the exodus from Egypt and in the desert. "There you saw how the LORD your God carried you, as a father carries his son, all the way you went until you reached this place" (Deut. 1:31 NIV).[8]

In fact, when Israel turned away from God, this too was cast in familial terms: the language of adultery where Israel prostituted herself to idols and false gods. The same imagery is used in the New Testament by Jesus and James when referring to a fickle people who turn away from the One they should love.[9]

Of course, our adoption would not be possible if it were not for God's true Son who, in humbling himself and coming to earth, identified with us and left his heavenly family. He bore God's estrangement in order that we might have fellowship with our Maker. Jesus' cry on the cross, "My God, my God, why have you forsaken me?" (Mark 15:34), echoes the disaffection Christ experienced so that we could become God's children. Our adoption was indeed costly. Through his death, we have been given

---

7. Deut. 32:6, 18; Jer. 3:4, 19; 31:20; Hos. 11:1; Deut. 14:1.

8. See the addendum to this chapter for a brief discussion about the objection to "father" in reference to God by those who deem the term chauvinistic.

9. Hos. 2:4; Ezek. 16:20; Mark 8:38; James 4:4.

the "full rights of sons." Biblical writers consistently refer to fellow believers as "brothers," and Jesus likewise calls believers "brother."[10]

The quintessential family term, "firstborn," is used both to describe Jesus and Israel. Commentator M. J. Selman notes the advantages accrued to the firstborn: "The accompanying privileges were highly valued, and in the Old Testament included a larger inheritance, a special paternal blessing, family leadership and an honoured place at mealtimes."[11] God calls Israel his firstborn (Exod. 4:22; Jer. 31:9), signifying the privilege the nation enjoyed above every other nation. This honored position was meant to be a sign to all people, ultimately culminating in the worship of the one, true God. The prophet Hosea looked forward to a time when a people not known as God's people would be called "my people" and "sons of the living God."[12]

While Jesus is peculiarly the "Son of God,"[13] for a variety of reasons he is also referred to as God's firstborn. He is the "firstborn among many brothers," the "firstborn of all creation," the "firstborn from the dead," and the firstborn the angels must worship.[14] All of these ways signify Jesus' preeminent position.

The Benefits of Family Membership

Adoption is only as good as the family doing the adopting, and what a wonderful family the children of God enter! The blessings and privileges are unparalleled, including guidance, affection, sense of belonging, and suitable discipline. We will briefly consider these benefits in four broad categories.

1. Receiving the Family Name

A name says everything. Consider American politics. If your last name is Clinton or Kennedy, there is an immediate cachet granted

---

10. Gal. 4:5; Rom. 10:1; Heb. 2:12, 14.

11. M. J. Selman, "First-born," in *New Bible Dictionary*, 369.

12. Hos. 2:23; 1:10 (KJV).

13. The coming Messiah is referred to as God's son (Ps. 2:7; 2 Sam. 7:14), which makes sense as this declaration concerning Jesus at his baptism—"You are my beloved Son" (Mark 1:11)—is the first public statement by the Father concerning Christ.

14. Rom. 8:29; Col. 1:15, 18; Rev. 1:5; Heb. 1:6. In the sense of privilege and position, believers comprising the church are called the firstborn (Heb. 12:23).

you. If you are in business and your surname is Rockefeller or Gates or Buffett, even if the name came from your great-great-grandfather, it immediately grants you access to the upper echelons of commerce. Paul says that believers get their name from their heavenly Father, and no earthly name compares. It is the "name above all names," a name to be hallowed. We become members of the "household of God."[15]

Worship and the Language of Adoption

Can you imagine if at any time you could drive to the White House and speak to the president of the United States? That would certainly be a privilege. Yet, as Christians, our privilege is far greater. In prayer, at any time and in any situation, we can approach the Creator of the universe with confidence (Heb. 4:16). When we pray, Jesus our co-heir promises that we will be heard (John 14:13).

As such, we can call the Lord of the universe "*Abba*, Father." This term of endearment portrays an intimate relationship between father and child, perhaps best rendered as "daddy" in our modern idiom. Originally used by Jesus, it is significant that Paul says believers may also use this term when addressing God.[16] Despite the fact that Jesus alone has a unique relationship with the Father, because of our faith in Christ and the indwelling of his Spirit, we too may enter this most intimate of relationships.

"Crawl up onto your Father's lap and enjoy his love and protection." That kind of talk makes certain evangelicals uneasy because it seems to detract from God's holiness and "otherness." Yet, is this intimacy not precisely what we as followers of God's Son presently enjoy? We are given the special provision of God, bold access to him in prayer, and the fatherly discipline that children need as they are lovingly yet firmly guided by him.[17]

In receiving the family name, the Roman adoptee lost all connection to his previous family. Past debts were cancelled, and he entered a new life with all the benefits of his newfound filial allegiance. John writes in

---

15. Eph. 2:19; 1 Tim. 3:15; 1 Peter 4:17; cf. Eph. 3:15.
16. Mark 14:36; Rom. 8:15; Gal. 4:6.
17. Matt. 6:32–33; 7:11; Eph. 3:12; Heb. 4:16; 12:5–10.

his first epistle that there will be clear evidence what family name you bear. He speaks of "children of God" versus "children of the devil." Paul exhorts us to be "imitators of God," and in so doing, we show the world who our true Father is.[18]

2. Receiving an Inheritance

I recently read an article that spoke about two wealthy men who will not leave any of their large fortune to their family when they die. One was the Chinese actor Jackie Chan. Chan plans to leave his entire $2.2 billion estate to charity. I am sure this comes as a surprise to those family members who were hoping for a piece of the pie, especially his only son. As Chan said, with what sounded like proverbial Chinese wisdom, "If my son is capable of making his own money, then he doesn't need mine. And if he isn't, then he'll just waste mine." There are many people who are hoping to inherit yet will be disappointed.

Not so when it comes to the family of our heavenly Father. Followers of Jesus become "fellow heirs" with God's Son and receive an inheritance that "can never perish, spoil or fade, . . . kept in heaven for you." Jesus says in the Sermon on the Mount that the meek shall inherit the earth. He further uses this inheritance language when he speaks of going to prepare a place for us where we can be with him forever.[19]

Note that inheritance is not wages. Wages are something earned for work performed. Inheritance, on the other hand, is something that comes in the future and is the result, not of work, but of relationship with the family head. This should help guard us against the idea of immediate gratification when we serve the Lord. Too often Christians look for a quick fix, instant payback from God when they exercise at times the littlest of faith. However, the New Testament emphasis is more on eternal rewards than temporal ones.

Related to this future inheritance is the Christian doctrine of hope. When we lose loved ones, for example, we do not mourn as those of the world mourn (1 Thess. 4:13). Why? Because we have genuine hope for a future with our Father.

---

18. 1 John 3:10; Eph. 5:1. Christians are supposed to imitate Jesus (1 Thess. 1:6) as well as other godly, Christian leaders (Phil. 4:9; 2 Thess. 3:7). There is a spiritual DNA that runs through all the members of God's household.

19. Rom. 8:17; 1 Peter 1:4 (NIV); Matt. 5:5; John 14:2–3; 1 Peter 3:22.

Biblical hope is never willy-nilly like, "I hope I win the lottery." Biblical hope involves a sense of surety and confidence, trusting in the promises of God because his character is one of faithfulness and trustworthiness. Because God makes the promises, and because God can never lie, we have a sure hope that whatever God has said he will do, he *will* do.

Part of this hope involves the redemption of our bodies (Rom. 8:23). I have a friend who has suffered from numerous physical ailments during her thirty-plus years of adult life, but she appears to never lose heart. "Lord, give me my resurrection body now!" she'll say with a twinkle in her eye. This is part of the glorious hope believers enjoy as God's children. Even though we "groan inwardly" as we currently experience the decay to which creation is subject (Rom. 8:23), Paul notes that our adoption brings with it the promise of life to our mortal bodies (8:11).

Still, we must not think that the whole Christian life is one of constant triumph. In that same chapter in Romans, the apostle makes it clear that sharing in the glory of Christ will involve sharing in his sufferings (8:17). However, rather than seeing suffering as a negative, as we are inclined to do given our fallen nature, we are meant to embrace it with joy.[20]

3. Receiving the Holy Spirit

As if assurance in the trustworthy nature of God is not enough, God gives us something *now* that guarantees our future inheritance: he gives us his Spirit. In several places Paul speaks of God's Spirit as a "deposit guaranteeing our inheritance" (Eph. 1:14 NIV; cf. 2 Cor. 1:22; 5:5). Much like a person who in buying a home puts money down as a statement of good faith that the remainder of the payment is coming, God provides us with a "down payment" of his Spirit as a pledge that he is good for the rest of the inheritance.

Roman adoption involved witnesses, and the Holy Spirit serves to testify with our spirit (Rom. 8:16), producing in us a surety of our salvation and a profound conviction that we are God's children. The idea that somehow before the foundation of the world God would adopt us (Eph. 1:5), only to later reject us, is entirely at odds with the biblical portrayal of salvation. Those who have the Spirit have him forever, otherwise Paul could not speak of a "guarantee."

---

20. Jesus, Paul, and James consider godly suffering as a blessed privilege (e.g., Matt. 5:11; Phil. 1:29; James 1:2).

Some Christians, though, object to this idea on the basis that if a person knows he cannot lose his salvation, it will drive him to complacency. However, when you read that God's Spirit is a guarantee, what is your natural reaction as a believer? Is it, "Oh, good, now I can sin as much as I want to and not worry about it!"? Or is it, "Wow, because of God's awesome faithfulness to his promises, I am going to live my life in humble gratitude for his grace shown to me"? If it is the first reaction, then perhaps you need to seriously reconsider the sincerity (or lack thereof) of your confession of faith.

Those who believe they can lose their salvation believe they can work to keep it, emptying the gospel of grace. Rather than drive us to complacency, this truth should provide believers with incredible comfort knowing that, despite our failures, God will never fail us.

A Roman adoptee was sealed with the gift of a ceremonial toga and signet ring, and believers are similarly "sealed" by the "promised Holy Spirit" (Eph. 1:13), signifying our rights to an inheritance from our heavenly Father. God has promised to never forsake us.

4. Receiving Spiritual Siblings

Jesus does not leave us as orphans (John 14:18), but instead he brings us into an expansive family network. Jesus refers to believers as his mother and brother and sister—all who do God's will (Matt. 12:46–50). With the new family come new siblings.

I am consistently struck during my travels how a bond is immediately created with other believers, regardless of the cultural, ethnic, and linguistic differences between us. In many respects, this bond is stronger than the biological bonds that exist between father and son, or mother and daughter. In fact, Jesus plainly says that his advent will break such biological bonds, and if we are not willing to forsake these natural relationships when necessary, we have no business seeking a supernatural relationship with Christ.[21]

As participants in the body of Christ, believers become members of one family with spiritual brothers and sisters around the globe. Not only do we relate differently to God, but we should relate differently to each other as well. This is true on the broad, ethnic level of Jew and

---

21. Matt. 10:35–36; Luke 14:26.

Gentile, where the two who once were at enmity have become one in Christ (Eph. 2:14–16). But it also affects us individually, as we begin to enjoy restored relationships with others in God's family.

When Paul says that those in Christ have "every spiritual blessing" (Eph. 1:3), the above list gives us a taste of why he can say that. The blessings are manifold.

We have considered some of the privileges we possess as believers, but there is much that can be said about our obligations as God's children, now that we have been taken from the children of the devil and adopted into God's family. Along with rights as sons, there are also responsibilities. This will be covered in chapter 10 on fruitfulness.

Conclusion

Do you want a sense of true identity, purpose, and belonging? All humans do. Conversely, estrangement and alienation regularly result in extreme depression and a slew of personality disorders. Humans were made for relationship, especially relationship with their Creator.

What does it mean to be saved? It means being brought into a family when you have no permanent home. It means receiving the love and discipline that come from a heavenly Father when previously your affiliation was to sin and Satan. It means looking forward to an eternal inheritance that can never perish, with the down payment of God's indwelling Spirit. It means moving from rejection to acceptance. Welcome to the family of God!

> See what kind of love the Father has given to us, that we should be called children of God; and so we are.
>
> *1 John 3:1*

Key Terms for Salvation Expressed in the Language of the Family

adoption, heirs, inheritance, children of God, discipline, Father, Abba, sons/daughters, orphans, family, household, firstborn, brothers/sisters

---

Questions for Group Discussion

1. If unregenerate people are not naturally part of God's family, then in whose family are they? What characterizes their membership in this family, and how are those different than the marks that characterize the children of God?

2. Do a simple survey of your small group or church. How many people enjoyed the benefits of growing up in an intact family? Is anyone willing to share his or her experiences about what it was like growing up in a family that was fragmented or broken?

3. Can you discern from Scripture what some of the responsibilities of God's adopted children might entail? Do you feel the sense not only of extreme relief in being brought into God's family, but also the duty of what it means to be his child in this fallen world? Explain.

Addendum: Patriarchal Language

Some people do not have a healthy relationship with their father, so certain scholars have expressed concern that to refer to God as Father might turn off these people. However, regardless of one's personal experience, everybody has a concept of a good father, otherwise images of "bad" fathers would have no benchmark against which to be measured.

Others are put off by the "patriarchal" terminology employed by the biblical authors. They attempt to provide balance by calling God our "mother," or by defusing this "chauvinistic" language with neutral terms like "divine parent."

The problem with this is twofold. The first is that it is offensive to God. In Scripture we are not dealing with the words of men who, in their fallible way, attempted to put to pen their thoughts about their Maker. We are confronted by the self-revelation of the Lord of glory. God is the One who has determined to portray himself as a "heavenly Father." Jesus spoke about him similarly. To deign to refer to God in "gender neutral" language is nothing more than arrogance on our part. We merely do not like the way God has chosen to reveal himself; we rather pick the way we find most suitable.

It is tantamount to me telling you that my name is Victor and yet you insisting on using a nickname unappreciated by me. Surely God has the right to choose how best to reveal himself to humanity. Is the slave entitled to call the master whatever he wants to call him?

The second problem with attempting to use gender-neutral language is that it ignores the cultural context in which the Bible originally came. In the case of adoption, in Roman times it was virtually unheard of for daughters to be adopted. When Paul speaks of "adoption as sons," he is speaking in terms understandable in first-century context. He is speaking of utmost privilege and position.

The beauty is that this adoption refers to all believers. Every Christian is adopted as a son, given the status reserved solely for those to whom the Lord of the universe has conferred it.

While the New Testament language of children is usually expressed in the masculine, "sons," it is not exclusively so. Notice how Paul speaks about sons in Galatians 3:25–29, but then immediately notes that coming to faith in Jesus is not gender determined.

> But now that faith has come, we are no longer under a guardian, for in Christ Jesus you are all sons of God, through faith. For as many of you as were baptized into Christ have put on Christ. There is neither Jew nor Greek, there is neither slave nor free, there is no male and female, for you are all one in Christ Jesus. And if you are Christ's, then you are Abraham's offspring, heirs according to promise.

The idea that Paul was a misogynist, and this allegedly proven by his use of masculine-oriented language, simply ignores the first-century context of the language Paul employed. In the apostle's reckoning, female believers also have the position of utmost privilege and relationship with God, in this first-century sense, becoming "sons of God."[22]

---

22. In quoting the Old Testament, Paul uses "sons and daughters" in 2 Cor. 6:18 to refer to believers, while God in speaking through the prophet Isaiah also refers to "everyone who is called by my name" as "my sons" and "my daughters" (Isa. 43:6–7).

4

The Language of the Marketplace
From Bondage to Liberation

REDEMPTION

You were *ransomed* from the futile ways inherited from your forefathers, not with perishable things such as silver or gold, but with the precious blood of Christ, like that of a lamb without blemish or spot.

1 Peter 1:18–19

There were few players more feared in the National Football League than Lawrence Taylor. Sports analysts credit Taylor with changing the outside linebacker's role and hence offensive line schemes in the NFL. It is no surprise that Taylor won a record three Defensive Player of the Year awards, an MVP, and led his New York Giants to two Super Bowl victories in five years.

However, Taylor's on-the-field achievements did not translate to off-the-field success. He ran into frequent bouts with alcohol, drugs, and the law. Taylor recounts these personal struggles in an autobiography, and one comment he made struck me. Taylor explains that his uncontrollable addiction to cocaine was so powerful that it consumed his every thought and desire. This MVP athlete, at the top of his profession, found his thoughts consistently wandering—even in the middle of huddles during a game—to the next line of cocaine he could snort. Taylor was enslaved by his addiction, and despite consistent attempts to break free, he could not. Subsequent events in Taylor's life have revealed that once again he is hitting the powder.

In stark contrast to Taylor is another NFL star, Deion Sanders. Sanders was a Pro Bowl defensive back in the 1990s who played on several Super Bowl champions including the Dallas Cowboys and San Francisco 49ers. Sanders likewise was addicted, but not to illegal substances. His was sexual addiction. Multiple partners and orgiastic participation were the hallmark of Sanders' enslavement, each sexual encounter requiring a greater sense of excitement and experimentation than the previous one.

However, unlike Taylor, Sanders recounts a conversion to Jesus Christ and complete freedom from his sexual addiction. His is a remarkable story that does not involve constant trips to rehab only to relapse into his compulsion. Rather, Sanders encountered the miraculous work of the Spirit of Christ in his life. He is frequently asked to speak at Christian events around the country, recounting how faith in Jesus set him free from the law of sin and death.

In this chapter, we come to an area that touches precisely upon the problem that plagued Taylor and Sanders. It involves a spiritual battle with evil forces we cannot defeat on our own. As we move to our fourth model of salvation, we must understand the reason why we needed to be redeemed, what kept us in bondage, and how through Jesus our freedom was purchased.

Christus Victor

Among evangelicals, salvation is most often expressed in our first two models, from death to life, and from guilt to acquittal. However, another biblical way of expressing salvation is from slavery to freedom, from bondage to liberation. It is what some refer to as the *Christus Victor* model of salvation, Jesus as a liberator. In fact, this understanding of Christian salvation has stronger support in the early centuries of Christianity than any other model.[1]

It is also the predominant Pentecostal picture of salvation, although it is regularly abused by envisioning "freedom from bondage" in wholly materialistic terms, e.g., Jesus promises freedom from the bondage of

---

1. Gustaf Aulén calls it "the ruling idea of the Atonement for the first thousand years of Christian history" (*Christus Victor*, 6).

financial debt or physical infirmity. Despite these abuses, evangelicals can learn a great deal from this biblically rich model of salvation.

Envision a prisoner in a dark dungeon. His hands and feet are tightly immobilized by chains, bound behind iron bars, guarded by a contingent of heavily armed strongmen whose sole purpose is to make sure he does not escape. However, the strongmen are overpowered by a deliverer, the key is placed in the lock, and the captive is released.

Things that restrain the sinner hinder his relationship with God. The redemption model envisions salvation as freedom from everything that binds sinners, so they can truly live as children of God.

The Greek words normally translated as "redemption" or "to redeem" bear this out. The noun *lutrōsis* and the verb *lutroō* both have the same root meaning "to loose." The Greek denoted ransoming prisoners of war, but it also was used when referring to the freeing of slaves. Other words seen in this context, *agorazō* and *exagorazō*, have the idea of purchasing in the marketplace (the *agora*). As such, it would be helpful to establish the first-century context of redemption before we investigate the way Scripture applies it to believers.

Slavery in the Roman Empire

The best first-century contrast for the privileges of adoption was the low status of slaves. In fact, Paul makes this distinction in his letter to the Galatians.

> So also, when we were children, we were in slavery under the basic principles of the world. But when the time had fully come, God sent his Son, born of a woman, born under law, to redeem those under law, that we might receive the full rights of sons. . . . So you are no longer a slave, but a son; and since you are a son, God has made you also an heir. (4:3–5, 7 NIV84)

Children had an extremely low status in Roman times and the children of slaves even lower. Slave children lived in fearful circumstances. They were the property of their parents' owners, to be done with as the master wished. The ruling class considered slave children as illegitimate and granted them virtually no rights. In the early days of Roman law and culture, slaves were not recognized as having legitimate families and relationships. Slave children were often subjected to heavy manual labor, sexual exploitation, and physical abuse, and were routinely separated from their parents.

Contrast this to the privileges of adoption enumerated in the previous chapter. Adopted sons had rights to the family name, possessions, and inheritance. To move from a position of slavery to adoption was a magnificent blessing as dramatic as moving from bondage in a dingy dungeon to living in a costly mansion.

Peter says that a man is a slave to whatever has mastered him (2 Peter 2:19). We will cover seven ways the New Testament speaks of the sinner's captivity. Bondage to sin, fear, and the law will be covered presently. Enslavement to Satan, false gods, and the principles of this world will be covered in chapter 5 on citizenship. Chapter 12 on participation will deal more with the problem of mortality, although we will briefly discuss it in our present chapter when we speak about the fear of death.

Bondage of Our Will

It is no accident that the New Testament authors chose the concept of slavery to express the human condition. A slave has no self-determination of his own. His will is totally subject to the will of his master. If the master returns home in the middle of the night and tells his slave to get up and serve him a meal, the slave cannot tell his master he would rather sleep and do it in the morning. The slave's will is always bound by the will of the owner.

Unfortunately, we have allowed a secular notion of human freedom to enter our Christianity. For some, it is as crude as fashioning humanity as a "tabula rasa," a Latin term meaning a clean slate or tablet. Pictured are people who need a gentle nudge toward the positive things in order to effectively contribute to society as a whole or to their own self-actualization. For others, it is a view that genuine human freedom involves making choices with no constraints. Salvation cannot be coerced by God. God must present the option to humans who can via unencumbered freewill make a choice for or against God's offer.

However, the biblical picture of sinners can hardly support the notion that humans stand unconstrained and able to make a choice for God. As we saw in our opening chapter, sin is an illness that produces spiritual death and the inability to make positive, spiritual choices.

Apart from Christ, the human will is spiritually incapable of producing anything good.

> For the mind that is set on the flesh is hostile to God, for it does not submit to God's law; indeed, it cannot. Those who are in the flesh cannot please God. (Rom. 8:7–8)

It is what I call "unwilling inability." Those controlled by the sinful nature are both unwilling and incapable of serving God. Evangelicals habitually concentrate on one aspect of our problem—our unwillingness to follow Christ—while ignoring the more fundamental problem—our inability to obey God apart from the Holy Spirit. Before our regeneration we were "*slaves* to various passions and pleasures" (Titus 3:3). This echoes the wisdom of the proverb that states: "The iniquities of the wicked ensnare him, and he is held fast in the cords of his sin" (Prov. 5:22).

We would do better to consider genuine freedom as the ability to act according to the manner in which the creature was originally created. Fallen nature inhibits humans from acting in the way commensurate with their principal design. We were created to glorify and serve God, but sin causes us to egoistically consider our own interests. Is this not the heart of all sin, human will selfishly placing itself above the will of God?

The end product is not a morally free being who can make unconstrained choices, but a morally dead being who displeases God. Sin has taken away the original design and with it, the original freedom of will. Fallen humanity is enslaved to sin and has no ability within itself to gain freedom.

The only people who have genuine free will are those who have been regenerated by the Holy Spirit. They now have the ability to serve and glorify God with their actions. They are able to produce the fruit of righteousness, whereas before their regeneration, they were objects of wrath solely producing works subject to that wrath.[2] It is an oxymoron to speak of free, unregenerate sinners. Unregenerate individuals are slaves to sin and act according to the power of that bondage. If your master is sin, then as its slave, you can do no other (John 8:34; 2 Peter 2:19).

People capable within themselves to wrestle free from the power of sin and death do not need a "deliverer" (Rom. 11:26). A deliverer

---

2. Rom. 6:20; Eph. 2:1–3; Titus 1:16.

is needed when people cannot do it themselves. This is why Scripture frequently speaks of sinners as "captives," and why Paul can speak of unregenerate humanity as "powerless" apart from Christ.[3] It is human ignorance or arrogance that speaks of unregenerate sinners as free beings, when Scripture consistently refers to us as dead and powerless hostages to a depraved nature.

Someone may object. "Do we not make free choices each and every day? Is this just a game played by God, who already has made all the choices for us?" However, we cannot pluck an individual out of history and then pretend that nothing has previously happened which affects that person's being.

In Adam all of humanity sinned (Rom. 5:12, 18–19). Human freedom is a fundamental part of the image of God found in human nature, but that nature has been corrupted. If we say that humans today have the ability to make free, spiritual choices apart from the regenerating work of God's Spirit, then we are basically ignoring the inherited condition of sin passed down from Adam.

However, we should clarify what this discussion of limited freedom is *not* saying. Humans make choices every day, like what to eat, or where to go, or when to sleep. Although our sinful nature affects everything we do, human freedom has not been lost in these areas. However, when it comes to the ability to make *spiritually* praiseworthy choices, no such aptitude is present in someone who does not have the indwelling Spirit.

Because Scripture speaks to believers as free to choose between good and evil, we make the mistake that this principle equally applies to the unregenerate. However, the only people who are capable of making positive spiritual choices are those who have been set free from their bondage to sin. As Jesus says, "That which is born of the flesh is flesh, and that which is born of the Spirit is spirit" (John 3:6). If you are not born again, you remain spiritually dead. Unregenerate humans cannot choose to follow God.[4]

---

3. Acts 8:23; 2 Tim. 2:26; Rom. 5:6.

4. The common mistake "seeker-oriented" churches make is to ignore this fact about the human condition. In an attempt to make church palatable for the unchurched— deemphasizing the "negative" aspects of Christianity (e.g., sin, hell, judgment)—these churches have unwittingly robbed the gospel of its power to save by removing the offense of the gospel. You can hardly speak of salvation when you do not speak about the things from which you are saved.

This talk about bondage of the will leads some to claim that sinners cannot be held accountable because they are under a power far greater than themselves. While some falsely claim "the devil made me do it," others will assert "God foreordained it." Those attempting to find sin's origin in God's preordination, thus dodging their own responsibility, appear to find kin in the audience for James' epistle.

> Let no one say when he is tempted, "I am being tempted by God," for God cannot be tempted with evil, and he himself tempts no one. But each person is tempted when he is lured and enticed by his own desire. Then desire when it has conceived gives birth to sin, and sin when it is fully grown brings forth death. (James 1:13–15)

Any talk of God's will somehow precluding human freedom is just a theological red herring. As Scripture makes clear, humans make willing choices and bear the consequences. People who attempt to skirt individual responsibility by appealing to the predetermining activity of God are fooling themselves.

It would be unfair if God created beings capable only of sinning, or coerced them to sin against their will, and then held them accountable.[5] However, neither of these is the biblical picture. Humanity's bondage of will is a direct result of humanity's rebellion against God. We have gotten ourselves into this mess, and we have no one else to blame for it, not Satan, and certainly not God.

All humans are in bondage to the fallen nature inherited from Adam. Only in the last Adam do we have genuine freedom of will, and this comes via a rebirth that occurs through the sovereign activity of God's Spirit. Every individual has one of two masters. Some are controlled by the sinful nature, others by God's Spirit.[6] The sole outcome of the sinful nature is destruction, while the Spirit is a gentle comforter who brings peace and purpose to our lives. Under his control, believers become "slaves to righteousness" (Rom. 6:18 NIV).

---

5. Paul foresaw these complaints in his discussion in Romans 9:14–21.

6. Romans 8 makes the distinction between two kinds of people, those controlled by the sinful flesh and those controlled by the Holy Spirit. There is no third, neutral position, any more than there can be a neutral position between being alive and being dead.

Bondage of Our Emotions

Not only is our will enslaved, but so too are our emotions. The New Testament emphasizes two kinds of fear. The first is the natural fear of death that all humans experience.

> Since therefore the children share in flesh and blood, he himself likewise partook of the same things, that through death he might destroy the one who has the power of death, that is, the devil, and deliver all those who through fear of death were subject to lifelong slavery. (Heb. 2:14–15)

I hate death. It oppresses me, to be honest. Everything around us has the stench of death upon it. It is the enemy of humankind, the great equalizer that befalls rich and poor, foolish and wise alike. It does not discriminate based on color or ethnicity, nationality or gender. All succumb to it and it is inevitable.

If you find this depressing, that's good! Death is a curse designed to humble us. It is a notification that we are not sovereign, that despite the lie the serpent gave Adam and Eve in the garden, we will not become like God if we eat the fruit. It is a reminder of our utter dependence upon God for life. It is the proof that puts the lie to our spiritual arrogance— that we do not need God, that we are the measure of all things.

For unbelievers, Christianity appears to have a morbid fixation with death. It is nothing more than a morose, guilt-ridden, fear-inflicting religion. However, we should not be fooled. Even atheists fear death, despite their brash statements to the contrary.

Hebrews 9:26 says that the God-man has appeared "once for all . . . to put away sin." I love that phrase, not simply for what it says Jesus did, but for what it says I do not have to do. I rightly deserve death, bearing the full weight of my guilt. The old covenant taught that death was required in order to cover sins. Blood must be shed. The new covenant says nothing different. Yet, Christians have the assurance that Christ has "abolished death and brought life and immortality to light through the gospel" (2 Tim. 1:10).

Death is an enemy that must be destroyed. Paul refers to the sting of death (1 Cor. 15:55), echoing an Old Testament prophet:

> I will ransom them from the power of the grave;
>> I will redeem them from death.
> Where, O death, are your plagues?
>> Where, O grave, is your destruction? (Hos. 13:14 NIV84)

We will all die one day, but there is a vast difference between dying with that burden entirely lifted, and dying while bearing your own sins. People will often say that the fear experienced in death is the fear of the unknown, but I think that is exactly backward. Is not the universal fear of death a sign that, deep inside, all humans implicitly know that judgment awaits them? It is fear of the known not the unknown.

Thus, there is a second kind of fear that Scripture repeatedly mentions, the fear of God. However, with this fear there is both a healthy aspect and an unhealthy one. While it is perfectly rational for sinners to fear God and his judgment, Christians are no longer expected to share this fear. John says in his first epistle,

> There is no fear in love, but perfect love casts out fear. For fear has to do with punishment, and whoever fears has not been perfected in love. (1 John 4:18)

Slavery to fear is another aspect removed by the redemptive work of Christ. As redeemed children, our relationship with our Maker is based on love, not fear of condemnation.

Bondage of Our Sinful Flesh

I opened this chapter with an illustration concerning two NFL players addicted either to drugs or sex. Humans are prone to various forms of addiction, and it is a powerful reminder that our struggle with the sinful flesh is all too real. Whether it be substance abuse, sexual obsession, or addiction to work or praise or money or body-altering procedures, or one of the countless temptations that look to entrap and enslave us, fallen humans have found myriad ways to tumble into compulsive, addictive behavior.

While I do not intend to engage the psychology of addiction, I will note that, biblically speaking, all sin finds its root in human will. No matter the problem, the source can always be boiled down to a sinner making a sinful choice. This is proved with statements made by Paul and James.

Witnessing and the Language of Redemption

In witnessing to someone under the grip of addiction, we should concentrate on the redemption model of salvation: "Jesus has come to set the captives free." Hammering an addict over the head about his sin might not be the wisest evangelistic tactic. Emphasizing his need for liberation—and the Liberator who alone can accomplish it—may be a far better approach.

James writes that people sin when they are "lured and enticed by [their] own desire" (James 1:14). In fact, he likens it to the birth process, from conception to delivery to growth to death. Sinful desire originates within us. If it did not, Satan would have nothing with which to tempt us. Paul concurs:

> No temptation has overtaken you that is not common to man. God is faithful, and he will not let you be tempted beyond your ability, but with the temptation he will also provide the way of escape, that you may be able to endure it. (1 Cor. 10:13)

Both James and Paul reason that sin is the result of our own stubborn refusal to obey God, not of an overbearing force outside ourselves that compels us beyond our control to do evil.[7]

However, in highly successful rehabilitation programs like Alcoholics Anonymous, the need for accountability partners and reliance on a "Higher Power" appear necessary in order to overcome one's addiction. This suggests that an addicted person is incapable of turning from his compulsion until help comes from outside himself.

So which is it, addiction is a coercion that cannot be helped, or merely a sinful choice a person could otherwise not make? The answer can be found in the basic difference between being saved and being an unbeliever.

A Wheaton College professor shared from his pre-conversion days that despite knowing his enslavement to drinking was destroying his

---

7. Jesus similarly notes that from the heart come evil thoughts, etc. (Mark 7:21).

body, he could not stop it. In a fit of despair, he committed his life to Christ. That very night he stopped drinking and never tasted alcohol again. A current student at the Bible college where I teach in South Africa has a similar testimony about the instant freedom from drug abuse he experienced at his conversion.

While I cannot give a precise answer why some Christians do not experience immediate victory, perhaps it is because God wants to teach us dependence upon him. I can only surmise that continued struggle with sin until we die is part of God's plan to break us and mold us into the image of Christ. God may allow Christians to wrestle with besetting sins for decades, simply to sever them from pride and spiritual self-reliance.

Immediate freedom from all sins for the rest of our days on earth might produce a spiritual arrogance in us. The enticement of spiritual self-reliance normally does not befall the young in the faith but the very old, those Christians who have walked for decades and are subsequently tempted to believe they are not as bad as others. I can see how fifty years of sinless living could produce spiritual pride rather than thanksgiving for what God did. As fallen humans, we are in the habit of forgetting the gracious acts of God.

Freedom from sin is only granted to Christians. Paul's statement in 1 Corinthians 10:13 tells believers that they have not been seized by any temptation that cannot be overcome. He is not talking to non-Christians, who Paul establishes elsewhere are controlled by the sinful flesh and cannot do anything spiritually pleasing to God (Rom. 8:7–8). The difference, as we have already established, is the indwelling of the Holy Spirit.

I foresee the objection that unbelievers do in fact receive freedom from addiction, as countless non-Christians can attest through successful rehab programs. But let's not confuse temporary freedom from a temporary addiction with the permanent fallen state of sinners. God, in his common grace, grants blessings to unbelievers (e.g., Matt. 5:45), but they still remain enslaved to their fallen condition. Christians alone are granted permanent freedom from the effects of the fall, now with a renewed will and, along with the assistance of God's indwelling Spirit, the ability to overcome every sin. Through God's grace unbelievers may overcome a compulsion here or there, but they still remain subject to the slavery of a fallen will and sinful flesh.

Paul juxtaposes the Spirit and the flesh when he writes,

> But I say, walk by the Spirit, and you will not gratify the desires of the flesh. For the desires of the flesh are against the Spirit, and the desires of the Spirit are against the flesh, for these are opposed to each other, to keep you from doing the things you want to do. (Gal. 5:16–17)

Again, this command is to Christians. Unbelievers cannot "walk by the Spirit." However, believers walking by the Spirit have the ability to "not gratify the desires of the flesh."

If this is true, that no temptation has ever come across a Christian that is not common to all, and that sin is nothing more than the Christian yielding to his fleshly desires, then how can addiction as commonly understood (i.e., uncontrollable urges and impulses) actually exist for believers?

James teaches us to "resist the devil, and he will flee from you," and Peter similarly commands believers to "resist him, standing firm in the faith."[8] This is an incredible image of Christians standing before a ravenous lion looking to devour them. Yet, in faithfully resisting Satan as Jesus did in the wilderness, believers will cause the beast to flee. This means that the devil is not an irresistible force, and if God always provides a way out for believers under temptation, then sin is not an irresistible force either.

Granted, sin can certainly feel irresistible, but perhaps it feels that way because we capitulate to it far too readily. We have not built up the essential perseverance to repel it. We have repeatedly said yes, and like muscles that have atrophied from disuse, our spirit has become weak because we have not exercised the fortitude to resist temptation as we ought.

This is the underlying assumption of Paul's argument in Romans 6 when he says:

- "Let not sin therefore reign in your mortal body, to make you obey its passions" (v. 12),
- "do not offer any part of yourself to sin" (v. 13 NIV), and
- "sin will have no dominion over you" (v. 14).

---

8. James 4:7; 1 Peter 5:9 (NIV).

Often Christians willingly submit themselves to the mastery of sin, and then claim they are under an uncontrollable urge or force.

We begin to get a picture of the extreme difference between the Christian and the non-Christian. Indwelled by the Holy Spirit and given the ability to turn away from sin, the believer is capable of resisting Satan and producing fruit pleasing to God. On the other hand, the unbeliever has a will that is spiritually dead. He has no ability to resist Satan. His loyalty is as a slave to the master of darkness, with no freedom to exercise any allegiance elsewhere. The contrast is unambiguous. A person is either capable of resisting temptation and the devil, or succumbing to both.

Christians alone have the ability to say "No!" to Satan and to temptation. Overcoming sin is the act of a regenerated will in cooperation with the restraining activity of God's Spirit, who helps us "put to death the deeds of the body" (Rom. 8:13).[9] There is no temptation too difficult for believers to withstand. If this were not the case, then of what value would the indwelling Spirit and a sympathetic God be to us?[10] Learning to say no (Titus 2:12) will help us become more like Christ.

Redemption Abused

Unfortunately, this Christ as liberator redemption model has been manipulated. The "prosperity gospel" teaches freedom from sickness or financial difficulty or lack of success in the workplace. Feminist theologians have used it to speak of female liberation from male supremacy. Even homosexual activists have utilized it to speak of the liberation of homosexuals from a heterosexual-dominated society.[11]

---

9. One of the qualities of character produced in believers as fruit of the Spirit is self-control (Gal. 5:23). This self-control becomes an act of cooperation as we yield to the Spirit's leading.

10. This seems to contradict the experience of the apostle Paul who in Romans 7 recounts his struggle with sin, doing what he does not want to do. However, there is much debate concerning Paul's spiritual state. Is he speaking about a genuine believer's struggle with sin, or an unregenerate Jew under the law of God, without the indwelling Spirit? The latter makes more sense in the entire scope of New Testament teaching on believers and sin, as well as chapter 8 where Paul then introduces the contrast between those controlled by the sinful nature and those controlled by the Spirit.

11. It has also been used in Africa to speak of freedom from white domination, such as during independence struggles against colonialism and apartheid.

The problem with these errant models is that they miss the main reason why Jesus came. However, one particular passage from the Gospels seems to support their position:

> The scroll of the prophet Isaiah was handed to him. Unrolling it, he found the place where it is written: "The Spirit of the Lord is on me, because he has anointed me to preach good news to the poor. He has sent me to proclaim freedom for the prisoners and recovery of sight for the blind, to release the oppressed, to proclaim the year of the Lord's favor." Then he rolled up the scroll, gave it back to the attendant and sat down. The eyes of everyone in the synagogue were fastened on him, and he began by saying to them, "Today this scripture is fulfilled in your hearing." (Luke 4:17–21 NIV84)

If taken out of context, the quotation from Isaiah appears to teach that the Messiah came to bring freedom from poverty, oppression, and physical ailment, much like prosperity gospel adherents proclaim. However, this confuses the temporary signs of Christ's messianic ministry with the eternal purposes of his coming.

In speaking to the Jews, Jesus says, "If you abide in my word, you are truly my disciples, and you will know the truth, and the truth will set you free" (John 8:31–32). The Jews respond that they are children of Abraham and have never been slaves to anyone, so how can Jesus promise them freedom. To which Jesus replies,

> I tell you the truth, everyone who sins is a slave to sin. . . .
> So if the Son sets you free, you will be free indeed. (vv. 34, 36 NIV84)

This is the kind of freedom Jesus envisions coming from his ministry. As miserable as poverty is—and after twenty years living in Africa I have seen firsthand how damaging it can be—it is temporary. There is a far greater oppressor, one that can keep a person in bondage not only in this life, but also in the life to come. The miraculous acts that Jesus performed over the physical realm—giving sight to the blind, healing the lame, bringing back the dead—were signs that pointed to an even greater power, the power to forgive sins. This is precisely what Jesus said when he healed the paralytic, proving that he had the authority to forgive sins by raising the crippled man to his feet (Luke 5:23–24).

As difficult as it is to be without sight—and as wonderful as it must be for a blind man to miraculously gain his vision—if the man dies without having the problem of his sins dealt with, it will matter little if he goes into the next life with healthy eyes or visionless ones. Of what benefit is temporary, physical sight when compared to eternal, spiritual blindness?

Similarly, as glorious as it was for Lazarus to be brought back from the dead (John 11), Lazarus eventually died. His resuscitation was temporary.[12] If Jesus merely came to give a dying man a few more years to live before continuing in his slavery to sin and death, of what value is being raised to life?

This corresponds with the whole sweep of salvation history. The greatest act of redemption in the Old Testament was the exodus of the Jews from Egyptian captivity, "out of the land of slavery" (Exod. 20:2 NIV).[13] This grand display of God's love for his people is used throughout the Hebrew Scriptures as the supreme proof of God's salvation for his people. Yet, the vast majority of Israelites who came out of Egypt died in the desert.[14] Why? Because the Israelites did not have faith.

Interestingly, most Jews in the first century made the same error the prosperity gospel makes today. The Jews expected a Messiah in the mold of a warrior-king, a Davidic ruler who would throw off Roman oppression and reinstate prosperity to Israel. Indeed, Jesus came to throw off oppression, but not the kind the Jews expected. He destroyed the work of the devil, crushed the power of death, and broke the rule of sin, problems far more severe than the temporary oppression of a temporary regime. Roman oppression became worse after Jesus, not

---

12. A resuscitation occurs when someone is brought back to life but dies later anyway. A resurrection occurs when someone is brought back to life, never to die again. Scripture states that Jesus is the first person to be resurrected from the dead (1 Cor. 15:20; Acts 17:31b).

13. Stephen (Acts 7) makes the connection between the exodus and Jesus, and Paul notes in 1 Corinthians 10 that the Old Testament accounts are replete with moral and spiritual significance and thus are examples for Christians to heed. Taking such instruction from God's Word engenders endurance, encouragement, and hope (Rom. 15:4).

14. 1 Cor. 10:5; Heb. 3:16–19.

better, and forty years after the ascension of Christ, Israel was obliterated by Roman armies.

Jesus says that in this world we will have tribulation, but we should take heart, because he has overcome the world (John 16:33). The prosperity gospel turns this into a false promise: "I have overcome the world, so you should prosper in it."[15] When we make temporal issues the sole reason for the coming of Christ, we lose sight of the momentous work that Jesus came to do. Consequently, we display a gross misunderstanding of the gospel.

The Benefits of Being Redeemed

In redemption, there is the person being redeemed and the price paid to redeem this person. The biblical authors envision a ransom paid on behalf of sinners, a payment that involves nothing less than the blood of the eternal Son of God.[16] In characterizing his own ministry, Jesus used this marketplace language:

> For even the Son of Man came not to be served but to serve,
> and to give his life as a ransom for many. (Mark 10:45)

Like modern kidnapping, that ransom was the payment for freedom, but it can also be understood as purchasing slaves for God's service. Christians are slaves to righteousness. We have not been purchased so we can merely go our own way. We have been procured to serve our Redeemer.[17] John speaks of the Lamb who "ransomed people for God"; others are considered "redeemed from mankind as firstfruits for God."[18] The picture is one of redemption with the purpose of service for God and his kingdom.

---

15. This is usually coupled with the teaching that difficulty in this life is the result of a lack of faith. However, Job, Jesus, and Paul with his "thorn . . . in the flesh" (2 Cor. 12:7) were righteous men purposefully subjected to suffering and physical turmoil by the express will of God. Their adverse condition was hardly the result of their lack of faith.

16. Acts 20:28, Eph. 1:7; Heb. 9:12.

17. "Redeemer" is used in the Old Testament to refer to God, but never to Jesus in the New Testament. This is probably because the one doing the redeeming is God the Father, while the Son serves as the payment for that redemption.

18. Rev. 5:9; 14:3–4.

> [Jesus] gave himself for us to redeem us from all lawlessness
> and to purify for himself a people for his own possession who
> are zealous for good works. (Titus 2:14)

Worship and the Language of Redemption

Much of Christian worship today is lifeless and listless. We offer passionless prayers or sing as if we are still captive people. But as redeemed men and women whose freedom has been secured by Christ's blood, our worship should be characterized by an evident joy in being liberated. While we do not look to falsely manufacture emotionalism, a genuine emotional response in worship should be expected as we celebrate the gracious freedom granted us in Christ.

Christians look forward to the "redemption of our bodies" (Rom. 8:23), but this is a future hope at the consummation of all things. Yet, believers experience present benefits. As redeemed people, we are able now to put to death the misdeeds of the body (Rom. 8:13), something that slaves to sin are incapable of doing. In fact, following Paul's example (1 Cor. 9:27), we should make our bodies our slaves, not the other way around.

> You are not your own, for you were bought with a price. So
> glorify God in your body. (1 Cor. 6:19b–20)

As Christians we must not abuse this newfound freedom. Peter commands, "Live as people who are free, not using your freedom as a cover-up for evil, but living as servants of God." Paul writes, "You, my brothers, were called to be free. But do not use your freedom to indulge the sinful nature."[19]

However, Paul states that Christ has redeemed believers "from the curse of the law." He rebukes the Galatians for wanting to turn back to the law, what he calls a "yoke of slavery."[20] How can the commandments

---

19. 1 Peter 2:16; Gal. 5:13a NIV84; also Rom. 6:12–13.
20. Gal. 3:13; 5:1.

God himself gave to his chosen people be considered a curse and yoke that must be removed?

The Galatians were being deceived by erring Jewish Christians ("Judaizers") who believed that in order to follow Jesus, a person first should become an adherent of the Jewish law. In other words, faith in Jesus coupled with strict adherence to the dos and don'ts of Jewish custom and ritual, especially circumcision, were necessary for salvation. Paul objects so strongly to this teaching that he declares it a false gospel deserving eternal condemnation (Gal. 1:6–9). However, because we are not first-century Gentiles being wooed by Jewish legalists, does this apply to us today?

The answer is yes, because Christians often make the same mistake. Christians who combine faith in Jesus with their self-made rules and regulations—no dancing or going to movies or playing with "face cards"— make the error of the Judaizers of Galatia. This legalism adds additional requirements to the new covenant that are completely unnecessary for salvation, much like the Pharisees did with the old covenant. We must be careful that our gospel is never a "Jesus plus" message. Legalistic systems inherently empty the gospel of grace, subject their adherents to boasting, and cause them to be slaves to fear with worrying if they have done enough to merit salvation.

> For this reason Christ is the mediator of a new covenant, that those who are called may receive the promised eternal inheritance—now that he has died as a ransom to set them free from the sins committed under the first covenant. (Heb. 9:15 NIV)

Further practical value of redemption is that we should be slow to judge unbelievers who are still held hostage and blinded by the god of this age (2 Cor. 4:4). Instead of looking down on unbelievers as many Christians do, we should be honest with ourselves. The adage is true, "There go I but for the grace of God." This knowledge of redemption should humble us; there is no room for spiritual arrogance in a gospel of grace.

More Than a Crutch

The detractors of Christianity say our faith is nothing more than a crutch, and there are some Christians who are embarrassed to admit even that. I, on the other hand, think the crutch analogy is a gross understatement. My problem is not that I am wounded needing the temporary assistance of a walking stick. I require a body cast in which every part of my being requires support and assistance. There is nothing about me that does not need freedom from this body of sin. I need a Liberator!

What does it mean to be saved? It means removing the chains that bind my will and emotions. It means having the ransom paid for my freedom from sin, death, and the devil. It means being set free to genuinely serve God. It means moving from bondage to liberation.

> Now the Lord is the Spirit, and where the Spirit of the Lord is,
> there is freedom.
>
> *2 Corinthians 3:17*

Key Terms for Salvation Expressed in the Language of the Marketplace

redemption, ransom, redeem, Redeemer, liberation, deliverer, freedom, purchase, slavery, bondage, captive, master

Questions for Group Discussion

1. If a person is spiritually dead and his will in bondage to sin, how can he exercise faith in Jesus? What must first happen before such a person is capable of believing the gospel?

2. How many believers are enslaved by legalistic notions of the Christian faith—self-made rules and regulations that falsely bind their consciences? Do legalistic Christians truly understand the gospel?

3. "The fear of the LORD is the beginning of wisdom" (Prov. 9:10): Yet, Christians need not fear God's condemnation. Discuss a healthy balance between fearing and not fearing the Lord, and how a Christian striving to live a holy life might achieve that balance.

4. Some Christians claim that for believers, uncontrollable addiction is not possible. What might you say to such a Christian, and how would you support your answer biblically?

5

The Language of Politics
From Satan's Kingdom to God's Kingdom

CITIZENSHIP

So then you are no longer strangers and aliens, but you are fellow *citizens* with the saints and members of the household of God.

Ephesians 2:19

As we consider our fifth model of salvation, we find the language of politics. There is no mystery when it comes to the plain meaning of the Greek words *sympolites* and *politeuma* translated "citizenship." Even someone who does not understand Greek can recognize that both words employ *polite* from which our English "politics" comes. In the first century, the word denoted a special privilege belonging to people who possess residency in a particular country.

The apostle Paul undoubtedly knew about the importance of citizenship. The Roman Empire granted special rights to its citizens. Paul appealed to this benefit when a Roman centurion was about to flog him in Jerusalem (Acts 22:25). Citizens of Rome were not subject to humiliating forms of public punishment such as scourging, flogging, and crucifixion. Whereas a random Jew could be grabbed off the street and degraded at the whim of a Roman soldier (e.g., Simon of Cyrene forced to carry the cross of Jesus), this should never happen to a Roman citizen. He had rights. Citizenship indeed had its benefits.

Our citizenship determines our allegiance, and from our allegiance comes our destiny. Citizenship in the wrong kingdom will bring certain doom; one kingdom alone will be eternally victorious.

The biblical authors have much to say about citizenship and what it means to live in one of two opposing camps. You are either a citizen of the world or a citizen of heaven. With this chapter, we are going to look at both sides of the situation—what it means to be at home in the world, and what it means to be a stranger in it.

Strangers in a Strange Land

There are few things more frustrating to a missionary than the reminder that you are an alien. As much as I want to believe I have become "African"—and after twenty years as a missionary on the continent I think I have to some extent—the fact is, I am still a stranger in a strange land.

There has always been an uneasiness with living overseas. You are constantly at the whim of those in power. Be in the wrong place at the wrong time (like I was one day in downtown Windhoek during an impromptu rally against white landowners!), and things can go badly very quickly. Depending on someone's mood or a random event, you may be asked to leave the country with twenty-four hours' notice. Missions history is littered with such incidences.

However, living as believers in this world is not simply being an alien in a foreign land. It is more akin to living as an illegal alien. This is not your permanent home and you have no business pretending that it is. Its customs, values, and belief systems are entirely different to your homeland's. What the people of this world want you do not want. What they strive for you consider insignificant and passing. While you have your mind set on eternal things, they have theirs set on the temporal. While you lay up treasures in heaven, their treasures are subject to moths, rust, and theft. Their worldview is not your own. Like a stranger speaking a foreign tongue, you will never fully be understood by the citizens of the world.

The author of Hebrews, in his great chronicle of the faithful men and women of the Old Testament, writes that these saints were "aliens and strangers on earth," people "seeking a homeland" who "desire a better country, that is, a heavenly one" (Heb. 11:13 NIV84, 14, 16a). The apostle Peter likewise reminds believers as "aliens and strangers in the world, to abstain from sinful desires, which war against your soul."[1]

Christians started as citizens of the world, but upon coming to faith in Jesus, our loyalty was dramatically altered. We used to vote for one party but now we throw our weight behind the other. In the past we fought in the army of one opponent, but presently we are enlisted with his enemy. Our allegiance has changed. We have made a declaration in the heavenly realms that we have switched our commitment from evil to good, from Satan to God, from the kingdom of darkness to the kingdom of light. We have declared war on Satan. Peter puts this new status in terms of ethnicity and nationality when he writes,

> But you are a chosen race, a royal priesthood, a holy nation, a people for his own possession, that you may proclaim the excellencies of him who called you out of darkness into his marvelous light. (1 Peter 2:9)

Our change in citizenship is not a cosmetic alteration. It actually involves an internal transformation that can be verbalized in the language of race. For example, Paul notes that in the church God determined to bring Jew and Gentile together, creating "one new man" (Eph. 2:15) out of the two. It is as if our skin color has changed. Our spiritual DNA is no longer the same. Whose citizen we are should be readily apparent, as much as it is when comparing a native of Africa with someone from Asia.

Witnessing and the Language of Citizenship

In the Great Commission (Matt. 28:18–20), Jesus commands his followers to make disciples of all nations. We can do this because Jesus as Lord and King has the authority to command obedience. It is his presence that guarantees fruit in our evangelism.

---

1. 1 Peter 2:11 NIV84. Depending on the translation, "alien," "foreigner," "exile," and "sojourner" are used in the New Testament to refer to believers as strangers in this world.

In chapter 4 we noted seven things the New Testament says enslave unbelievers. Three of these will be covered in the present chapter: Satan, false gods, and the principles of the world. This all has something to do with which citizenship we possess.

The West versus the Rest

Talk about Satan is falling out of favor in Western Christianity. While the rest of the world embraces belief in the demonic realm with its principalities and powers of spiritual evil, Western Christians are becoming more materialistic in their approach. While I cannot take my own anecdotal experience as a rule, I know that only after coming to Africa at the age of thirty did I begin to take demonic forces seriously, even though Jesus and the New Testament authors consistently speak of them. I wonder why I previously overlooked this important aspect of the biblical worldview. Christians in the West are moving away from a biblical worldview that embraces the reality of a demonic presence, while ironically the non-Christian world increasingly adopts a neo-pagan view of the spiritual realm.

I had a conversation with a relative who believes in God but claims that belief in angels and demons is "primitive thinking from a primitive age." I asked why he believes in the "big spirit" but not in the little ones? There seems to be an inconsistency that he is unwilling to admit. Of course, denying the existence of angels and demons is one step away from full-blown naturalism and atheism.

My father-in-law serves as a missionary in Uganda. There he works with various church leaders in Discipleship Training Ministries, in which they have taught hundreds of pastors in East Africa about making disciples and not simply converts.

He asked me to read through the material. It is straightforward and biblical, making it useful for any culture. However, there was something that made this course decidedly African. In the fourth lesson was a small comment about how those leading the discipleship groups should not worry about curses placed on them by those who oppose Christianity. Surely this would not be included in a discipleship training course in America.

This little example accentuates the differences between cultures and how they view salvation. One culture may be oblivious to something in the Bible that another culture recognizes immediately. In this case, the presence of black magic and witchcraft is all too real in Africa. Yet it is a contextual problem few people in the West will ever encounter.

Through years of teaching African seminarians, I have been amazed with the spiritual forces of darkness they confront. A woman talks for several hours in the middle of the night with her grandmother who has been dead for six months. A man walks to a village and is met along the way by an old friend he has not seen for quite some time. Upon entering the village he learns that his friend died months earlier. The stories can be multiplied a thousandfold.

At first I found the accounts unbelievable, almost silly. "Surely they can't believe these things have happened?" I asked myself. Had I not come with a mind willing to learn from cultures that were foreign to me, I would not have grown in my faith in this respect.

Readers from the West will typically find these accounts unrealistic, and they will look for naturalistic explanations. Their consternation is matched by my African students when I tell them that Americans normally do not have similar experiences. They are amazed when I state that once my grandfather died, I no longer was concerned about him. I did not worry about him coming to me at night in my dreams, or sending calamity upon my family should I not follow his traditions. When he died, as far as I was concerned he permanently left this world for the next.

Don't get me wrong. There have always been people in the West who have embraced spiritism. Recently some people claimed to contact the spirit of assassinated Beatles legend John Lennon. Whether or not this was a gimmick misses the point. You do not make up things that have no chance of being believed. Counterfeit money is only good if real money is circulating. In the scientifically inclined West, we have people who go to gravestones and speak to their departed loved ones, or who believe that Uncle Bill is watching from heaven. We have séances and fortune-tellers and necromancers and clairvoyants, but they generally appeal to a small minority. They are certainly not as widespread as, say, in Africa or other parts of the world where spiritism holds sway.

Given their cultural context, Christians raised in Africa have an immediate connection with the Bible when it reports demonic activity and influence. We in the West need to learn from this, gaining a more balanced view.

For clarity, I am not saying that we must believe in fairies and vampires, no matter how popular television and cinematic portrayals of these beings may be today. Conjuring up orcs and elves is not necessary, but a recognition that Satan and his minions are real is. For starters, Jesus regularly encountered these beings. It is time we in the West stop pretending that Satan does not exist.

The Kingdom of Satan

We noted in our chapter on adoption that unbelievers are outside the family of God. Something similar can be said with respect to citizenship. Paul's commission to the Gentiles given by the risen Lord on the road to Damascus was "to open their eyes, so that they may turn from darkness to light and from the power of Satan to God" (Acts 26:18). The biblical picture of the state of unbelievers is bleak. Apart from Christ, they are blind and under the power of darkness.

If we couple this with Paul's comments in another epistle, the situation is graver still. Note what Paul says about Gentile unbelievers and their status prior to their citizenship in God's kingdom:

> Remember that at that time you were separate from Christ, excluded from citizenship in Israel and foreigners to the covenants of the promise, without hope and without God in the world. (Eph. 2:12 NIV)

Gentiles, not originally part of the chosen people of God, were "without hope and without God." This is a remarkable statement considering the polytheism of the Gentile nations around Israel. Despite their plethora of gods and idols, the apostle can say they were without God. The same applies to unbelievers today. Apart from Christ they are excluded from the promises of God. If they do not have faith in Jesus, they are without God and without hope.

This biblical truth is despicable to our pluralistic world. As a result, there is a constant pull within particular Christian circles to paint a rosier picture. Evangelicals, especially in academia, are becoming more open to non-Christian religions as vehicles of salvation. Adherents of other religions who are morally upright and coincidentally follow part of Jesus' teaching, despite not knowing specifically about Christ, are referred to as "anonymous Christians," implying they are justified by him nonetheless. This kind of inclusive approach to Christianity tends to downplay the demonic activity found in other faiths.

We often envision "spiritual warfare" as dealing with overt satanic activity such as demonic possession, but false doctrine is as much an element of spiritual warfare as are witchcraft and Ouija boards.[2] It just is not as sensationalistic; it is far more subtle.

I wrote in the initial draft of my doctoral dissertation that non-Christian religions were inspired by the devil. Paul, for example, speaks of "seducing spirits and doctrines of demons."[3] But I was told that I needed to tone down this language. I am certain that the first individuals happiest about muting talk about demons are the demons themselves.

There are two equally harmful positions Christians can take when it comes to our enemy the devil. Some utterly ignore him. They doubt very much that he exists, or if he does exist, they attribute little to his activity. Satan was fine during the time of the Bible, but now he is nowhere to be seen. Many border on calling him a myth, and the popular depiction of Satan dressed in red tights sporting a pitch fork, horns, and a tail adds to the lore.

Consequently, those who ignore the existence of an enemy are caught off guard when that enemy attacks. Every author of the New Testament portrays the devil as personal and real. The Gospel writers, Peter and John in their epistles, James, Jude, and Paul all describe the devil not as a "force" or as a metaphorical depiction of the evil within human beings, but as a living, personal being.[4]

Consider this sampling of New Testament statements about him:

- He is the ruler of this world (John 12:31) and the god of this world who has blinded the eyes of unbelievers (2 Cor. 4:4).

---

2. We will deal more with spiritual warfare in chapter 13 on the language of the military.

3. 1 Tim. 4:1 ASV. James 3:15–16 likewise speaks of demonic wisdom that yields jealousy, selfish ambition, disorder, and vile practices.

4. I recently heard this apropos comment by a Bulgarian pastor during a visit I made to his country: "There are some people who claim to believe in God but do not serve him; there are others who do not believe in the existence of Satan but serve him." This echoes a sentiment made by the Puritan father Cotton Mather in his *The Wonders of the Invisible World* (1692): "That there is a Devil, is a thing doubted by none but such as are under the influences of the Devil."

- He holds the power of death (Heb. 2:14).
- Paul was hindered by Satan from visiting believers in Thessalonica (1 Thess. 2:18).
- Satan can perform counterfeit signs and wonders (2 Thess. 2:9) and can pose as an angel of light (2 Cor. 11:14).
- Believers, if they are not careful, can fall into the snare of the devil (1 Tim. 3:7) and be captured by him (2 Tim. 2:26).
- Paul speaks of handing over false brothers to Satan "to be taught not to blaspheme" (1 Tim. 1:20 NIV).

On the other hand, there are those who are fixated on Satan and his demons of darkness. Day and night they dwell on them. In their prayers to God they pause to rebuke Satan and at times one wonders to whom they are praying. Every rock, every tree, every bush has a demon hiding behind it. If their car breaks down during rush-hour traffic, it was the work of the devil. A person who opposes their position in a church meeting is being used by Satan. Books they read, lectures they attend, thoughts they entertain are obsessed with Satan and his minions, and the lordship of Christ is swallowed up in their fascination with the forces of evil.

Both positions are equally damaging. In the first place, those who ignore Satan are ill-prepared for his attacks, while those who are fixated on him give Satan too much credit and live lives outside the victory won by Christ.

What we need to know about our enemy is that he is alive and active. Scripture calls or compares him to a lion, a dragon, an accuser, a deceiver, a murderer, a liar, a destroyer, and a tempter.[5] Jesus confronted him personally in the wilderness. He is pictured in the book of Job as having access to the throne of God. He is the accuser of the faithful. Peter implores us to be alert because our enemy "prowls around like a roaring lion, seeking someone to devour" (1 Peter 5:8). This is why John commands us to not believe every spirit but to "test the spirits to see whether they are from God" (1 John 4:1).

But he is also defeated. Jesus saw him fall from the sky like lightning as his disciples spread the Good News (Luke 10:18). Satan's hold on sinners was crushed by the atoning work of Christ on the cross, and

---

5. 1 Peter 5:8; Rev. 12:9–10; John 8:44; Rev. 9:11; 1 Thess. 3:5.

when Satan thought he had the very Son of God in his grasp, Jesus broke the gates of hell and rose from the dead!

> The reason the Son of God appeared was to destroy the works
> of the devil. (1 John 3:8b)

Our enemy is alive but fatally wounded, which makes him especially dangerous. His time is short and he knows it, and he will attack the children of God with a vengeance.

Christ's victory over the devil is not solely found in his death, but is established through his whole life, which was a constant struggle with Satan (Luke 4:13). Of course, the final and decisive battle was at the cross (Col. 2:15), but we should not view the ministry of Jesus in a minimalistic manner, concentrating on the last week of his life, as if the other thirty-three years are of little significance. From virgin birth to crucifixion and resurrection, Christ engaged the powers of evil and won decisively. He entered under the conditions of law and death to take up the conflict with the forces of darkness. No power was able to subdue these forces other than God himself becoming a man.

The Devil's Playground

Scripture makes it clear that Satan's power is mainly expressed through the world and its systems that are contrary to God.

> We know that we are from God, and the whole world lies in
> the power of the evil one. (1 John 5:19)

As I am writing this chapter, the Hollywood blockbuster *Noah* is in cinemas. While this movie is nowhere near being faithful to the biblical account, it still can serve as a sober reminder of what standing up against the world involves.

Noah was the only man in his day who was considered righteous by God. Imagine if that were your situation, the lone believer on the entire planet. How difficult would your struggle be against a world completely devoted to wickedness and evil ways? Yet, as believers, we do experience this struggle.

The great Old Testament themes of slavery and exile, leading to exodus and freedom, are met in the New Testament with the idea of

God's people as spiritual strangers in a world ruled by Satan and hostile to Christ. In this sense, Jesus can say to the corrupt Jewish religious leaders, "You are from below; I am from above" (John 8:23).

The world hated Jesus, therefore it will hate his followers (John 17:14). Believers are frequently singled out or persecuted for biblical views that are contrary to the reigning paradigms of the world. Christians in academia who disagree with the naturalistic theory of evolution are openly mocked. Take a stance against gay marriage or abortion and expect to be ridiculed and slandered. Such pressure can cause weaker believers to wane in their conviction.

Paul names six men in his second letter to Timothy who had forsaken the Christian faith.[6] Of particular note is Demas, who deserted Paul because he "loved this world" (2 Tim. 4:10 NIV). In Colossians 4:14 Paul notes that both Demas and Luke are ministry companions. Perhaps the ministry was too difficult, or there were better opportunities for Demas back in Thessalonica.

Today the pressure to conform to the world's standards has tempted Christians to dress a certain way, listen to ungodly music, even to adjust Christian worship to imitate worldly standards of entertainment in an attempt to appear suitable to the world. Yet, acceptance by the world means we have denied the gospel.

Worship and the Language of Citizenship

Like any citizens of a country, Christians speak their own language, the language of heaven. Many churches, in a desire to reach the unreached, have changed the language of Christian worship, making it conform more to the world's standards. By excising the biblical offense of the gospel and replacing it with worldly ideals of tolerance, they preach a "gospel" that cannot save. Worship that is not biblical is worldly worship. As our citizenship is heavenly, so should our worship be.

---

6. The six men are Phygelus and Hermogenes (1:15), Hymenaeus and Philetus (2:17), Demas (4:10), and Alexander the metalworker (4:14). Paul says everyone in the province of Asia deserted him. "At my first defense, no one came to my support, but everyone deserted me" (2 Tim. 1:15; 4:16 NIV).

> You adulterous people! Do you not know that friendship with
> the world is enmity with God? Therefore whoever wishes to
> be a friend of the world makes himself an enemy of God.
> (James 4:4)

Paul writes that Jews and Gentiles apart from Christ were enslaved to the "basic principles of the world" (Gal. 4:3 NIV84). We have already seen that Satan is the ruler of this world, so it stands to reason that its principles come from him, in collusion with fallen human nature. In this same Galatian passage, Paul later speaks of Gentiles formerly being "slaves to those who by nature are not gods" (v. 8 NIV). This is a reference to the idolatrous practices of pagan religions, which Paul connects elsewhere to demons.[7]

Jesus came to free us from enslavement to the world's principles. In fact, only in Christ do we have this freedom. However, Paul warns believers to not fall back into their previous captivity. "See to it that no one takes you captive by philosophy and empty deceit, according to human tradition, according to the elemental spirits of the world, and not according to Christ" (Col. 2:8). Paul is speaking to believers who must be vigilant in guarding the faith. Visit a local Christian bookstore to see how many Christians have imbibed the world's principles, creating a monstrous combination of biblical and nonbiblical philosophies.

Every other religious system finds its source in Satan and the patterns of this sinful, fallen world. We would be foolish to emulate values and behaviors that are contrary to Christ.

> If then you have been raised with Christ, seek the things that
> are above, where Christ is, seated at the right hand of God.
> Set your minds on things that are above, not on things that
> are on earth. (Col. 3:1–2)

When Paul says that Christ is seated at the "right hand of God," this phrase speaks of his power and authority. All authority in heaven and on earth has been given to him (Matt. 28:18). We call him Lord because he is the sovereign ruler of the kingdom.

---

7. 1 Cor. 10:20. The idolatrous Israelites similarly "sacrificed to demons" (Deut. 32:17; Ps. 106:36–37).

He who is the blessed and only Sovereign, the King of kings
and Lord of lords. (1 Tim. 6:15)

The Greek for "sovereign" is where we get our English "dynasty." It is
kingdom language. Jesus is the long-awaited Davidic king whose throne
will be established forever. This is why the angel Gabriel told Mary that
the child she carried "will reign over the house of Jacob forever, and of
his kingdom there will be no end."[8] However, Jesus is not merely King
of the Jews. He is the sovereign King above all kings. As such, every knee
shall bow to him.[9]

We are told elsewhere that other things currently reign in this
world, like sin and death (Rom. 5:14, 17, 21). Thus we see two kingdoms
in conflict. Jesus told Pilate that his kingdom is not of this world (John
18:36). A supreme contrast between the values and ideals of the world
and those of the citizens of heaven is found in Jesus' words in the
Sermon on the Mount, where he juxtaposes treasures laid up in heaven
with treasures on earth (Matt. 6:19–20). There the values of the world
(e.g., hatred, lust, oath breaking, retaliation, divorce) are contrasted
with the ideals Jesus lays before the citizens of God's kingdom. Those
citizens are peacemakers, pursuers of righteousness, humble people of
integrity. They do not retaliate when harmed, they rejoice in persecution
for Christ's sake, they love their enemies and pursue heavenly treasures
of eternal consequence and value.

In Paul's letter to the Galatian believers, he contrasts the fruit of the
Spirit with the characteristics of the citizens of the kingdom of Satan.

Now the works of the flesh are evident: sexual immorality,
impurity, sensuality, idolatry, sorcery, enmity, strife, jealousy,
fits of anger, rivalries, dissensions, divisions, envy, drunkenness, orgies, and things like these. I warn you, as I warned
you before, that those who do such things will not inherit the
kingdom of God. (Gal. 5:19–21)

John writes, "The world is passing away along with its desires"
(1 John 2:17). Unfortunately, Christians often trade the things of
God for the things of the world. Therefore, they forfeit the blessings

---

8. 2 Sam. 7:16; Luke 1:33.
9. Matt. 2:2; 27:11; John 1:49; Rev. 17:14; 19:16; Phil. 2:10.

of the kingdom of God. Christians should bring glory to their King. The primary way we do this is by living a holy life that is set apart and glorifies a holy God, not a life that reflects the ideals and practices of the world. What do we watch on television or videos online? What do we have our minds or hearts set on? Are our values and desires the same as those of our unbelieving neighbors? We cannot be salt and light to the world when we look just like the world.

Satan is the ruler of this world. When we reflect the standards and ideals of the world, are we not proclaiming him as our father? Rather, God is glorified when we live counter to the world's ideals.

> Do not love the world or the things in the world. If anyone loves
> the world, the love of the Father is not in him. (1 John 2:15)

The Benefits of Heavenly Citizenship

The benefits of our new citizenship are quite remarkable, both in the here and the hereafter. Evangelicals usually think only of the rewards awaiting them in heaven, but even now believers benefit from their new citizenship. To be sure, with it comes hatred from the world and the ensuing persecution that everyone who truly follows Christ will endure. But Jesus has promised that he has overcome the world and in so doing, the world will ultimately become his kingdom.[10]

In the here and now, the benefits of our citizenship involve things enumerated in previous chapters: access to the throne of God; freedom from the burden and power of sin; adoption into God's family and the privileges of sonship; the fruit and gifts of God's Spirit.

Yet, there is a New Testament emphasis on the kingdom that is to come. We presently experience the down payment, a small portion of the heavenly blessings that await us. For this reason, Paul's hope is that he will be rescued into God's "heavenly kingdom." He writes that believers should not have their minds set on earthly things because "our citizenship is in heaven, and from it we await a Savior, the Lord Jesus Christ." There is a forward-looking emphasis throughout the Christian epistles, as we raise our eyes heavenward and away from this fading world. In fact, believers will judge the world and sit with Jesus on his throne.[11]

---

10. 2 Tim. 3:12; John 16:33; Rev. 11:15.
11. 2 Tim. 4:18; Phil. 3:20; 1 Cor. 6:2; Rev. 3:21.

> Then comes the end, when he delivers the kingdom to God the Father after destroying every rule and every authority and power. For he must reign until he has put all his enemies under his feet. (1 Cor. 15:24–25)

From an eternal perspective, the contrast between heaven and hell cannot be more clear-cut. Heaven is pictured as a wondrous place filled with the light of the glory of God, with "innumerable angels in festal gathering." In heaven there will be no more sorrow or crying or pain,[12] while in hell the exact opposite is true. Jesus frequently warns of the turmoil of hell. It is a place where there is weeping and gnashing of teeth, where "their worm does not die and the fire is not quenched," a place of "eternal fire." For those who reject the gospel concerning Jesus, they will "suffer the punishment of eternal destruction."[13]

Praise be to God who has granted us citizenship in his Son's kingdom! He has defeated the devil and given us eyes to see how empty the ways of the world are, so that we may concentrate on matters of eternal significance.

What does it mean to be saved? It means being delivered from the powers of darkness and brought to the light that is in Christ. It means overcoming the temptations of the world and submitting your allegiance to Jesus our sovereign Lord and King. It means changing your citizenship from the kingdom of Satan to the kingdom of God.

He has delivered us from the domain of darkness and transferred us to the kingdom of his beloved Son.

Colossians 1:13

Key Terms for Salvation Expressed in the Language of Politics

citizenship, foreigners, aliens, exiles, strangers, kingdom of God, kingdom of light, kingdom of Satan, kingdom of darkness, heaven, hell, king, lord, sovereign, authority, right hand of God, reign, throne

---

12. Rev. 21:23; Heb. 12:22; Rev. 21:4.
13. Luke 13:28; Mark 9:48; Matt. 25:41; 2 Thess. 1:9.

Questions for Group Discussion

1. Do you see clues in the world that humanity apart from Christ is part of the "kingdom of darkness"? Explain.

2. In what ways do you potentially deny the existence of Satan, or at least downplay his activity in the world or in your life? Is it possible to overemphasize the involvement of the spiritual realm in our physical world? How?

3. As a citizen of heaven, what are your responsibilities in light of the fact that Jesus has all authority in heaven and on earth? What evidence is there to suggest that you are an active citizen of his kingdom?

6

The Language of the Temple

From Retribution to Propitiation

Therefore he had to be made like his brothers in every respect, so that he might become a merciful and faithful high priest in the service of God, to make **propitiation** for the sins of the people.

Hebrews 2:17

In Namibia there is a thoroughfare intersecting two main streets in the capital city, Windhoek. It is here on Post Street Mall that hawkers ply their wares as a large number of people stroll past their booths each day.

Years ago it was not uncommon for this area to be targeted by Christian evangelists looking to share their brand of Christianity. Bolder people than I stood in the mall and proclaimed their message. One crowded Saturday morning there was a young man screaming at people as they went by. He wanted to warn them of the fires of hell—and warn them he did—but it was obvious that his approach was not producing his hoped-for results. In fact, he was more a sideshow than anything else, and I stood and watched for ten minutes as he warned young ladies that in their promiscuity they were "opening their legs for the devil." Such was the tone of his message.

This approach to witnessing is easy to mock. In the video *Bullhorn* by influential American figure Rob Bell, an obnoxious Christian—playing the part of the "typical" evangelical—stands on a street corner screaming through a megaphone at passers-by that they are going to hell.[1] In fact, *Bullhorn* levels all mass evangelism to this type, stating that what we really need is relationship evangelism, not "proclamation" evangelism. While bullhorn man is clearly insufferable, this overgeneralization about evangelicals is unfair.

Consider the opposite end of the spectrum. In the 1990s a prominent television evangelist and pastor of a large church in California was loathe to ever speak about hell, or God's wrath, or sin, for fear it would turn people away from the church. It was estimated at the height of this seeker-sensitive speaker's popularity that 10 million people worldwide heard him preach each week. Much like modern-day prosperity preachers, his feel-good messages attracted listeners with itching ears.

While bullhorn man's approach is unbearable, the fact is that his message contains a truth that Jesus did not shy from declaring. An impending judgment is coming, and from the heavenly Father no less. The call to repentance is a biblical one. However, the feel-good pastor's message has half the truth. In excising the unpalatable parts of the biblical message, his approach cannot produce a clear presentation of the gospel.

Jesus spoke more about hell and God's judgment than anyone in the Bible. While I am sure he did not do it to scare people into heaven (a common caricature of bullhorn men), he certainly did it because Jesus was dedicated to speaking the truth. I am amazed at speakers who think they can improve on the message of Jesus. If only Jesus hadn't included that intolerant, uncomfortable stuff about God!

It makes little sense to speak about salvation without telling people from what they are being saved. "Jesus saved me from my sins" is an answer that lacks theological accuracy, which can result in confusion. I am a theological nitpicker. While some people think "fuzzy" is good, I think it is the fountain from which heresy flows. Rather than saying Jesus saves us from our sins, I prefer to speak about Jesus saving us from

---

1. Rob Bell, *Bullhorn: Nooma*, 009, produced and directed by Flannel (Grand Rapids: Zondervan, 2005), DVD. This thirteen-minute video can be seen on Vimeo at http://vimeo.com/46266590 (accessed December 18, 2014).

the *consequences* of our sins. Biblically speaking, those consequences involve the wrath of God.

Witnessing and the Language of Atonement

Sharing our faith with people distraught over their sin will involve being gentle with them, taking into consideration their tender soul. But with those who flaunt their sin and brag about their active rebellion against God, a more stringent approach might be wiser. The temporary sting of a verbal slap in the face is worth the potential fruit of startling sinners out of their rebellious malaise.

In the previous chapters, we saw that biblical salvation involves God saving sinners from phenomena outside themselves (Satan, death) and elements from within (sin, fear). This makes good sense, that God rescues us from forces that harm us. However, with our present model of salvation, the person from whom we need saving is God himself. God is angry and he must be appeased. In the words of A.W. Tozer, "We must take refuge from God in God."[2]

Many of us are perplexed by the notion of an incensed God who demands reprisal. For others, though, the idea engenders anger. It seems to make God unloving, peevish, and cranky. A God of retribution is beneath the formulation of those who desire a more loving, tolerant, and forgiving portrait.

With this chapter, we will investigate the biblical teaching on atonement, seeing how God has provided a way by which he can turn from his fair retribution against sinners to being propitious toward them, without violating his own holy nature. We will consider the relationship between the wrath of the Father and the blood of the Son who makes atonement possible. Lastly, we will note the practical implications of the high priestly ministry of Jesus as he intercedes for us.

---

2. Tozer, *Knowledge of the Holy*, 107.

How Are Atonement and Propitiation Related?

The New International Version, the most widely read English Bible in the world over the past several decades, renders Romans 3:25 this way: God presented Jesus as a "sacrifice of atonement, through faith in his blood" (NIV84). In the English Standard Version, it reads that God put forth Jesus as a "propitiation by his blood, to be received by faith" (ESV). Although both translate identical Greek words, the NIV uses "sacrifice of atonement" while the ESV renders "propitiation."

While atonement is a familiar word to Christians as it appears regularly throughout the Bible, the idea of propitiation unfortunately is not as recognizable. It is a word that has fallen out of popular English, even though it was preferred by the King James Version that dominated the English-speaking world for four centuries.

At issue is the Greek *hilastērion*. Up to this point, we have seen the New Testament authors choosing common words from everyday Roman life to portray Christian salvation. However, with our present term, instead of looking to the Roman marketplace or court of law, they reached back into the Jewish sacrificial system.

Hilastērion is a noun that signifies the "mercy seat," the golden cover of the ark of the covenant on which the blood of the levitical sacrifice was sprinkled on the Day of Atonement.[3] The verb form is seen in the quotation at the opening of this chapter. The New Testament idea signifies that by which God covers, overlooks, and pardons the penitent and believing sinner because of Christ's death.

The word "atonement" has sixteenth-century, Anglo-Saxon roots and means "to make at one." In this sense, it is a reconciliation term, and we will see this intimate connection in our next chapter.[4] We tend to use it today to speak of making amends or making things right or appeasing a given situation.

The biblical term, though, goes considerably deeper and is related to the interaction between the sins of humans and the holiness of God. Because our sins put us at odds with God, they must be dealt with.

---

3. Exod. 25:21–22; Lev. 16:14; Num. 7:89; Heb. 9:5.

4. Compare Hebrews 2:17 ESV ("make propitiation") with KJV ("make reconciliation").

Otherwise, God's holy wrath—understood as God's hatred of sin—could not be removed. This is why John writes:

> Whoever believes in the Son has eternal life; whoever does not obey the Son shall not see life, but the wrath of God remains on him. (John 3:36)

A common misunderstanding today is that God's wrath comes upon people if they reject Jesus. However, his wrath is *already* upon sinners, and the sole way it can be removed is through faith in God's Son and his atoning work on the cross.

Atonement makes God propitious toward sinners. His wrath is removed. Christ is "the propitiation for our sins, and not for ours only but also for the sins of the whole world" (1 John 2:2; see also 1 John 4:10).

The death of Jesus Christ is set forth as the ground on which a righteous God can pardon a guilty and sinful race without in any way compromising his righteousness.[5]

> For our sake he made him to be sin who knew no sin, so that in him we might become the righteousness of God. (2 Cor. 5:21)

This is why Jesus is referred to as the "Lamb of God" (John 1:29, 36). This echoes the Passover lamb of the exodus, and Jesus recapitulates this event when at the Last Supper he takes the Passover meal and equates it with his own flesh and blood.[6] Subsequently, the author of Hebrews can say that "a death has occurred that redeems [sinners] from the transgressions committed under the first covenant" (Heb. 9:15).

Christians gain great comfort in knowing that "if God is for us, who can be against us?" However, consider the opposite. If God is against us, who can possibly be for us? As the psalmist writes, "God is angry with the wicked every day."[7] As such, propitiation is necessary.

> For the wrath of God is revealed from heaven against all ungodliness and unrighteousness of men, who by their unrighteousness suppress the truth. (Rom. 1:18)

---

5. Rom. 3:25–26; Heb. 9:15.
6. Matt. 26:26; Mark 14:22; Luke 22:19.
7. Rom. 8:31; Ps. 7:11 KJV.

However, what appears to be solid biblical teaching is not readily acceptable to some. There are several objections to this formulation of atonement, many coming from a growing group of evangelical scholars. Four of the main complaints we will tackle are:

1. Talk of God's wrath is more Old Testament than New and thus obsolete. With the coming of Jesus, we should highlight the love of God more than his wrath.
2. The idea of Jesus turning away the wrath of the Father creates an unhealthy tension in our doctrine of the Trinity.
3. Speaking about God's wrath turns unbelievers away from Christianity. Concentrating on the love of Jesus is more appealing.
4. Emphasizing the wrath of God makes Christians prone to violence, since God is prone to violence.

The Holiness of God Requires Atonement

Let's be honest. We hate the judgment of God. It puts the lie to human autonomy. It exposes our despicable wantonness toward the holiness of our Maker.

Is it any wonder that the judgment of God was one of the first doctrines to be questioned in the garden of Eden? As the serpent lisped his seductive lie, "If you eat the fruit you will not die," he was appealing to humanity's desire to be autonomous and self-governing, to "be like God" (Gen. 3:5). The best route to this goal is to reject God's judgment, for it reminds us of our utter dependence upon him, while we prefer to bask in self-love and self-reliance.

Two questions I have been asked by skeptics and unbelievers involve God's judgment. One is, "Are you one of those people who think salvation is only through Jesus?" The other is, "Do you really think God will send people to hell who have never heard about Jesus?" In fact, this second question is often asked by Christians who are struck by the seeming unfairness of God condemning people ignorant of the gospel. We already touched upon this problem in chapter 2 in our discussion about biblical grace.

The "all ways lead to God" pluralism of today is nothing new. The objection against Jesus as the only way has at its core the age-old rejection of God's judgment. The serpent sold that lie to our first parents, and humanity has been buying it ever since.

I once had a conversation with a man who disapproved of his wife's recent conversion to Jesus. I have encountered few people who had more hatred for Christianity than this man. His main objection was that the biblical God was too judgmental. "If your child did something against you, would you eternally punish him with fire?" he asked. He preferred a "loving God," which was another way of saying a God who never judges.

I noted that his God is devoid of justice, one who will put up with anything. You can murder, steal, or sell children into slavery; it does not matter. His God will do nothing about it. Rather than a loving God, his is an indifferent one.

Further, his analogy was faulty. "Suppose you had a child," I asked, "who was relentlessly harming your other children. In fact, his actions put their lives in constant danger. Is there anything your child could do that would eventually get you to say enough is enough?"

This man's view of God was deficient on several levels. He might say he favors a god like this, but he does not understand the consequences. The next time someone breaks into his house, or tries to harm his wife and children, he might understand what the lack of justice engenders. A god who winks and nods at evil is no god at all.

One argument used against the traditional understanding of the wrath of God being poured out on unrepentant sinners is that this view encourages Christians toward violence. Since God violently stomps out evil, his followers may be inclined to imitate him.

However, a contrary argument is possible. Is not the violence we see in the world in large part because we *deny* that a just God will rightly avenge evil? We rather take the retribution into our own hands. Even some Christians ignore the teaching of Scripture that clearly tells us to leave vengeance to God (e.g., Rom 12:19). A disbelief in the justice of God causes sinful humans to mete out the justice themselves.

Unfortunately, we have lost something of the fear of the Lord in our churches today. God—and more often Jesus—is seen as a buddy or pal, not the Lord of glory that he truly is. In quoting the psalmist, Paul says that a lack of the fear of God is the root cause of humanity's wickedness (Rom. 3:18). Once you lose the fear of the Lord, you lose godly wisdom.

God is love, but he is also a consuming fire (Heb. 12:29). Subsequently, a holy fear of God is the sanest response a sinner can have. Sinners who believe they can saunter up to God and pat him on the back have no concept of his holiness. As sinners, we have every reason to fear God's wrath. Things that are unholy are consumed when put in the presence of that which is holy.[8]

A Schizophrenic God?

The wrath of God is not an ancillary or optional aspect of the nature of the biblical God. It is indispensable. Rather than contradicting God's loving nature, as if God is schizophrenic, the wrath of God is the necessary corollary to his love. A loving God must hate evil. Systematic theologian Wayne Grudem draws out the necessary implication: "There is an eternal, unchangeable requirement in the holiness and justice of God that sin be paid for."[9]

Given the dozens of times the Bible speaks about the wrath of God, how can people downplay or outright ignore it? How can they formulate theological systems that appear to make the judgment of God virtually nonexistent? The answer is found in the belief that in Jesus a new age has come, making God's wrath a vestige of a bygone era.

A common misconception floats around various churches today: "God is a God of wrath in the Old Testament but a God of love in the New." God was harsh and judgmental in the past, whereas by the time of Jesus he has mellowed considerably. It pits the forgiving, merciful character of Jesus against the stern, condemnatory personality of God in the Old Testament.

To be sure, things are new in Christ. The old covenant has been replaced with a covenant that brings with it blessings on a far greater scale, so that the author of Hebrews can say the old covenant is obsolete and deficient now that the new has arrived. However, this should not be confused with the idea that the very nature of God has changed.[10]

The new covenant is not something created from scratch. It finds its root in the old covenant. To imply that the new covenant is unique to the old is like saying a flower is of a different substance than the seed from

---

8. The concept of holiness will be investigated in greater detail in chapter 9 on sanctification.

9. Grudem, *Systematic Theology*, 575.

10. For God's unchanging being, see Num. 23:19; 1 Sam. 15:29; Mal. 3:6; James 1:17. Similar language is used for Jesus (e.g., Heb. 13:8).

which it bloomed. However, it is the same plant in different form. God's plan of salvation has not changed. Rather, it has blossomed.

Our Trinitarian convictions—there is one God who exists in three equally divine persons—lead us to the conclusion that the character of Jesus is precisely the same as the character of God revealed in the Old Testament. To say otherwise implies ontological differences between the persons of the Godhead, or changes in their being over time. Questioning the immutability of God yields a God who today could be better than he was yesterday, or the opposite, a God who can get worse. Both are at odds with the self-revelation of God found in his Word.

In the same way, if we fashion the character of Jesus as gentler or less austere than the character of God revealed in the Old Testament, we have created a Godhead in which the persons of the Trinity are not identical in their being. This monstrosity is more akin to polytheistic systems like Hinduism or the Roman and Greek pantheon than to the God of the Bible.

The falsehood that God has softened up in the New Testament is disproved in two ways. First, we must show that God as revealed in the Old Testament was consistently a God of grace and mercy. Second, we must prove that his wrath is taught in the New Testament, coupled with the wrath of God's Son. We will start with the latter.

The Wrath of the Father and the Son

The book of Acts gives us a glimpse into the early decades of the spread of the Christian faith. A picture of God's instantaneous judgment is seen in the episode of Ananias and Sapphira in Acts 5. The couple are Christians who are struck dead by God for their lying and greed. This act of judgment is parallel to numerous Old Testament accounts where God likewise judged his people.

In Acts 12 we see the judgment of Herod who, rather than give praise to God, accepted the praise of men as if he were a god (v. 22). This story closely parallels events recorded in Daniel 4 concerning the life of Nebuchadnezzar, who similarly took praise upon himself and did not acknowledge God (v. 30). In fact, whereas Herod was struck dead, Nebuchadnezzar was eventually restored after seven years of insanity. In this case, God in the New Testament appears more severe than in the Old.

We need not conclude that since there are more judgment episodes in the Old Testament than in the New that God was more severe before Christ. Old Testament history spans several millennia, while Acts covers roughly thirty-five years. We should expect more portrayals of God's wrath over a period one hundred times longer than the time recorded in Acts.

The modern depiction of Jesus as a tolerance-loving flower child runs contrary to his own teaching that habitually was characterized by extreme talk of the wrath of his heavenly Father. Various parables end with the judgment of God,[11] and numerous sermons speak about hell, his Father's wrath, judgment of sin, and other negative topics modern readers (and certain popular preachers) rather ignore.

Both the Sermon on the Mount (Matthew 5–7) and the Olivet Discourse (Matthew 24–25) speak of judgment that will come during the last days. In the latter discourse, Jesus uses the quintessential Old Testament example of God's universal destruction, the flood in Noah's day, as a template for the coming judgment during the end times (Matt. 24:37–39). Evidently Christ was a firm believer in the wrathful God revealed in the Hebrew Scriptures, ironically more than certain Christians today. Jesus equates the flood with the judgment accompanying his second coming: "so will be the coming of the Son of Man" (v. 39).

Paul speaks in equally blunt terms about what the second coming of Jesus will involve, as he comforts Thessalonian believers who are undergoing persecution because of their faith.

> God considers it just to repay with affliction those who afflict you, and to grant relief to you who are afflicted as well as to us, when the Lord Jesus is revealed from heaven with his mighty angels in flaming fire, inflicting vengeance on those who do not know God and on those who do not obey the gospel of our Lord Jesus. They will suffer the punishment of eternal destruction, away from the presence of the Lord and from the glory of his might. (2 Thess. 1:6–9)

---

11. At least a dozen have strong elements of judgment, e.g., the parables of the sheep and goats, invitation to a wedding banquet, unmerciful servant, wicked tenants, and wheat and weeds.

Any idea that Jesus is all about love, love, love, while God of the Old Testament is wrath, wrath, wrath, is obliterated when we come to the last book of the New Testament, Revelation. The awe-inspiring picture of Christ—a sword coming from his mouth, feet of burnished bronze, and eyes ablaze—accentuates the judgment that accompanies him. So fearsome will this judgment be that "the kings of the earth and the great ones and the generals and the rich and the powerful" will flee from him. For those expecting a meek and mild Jesus, the paradoxical "wrath of the lamb" will be something of a surprise.[12]

Worship and the Language of Atonement

When is the last time you sang a song in a worship service that spoke about God's wrath? Modern Christian hymnody is skewed toward the love and forgiveness of God. Understandably so, as singing about judgment and wrath does not normally have the same positive emotional effect as crooning about God's grace. Yet, we must attempt better balance in our worship.

That there is no contradiction in the two Testaments concerning God's character is moreover proven from depictions of God as gracious and loving. A frequent description of God in the Old Testament is, "The LORD, the LORD, a God merciful and gracious, slow to anger, and abounding in steadfast love and faithfulness" (Exod. 34:6).[13]

A cursory reading of the Old Testament bears this out, especially surrounding the wilderness wandering of the Israelites in the book of Exodus and the history of the Judges, where "everyone did what was right in his own eyes" (Judg. 21:25). The reader cannot help but be struck by the consistent patience of God in dealing with an unbelieving, stiff-necked people. To say that the Old Testament solely, or even predominantly, depicts a God of wrath is to reveal a highly skewed reading of the Hebrew Scriptures. Both Testaments speak of a God who is at once angry at sin and patient with sinners.

---

12. Rev. 1:14–16; 2:15–16; 6:15.
13. Also Num. 14:18; Neh. 9:17; Ps. 86:15; 103:8; 145:8; Joel 2:13; Jonah 4:2.

At the Cross

Mel Gibson's 2004 movie artistically portraying the last hours of the life of Jesus, *The Passion of the Christ*, was assailed months before it was released, its detractors speaking of its supposed anti-Semitism and over-the-top violence. To be sure, the movie was graphic in its depiction of the scourging and bloody crucifixion of Jesus, but what do you expect with a more or less authentic Roman crucifixion?

Of course, Jesus had to endure the jeers of the Jews and the torture of the Romans during his crucifixion. What is usually missed is that his suffering came not merely from these two evil forces, but also from a third cause—the wrath of the Father poured out upon him.

This is a difficult concept to swallow. We accept that the blameless Jesus endured unfair treatment from sinful men. However, when we speak of the Son bearing the wrath of an incensed, holy God, we flinch. Yet, is this not what is involved when Jesus became sin for us (2 Cor. 5:21)?

The biblical portrayal of hell is not pretty. A place of gnashing teeth and unquenchable fire properly causes the sympathetic to squirm.[14] Apart from these direct statements about hell's characteristics, the crucifixion gives us a glimpse into it. Hell is the place where sinners bear their own punishment, where the unregenerate spend eternity under the weight of God's wrath.

This is precisely what Jesus endured when he took our sins upon himself. It involved obvious physical pain but also the less evident emotional anguish ("My God, my God, why have you forsaken me?" Matt. 27:46). Is this not the exact portrayal of the agonies of hell? It is no coincidence. Both in the crucifixion and in the inferno, God's wrath is poured out. When Jesus became sin, this was the inevitable outcome. When we look at the cross, we gain insight into hell's torments.

Again we see that the wrath of God is the very thing from which God saves us. Paul writes that Jesus rescues believers from the coming wrath. Clearly this wrath comes from God himself.[15] Yet as followers of Jesus, we are shielded from it.

> For God has not destined us for wrath, but to obtain salvation through our Lord Jesus Christ. (1 Thess. 5:9)

---

14. Matt. 25:41; Mark 9:48; Luke 13:28; 2 Thess. 1:9.
15. 1 Thess. 1:10; Rom. 5:9.

Note that salvation is juxtaposed with God's wrath. Those who find a wrathless view of God more pleasant and congenial unwittingly empty the cross of all meaning. Without God's wrath there can be no salvation. In *Jesus and Judgment*, New Testament professor Marius Reiser notes this requirement: "Judgment is the obverse of salvation, and its necessary precondition."[16]

Avoidance Mechanisms

Our investigation in chapter 4 on biblical redemption showed us that sin is a death sentence from which there is no escape in our own power. Atonement puts the burden of salvation squarely on the shoulders of someone who can atone for that sin.

To be sure, there are would-be Christians who believe they can do the atoning themselves. Talk of "sin" is not a common habit among such people. Terms like "shortcomings" or "errors in judgment" are preferred, for no other reason than it allows for self-atonement. As long as we treat sin as a minor category, we will always question the atoning death of the God-man to solve our problem. Show me a person who questions the incarnation and you have shown me a person who takes the categories of sin and God's holiness rather lightly.

This has been a problem from the beginning. When Adam and Eve ate the forbidden fruit and were exposed, they took fig leaves to cover their shame. I had two fig trees in my yard while living in Namibia. Once the leaves fall to the ground, they immediately become brittle and crumble. That our first parents chose this leaf as a covering for their bodies is almost comical. God had to later present them with proper attire (Gen. 3:21).

Today we continue the big cover-up. The first step is to minimize our own sins by concentrating on the ones we have not committed. Because we have not murdered or committed adultery, it is argued that we are good people, and good people do not need others to atone for them. We attend church, or we give to charitable causes, and this sort of spiritual self-congratulation is quite adequate to cover over our inadequacies which, by the way, are not nearly as bad as our neighbor's. By trivializing sin, we have trivialized atonement.

---

16. Reiser, *Jesus and Judgment*, 255.

The second step is to belittle God. The biblical picture of God banishing Adam and Eve from Eden for eating a piece of forbidden fruit is replaced with a God who will basically put up with anything. He is a God more interested in sincerity than holiness, content to tolerate anything we do because he has a love affair with human free will. God does not send people to hell, we are told, people willingly go there themselves, and thus any notion of God's judgment against sin is muted. Hell is a destination of our own choosing, not a place where rebellious sinners are tormented by an incensed Judge. God would never do that.

The idea that God is angry but can be appeased through proper sacrifice strikes many today as unsophisticated and outdated. This being the case, the wrath of God has been relegated to the backseat of their theology, if not the trunk! My doctoral dissertation was spent in large part covering this new kind of evangelical—one who speaks so often about the love of God that any talk about God's wrath is washed away in a sea of warm waves and fluffy foam. I spent the better part of seven years reading book after book by the new, open-minded variety of evangelical Christian, ones who have "emerged" from the hateful kind of evangelicalism that tells people they are sinners destined for hell if not for the grace and kindness of God in Jesus.

These postmodern Christians believe that the unsavory, archaic view of God's wrath must be eliminated. Modern man is more cultured and refined than primitive man and hence, requires a more genial Maker. You will be hard-pressed to find two pages worth of material covering sin against a holy God in all their writing.[17]

Once we have neutered God of the attribute of his holy wrath and toned down talk of sin by minimizing its dastardly effects—fashioning ourselves as good people who occasionally err—we have effectively removed the requirement for atonement. It is then a short step to

---

17. A prime example is pastor and prolific, best-selling author Brian McLaren, who frequently scolds evangelicals for their harsh views about God. In *A New Kind of Christianity* (2010), McLaren notes in chapter 11, "From a Violent Tribal God to a Christlike God," that the God of the Genesis flood is "hardly worthy of belief, much less worship" (110), while McLaren bends over backward to appear open-minded and warmhearted to those of non-Christian faiths. His more recent work, *Why Did Jesus, Moses, the Buddha, and Mohammed Cross the Road? Christian Identity in a Multi-Faith World* (New York: Jericho Books, 2012) continues the theme.

questioning the incarnation. Why insist on God becoming human and solving a problem we are quite capable of solving ourselves? The modern propensity to downplay the divinity of Jesus is tied to a watered-down version of what constitutes sin, and a wishy-washy portrayal of a God too tolerant and friendly to worry about it. At the heart of this comes a faulty understanding of atonement.

While I am not one for standing on the street corner with a megaphone screaming at sinners destined for hell—the "turn-or-burn" approach to evangelism—I do believe at times we should be forceful in our declaration of the truth. It is what the Old Testament prophets did when speaking to the stiff-necked lawbreakers of God's covenant; it is why Jesus called the Pharisees and teachers of the law "blind guides"; and it was how Paul dealt with those who warped the gospel for personal gain.[18]

Propitiation Is God's Idea

In recent years, there have been evangelicals who have called for a rethinking of propitiation, on the understanding that it appears to make God the Father at odds with his Son. Pictured is the Father ready to strike sinners, but Jesus stepping in and defending them. An unacceptable tension within the Godhead seemingly exists, with the Son opposing the righteous anger of the Father.

If indeed this were a true picture of propitiation it would be unacceptable. The biblical atonement necessary to turn away wrath has always come by the will of God who graciously provides the means by which the sins of humans may be atoned. There is no opposition within the Godhead, as if the Son placates a Father who otherwise wants to wipe out humanity. On the contrary, Jesus makes it abundantly clear that he is *only* doing the Father's will and nothing else.[19] We cannot speak about the love of Jesus without first speaking about the Father's love.

Even before the giving of the Mosaic law, there were hints of this. For example, after Adam and Eve sinned, God provided a proper covering with animal skins. When Cain brought his unacceptable sacrifice, God told Cain the way he could be accepted. It is Cain's refusal to do things God's way that ultimately led to the murder of his brother Abel. Similarly

---

18. Jer. 7:4, 11, 20; Matt. 23:16, 24; Gal. 1:9; 5:12.
19. For example, see Matt. 26:39; John 4:34; 6:38.

with the Old Testament sacrifices, God was the one who designed the system, not man.[20]

This is why the incarnation is crucial to Christianity and sets it apart from other religions. The atrocity of sin cannot be smoothed over by a few dos and don'ts, nor can it be ignored. Sin against a holy God must be dealt with, yet sinners cannot deal with it themselves. This is why the deity of Jesus is vital to our faith. God alone can turn away God's wrath.

Only the God-man can properly remove the blight of sin. The blood of bulls and goats could never atone for human sins, and finite sinners could never atone for sins against an infinite God. Yet the God-man can do both: stand in the stead of sinful humans and absorb the eternal wrath of a holy God. The Christian faith takes sin seriously, and then prescribes a remedy that is powerful enough to cure it. The God-man performs this miraculous work of grace.

It is for this reason that evangelicals have traditionally spoken of Christ's atoning work as substitutionary and vicarious. Jesus does what we cannot do. He takes our place and bears our penalty. The apostle Peter tells us, "He himself bore our sins in his body on the tree, that we might die to sin and live to righteousness." The vicarious atoning work of the Messiah was prophesied in Isaiah where we are told "he bore the sin of many, and makes intercession for the transgressors." Paul continues this theme when he writes that our trespasses were nailed to the cross.[21]

It is because Jesus has borne the wrath of God that Paul can state, "There is therefore now no condemnation for those who are in Christ Jesus" (Rom. 8:1). Once we remove any notion of God's wrath and the need for him to be propitiated, it is a small step to removing the ultimate sacrifice of his Son on the cross.

The Lifeblood of Our High Priest

There are more references in the New Testament to the blood of Jesus than there are to the cross or his death. It is a central New Testament focus when describing the importance of his work. As blood was required for atonement under the old covenant (Exod. 24:8), it is

---

20. Gen. 3:21; 4:6; Lev. 17:11.
21. 1 Peter 2:24; Isa. 53:12; Col. 2:13–14.

required under the new. Hebrews 9:22 says, "Without the shedding of blood there is no forgiveness of sins."

The law says that life is in the blood (Lev. 17:11). The sixteenth-century English word "lifeblood" was coined for this concept.[22] Since life is in the blood, and because the wages of sin is death, blood is essential for atonement. The only way to atone for your life is by giving it up.

Jesus does this on our behalf as our high priest. The verse from Hebrews quoted at the head of this chapter makes a connection between the incarnation, the sin of humanity, and the priestly ministry of Christ. As our high priest, Jesus has made propitiation for the sins of believers by shedding his blood.[23]

Since "the law made nothing perfect" (Heb. 7:19), a new covenant with a superior priest was required. The priesthood of Jesus is greater than the levitical priesthood because Jesus came from heaven, is a sinless intercessor, has the "power of an indestructible life," saves completely those under his care, sacrificed for the sins of his people once for all, and intercedes for them forever.[24]

> Christ was sacrificed once to take away the sins of many; and he will appear a second time, not to bear sin, but to bring salvation to those who are waiting for him. (Heb. 9:28 NIV)

What does it mean to be saved? It means having the blood of Jesus atone for your sins, thus turning away God's righteous wrath. It means having your high priest, Jesus, eternally intercede for you before the throne of God. It means moving from retribution to propitiation.

Since, therefore, we have now been justified by his blood, much more shall we be saved by him from the wrath of God.

Romans 5:9

---

22. See Gen. 9:5; Isa. 63:3; Jer. 2:34.

23. Heb. 2:17; 7:27. Scripture says that the blood of Jesus also cleanses our consciences (Heb. 9:14), defeats Satan (Rev. 12:10–11), and gives us confidence to approach God (Heb. 10:19).

24. Heb. 4:14–15; 7:16, 25, 27; Rom. 8:34.

Key Terms for Salvation Expressed in the Language of the Temple

atonement, sacrifice, Passover Lamb, blood of the new covenant, propitiation, vicarious, substitutionary, high priest, intercession, wrath, holiness, retribution, vengeance, justice, condemnation

---

Questions for Group Discussion

1. If God has turned from retribution against sinners to being favorable toward them, how might this work out in the life of a Christian living in a world disposed against believers?

2. Is your picture of God skewed more toward his grace and love, or his wrath and judgment? How does either inclination affect a Christian's walk?

3. More evangelical scholars are beginning to question the substitutionary atonement of Jesus. However, if Jesus does not take our place, what does that imply about salvation and our responsibility?

4. Do you think speaking about the wrath of God is a good evangelistic tactic? Explain why or why not.

7

The Language of Diplomacy
From Enmity to Friendship

For if while we were enemies we were ***reconciled*** to God
by the death of his Son, much more, now that we are reconciled,
shall we be saved by his life.

Romans 5:10

In 1994 my wife and I left the United States and went to Namibia as missionaries with Africa Inland Mission. It was four years after Namibian independence from the South African apartheid regime, and as you can imagine, the structures of society did not change overnight. Towns were still largely segregated according to color and race, and a level of animosity continued to exist between the people groups.

For nine years we lived in what were formerly known as "black locations," areas where blacks had been forced to live during apartheid. Our neighbors were very welcoming, despite the fact that our skin color made us conspicuous in the community. The most resistance we experienced was not from blacks but from whites who viewed us with suspicion. For a white person to voluntarily move to a black location was at best strange, at worst just plain crazy.

In time I had opportunities to preach in different churches, and one was in the coastal town of Swakopmund, a beautiful oasis in the middle of the Namib Desert. One Sunday I preached an evening sermon on the ministry of reconciliation as taught by Paul in 2 Corinthians 5. Because the service was more informal than in the morning, I decided to open with an example of reconciliation and then ask if anyone wanted to share one from their own life.

The pastor's mother stood up, a white woman in her seventies, and recounted how she had been a Christian her whole life, but it was not until recently that she confronted her own racism toward blacks. She noted that it had only been several years ago that she shook a black person's hand in church. While recounting the event, she began to weep. It was a moving account of someone whose heart had been softened by God's Spirit.

When we fully understand what biblical reconciliation involves, our hearts should likewise be warmed. With this chapter, we will investigate the unique way Scripture envisions reconciliation between God and humans, what the problem is that necessitates reconciliation in the first place, and what practical effects a restored relationship with God can produce in the lives of believers.

Reconciliation as Biblically Understood

In ancient Greek, two words normally expressed the idea of reconciliation. One word, *diallassō*, described a relationship where both parties were offended and required restoration. The other, *katallassō*, was used when just one of the parties was affronted. This is the word chosen in the New Testament—a term unique to Paul—to speak of the reconciliation that takes place between God and man.

Originally, *katallassō* was a monetary term. It meant to change or exchange money. However, it came to be employed as a diplomatic term, first in the context of marriage, then later more broadly, where one party was changed from an enemy to a friend. Paul uses the verb six times (and the related noun *katallagē* four times) in his epistles, once in reference to marriage (1 Cor. 7:11), the other five times with respect to the broken relationship between God and man.[1]

---

1. For the noun, Rom. 5:11; 11:15; 2 Cor. 5:18–19 (one time in each verse), and for the verb, Rom. 5:10; 2 Cor. 5:18–20 (one time in each verse).

The English word "reconcile" comes from Anglo-French and Latin origins, meaning to restore to friendship or harmony, and is a perfect translation for the Greek in Paul's usage. The uniqueness of Paul's handling of the Greek word is that it had never been used in ancient literature to refer to the religious relationship between man and God.[2]

Biblical reconciliation is a one-way street. In normal situations with mediation, both parties leave something on the table in an act of compromise. However, with biblical reconciliation, there are not two, equally offended parties. There is one side who has produced all of the offense (sinful humans) and the other side who is entirely wronged (a holy God). Man is the felonious party, God the offended. As such, biblical reconciliation is one-sided, originating from God.

"We love because he first loved us" (1 John 4:19). If God had not made the move toward reconciliation, there would be no resolution. Humanity would remain in active rebellion against an incensed God.

Enemies of God

"God is your enemy." When you read those words, what is the first thought that pops into your mind? Is it one of indignation that God opposes you, or comfort in knowing that this *used* to be true but no longer is? Or is it fear?

In our pluralistic world, the first reaction is the most common. How can God be my enemy when he loves everybody? Usually coupled with this universal love of God is the modern notion that God is quite willing to tolerate virtually any belief a person may have, as long as that person is sincere about it. It is the democratization of God, that he ought to treat everyone equally. Therefore, to speak of God as our enemy will frequently produce looks of disdain from non-Christians.

However, the first thing we must banish is the belief that God relates the same way to all people. While this might be a popular view today, it is hardly the biblical one. God does indeed relate differently to a wicked man versus a righteous one (e.g., Noah); to a self-righteous man versus a humble one (e.g., Luke 18:14); to the one with whom he is pleased

---

2. Kittel, *Theological Dictionary of the New Testament*, 1:254–58.

versus those he is not (e.g., Luke 2:14); to the wise and learned versus little children. As Jesus declares,

> I thank you, Father, Lord of heaven and earth, that you have hidden these things from the wise and understanding and revealed them to little children; yes, Father, for such was your gracious will. (Matt. 11:25–26)

God is a God who both reveals and conceals. He is the one who sovereignly chooses. "Jacob I loved, but Esau I hated" (Rom. 9:13; also Mal. 1:2–3). Of all the nations of the world, God chose *one* through whom his redemptive blessings would come (i.e., Israel). He chose one man from the pagans in Ur of the Chaldeans in order to create this nation (i.e., Abraham, Gen. 11:31; Josh. 24:2–3). Even though God sends rain on both the just and the unjust (Matt. 5:45), he withholds his forgiveness from those outside the blessings of Christ (John 20:23). Revealing the Father to others is left to the choice of the Son. Jesus says, "All things have been handed over to me by my Father, and no one knows the Son except the Father, and no one knows the Father except the Son and anyone to whom the Son chooses to reveal him" (Matt. 11:27).

Why are people considered enemies of God? Once again, sin is the problem. Paul makes this connection unambiguous in Romans 5 with three "while we" comments.

- "For while we were still weak, at the right time Christ died for the ungodly." (v. 6)
- "God shows his love for us in that while we were still sinners, Christ died for us." (v. 8)
- "For if while we were enemies we were reconciled to God by the death of his Son, much more, now that we are reconciled, shall we be saved by his life." (v. 10)

Ungodly. Sinners. Enemies. These words describe unregenerate humanity.

Witnessing and the Language of Reconciliation

The plethora of religions in the world proves that humanity perceives its need for reconciliation with God. Frequently, we expect hostility from sinners when we share the gospel, but more often than not, people already know they are in trouble. Our task is to show them that only in Jesus is genuine reconciliation with our Maker possible.

An enemy is not someone who comes a little short of being a friend. An enemy is diametrically opposed to another. In saying that humans are enemies of God, Paul is declaring that as sinners in active and willful rebellion against a holy Lord, we can expect the vigorous opposition of God against us.

To get the weightiness of what the Bible means when it uses the word "enemy," consider these other usages in the New Testament. The word speaks of the devil and death, of someone opposed to righteousness, people who were pitted against Jesus during his earthly ministry, and even of Christians who become "friends with the world."[3] To say unreconciled sinners are enemies of God is no small point to make.

We often envision sin as merely a mistake. I was walking along the road and, oops! I blundered. But Scripture pictures sin as hostility toward God. In an earlier chapter we saw how this works out in the sinner's mind. "The mind that is set on the flesh is hostile to God" (Rom. 8:7). Similarly, it works out in the sinner's actions. Paul couples both of these influences in speaking to the Colossians:

> And you, who once were alienated and hostile in mind,
> doing evil deeds, he has now reconciled. . . . (Col. 1:21–22)

A hostile mind yields hostile behavior. What we think ultimately produces what we do.[4] Sinners do not simply make mistakes, they make willfully antagonistic choices against God. Consequently, Scripture is correct in calling us God's enemies. That enmity must be removed if we are to ever have a relationship with God again.

---

3. Matt. 13:39; 1 Cor. 15:26; Acts 13:10; Matt. 13:25, 28; James 4:4.

4. As the saying goes, "Sow a thought, reap an action; sow an action, reap a habit; sow a habit, reap a character; sow a character, reap a destiny."

The Mediator of a New Covenant

As is often the case with two factions at odds with each other, a mediator is required to attempt a reconciliation.[5] Both sides recognize that mediation is needed and an agreed upon mediator is selected.[6] However, this is not the case with biblical reconciliation. Sinners are quite content to remain in their rebellion. They have no concern for reconciliation nor are they capable of initiating it. Therefore, God must start the process.

Ideally, a mediator fairly represents both parties involved. But in the case of fallen humanity, a mediator can hardly come from man's side alone, since it is man who is entirely at fault. As his rebellion is an affront to God's sovereign rule, man cannot make restitution himself. Thus, a very special kind of mediator is necessary for the reconciliation between God and man, one who comes from God's side yet still represents mankind.

The beauty of the incarnation is that in Jesus Christ, the God-man, a mediator exists who can properly represent both sides. This is why the author of Hebrews connects the mediatory role of Jesus to him being made like us (Heb. 2:14). Yet, this mediator does something most incredible. He dies on behalf of those he came to represent.

The penalty for sin is death. Only the blood of humans can rightly atone for human transgressions. The death of rams and goats could not atone for human sins and was just a temporary measure until the reality of the ultimate sacrifice came (Rom. 3:25; Heb. 10:4). However, someone who is solely human in nature could never overcome death, let alone the devil who holds the power of death. However, the God-man who has life in himself and is also fully human can overcome both the power of death and the devil, while atoning for human sin, thus making his mediation complete.

As we saw in the previous chapter, atonement is the ground upon which reconciliation is built. If our sins have not been atoned for, there is no possibility of reconciliation with God. Each model of salvation can stand on its own right as a valid way to describe biblical salvation. Yet,

---

5. The Greek word translated "mediator" can have the idea of a reconciler, and this is most appropriate for our purposes in this chapter.

6. "Intercessor" is another term used in mediation, but it is covered in chapter 2 on justification because it is also a legal term.

the models are interrelated, much like the overlapping circles on the cover of this book.

Reconciliation requires a mediator. This mediator atones for sins by shedding his blood. This atonement turns away the wrath of God. By participating in death he conquers death on behalf of sinful humans. The payment for the redemption of sinners is the mediator's blood. And so on.

More diplomatic language is used when we read that the shedding of the mediator's blood inaugurates a new covenant. In both the Old Testament and the New, the idea of a covenant involves the forming of a treaty or alliance.[7] God made covenants with Noah, Abraham, and David, called the Noahic, Abrahamic, and Davidic covenants, respectively.[8] He made another with the Israelites through the mediation of Moses, known as the Mosaic covenant, what is commonly referred to as the law of Moses.

Whenever the New Testament contrasts the old covenant with the new, it is speaking about the Mosaic covenant versus the new one inaugurated by Jesus. This new covenant is what Jesus referred to at the Last Supper when he spoke of the cup as "the new covenant in my blood" (Luke 22:20). It is the covenant to which the prophet Jeremiah looked forward, written on the hearts of God's people (Jer. 31:31–34). Note that this new covenant deals properly with sin: "For I will forgive their iniquity, and I will remember their sin no more" (v. 34).

The author of Hebrews writes extensively about the superiority of the new covenant over the old, and we covered much of this in chapter 6 on atonement and the role of the high priest. However, Hebrews uses two different Greek words when saying that this covenant is "new." The one word, *kainos*, connotes chronology. The new covenant is new in terms of time, i.e., it follows after the old one. The other Greek word, *neos*, connotes a *qualitative* difference. The new covenant is superior to the old by degree.

In fact, it is not merely a new covenant, but it is also the last one. There is no need for an additional covenant. In this sense, then, the new covenant lasts forever. The old, temporary covenant and everything in it was pointing forward in time, chronologically, to a new covenant, and

---

7. "Testament" is another term of diplomacy and is a synonym for "covenant."
8. Gen. 9:12; Gen. 12:1–3; 2 Sam. 7:11–16.

qualitatively, to an eternal covenant. While the old was one of shadows, the new is one of substance (Heb. 10:1).

In Paul's second letter to the church at Corinth, he similarly contrasts the old covenant with the new. Paul calls the law of Moses a "ministry of death, carved in letters on stone" and a "ministry of condemnation." The law condemns; the law brings death; the law could never save. But in Jesus Christ as the "mediator of a new covenant," Paul can speak of a "ministry of righteousness" that brings life and is permanent, thus making the old one obsolete.[9]

Damaged Relationships Restored

Three relationships were damaged when Adam and Eve ate the forbidden fruit. This puts the lie to the notion that sin is a private affair. Regardless of the infraction, sin always has a public effect, impairing the life not only of the one committing the transgression but also the lives of those around him.

In the case of Adam and Eve, the first damaged relationship was the most fundamental, their bond with God. Prior to the fall, Adam enjoyed an unencumbered connection with his Maker. There was communication and fellowship. However, as soon as our first parents ate from the tree of the knowledge of good and evil, their initial reaction to God's presence was anything but warm. They were afraid and hid from him (Gen. 3:8, 10).

Is this not the case for us today when we sin? Does it not cause us to flee from God's presence? Is it not an impediment to a vibrant prayer life, to eager reading of God's Word, and to the desire for fellowshipping with God's people?

The second relationship damaged by the fall was the bond between Adam and Eve. Prior to Eve's creation, Adam was without a suitable partner. As we established in chapter 3 on adoption, humans were created for relationship. Despite his unrestricted relationship with God, Adam was alone, unable to find a suitable partner, something that was not good. Knowing this, God made a woman from Adam's body, "bone of my bones and flesh of my flesh" (Gen. 2:23). Adam was ecstatic!

---

9. 2 Cor. 3:6–11; Heb. 9:15. "Ministry" and "minister," as cognates of "administration," are political terms for those serving in government.

However, his elation was short-lived. Upon eating the fruit and his post-fall confrontation with God, Adam became a master of avoidance. When hiding from God did not work, he moved to avoidance mechanism number two, the blame game. "The woman whom you gave to be with me, she gave me fruit of the tree, and I ate" (Gen. 3:12). Apparently the honeymoon was over!

Incredibly, Adam finds a way to blame both Eve and God, and this is perhaps the most insidious aspect of our sin. We regularly lay the blame at God's feet. "If only you had done something differently, God, I wouldn't have acted that way." "If my circumstances were changed I could more easily serve you." Adam exposes a tendency in all sinners, to skirt responsibility and find another to accuse.

Can you imagine the conversations between Adam and Eve that took place at the dinner table after that fateful day in the garden? In fact, that was their last day in Paradise, as God immediately banished them from Eden (Gen. 3:23). With the eating of forbidden fruit came pain in childbearing for the woman, and the way she related to her husband was affected (Gen. 3:16). Subsequently, all human relationships have been spoiled by the fall.

The third damaged relationship is that between humans and their environment. Prior to the fall, Adam was placed in the garden where he was given the task of tending it (Gen. 2:15). Already it was established that dominion over this created world was given to humans. The naming of the animals is one sign of this authority (Gen. 1:28; 2:19–20).

However, after the fall, both the serpent and the ground are cursed (Gen. 3:14, 17–19). Of course, we might not care much that the serpent was punished, given his role in the temptation and downfall of humanity, but even the ground is afflicted because of Adam's rebellion. Working the ground will now be "painful toil" (v. 17 NIV).

The beauty of the mediatory work of Jesus is that all three relationships can be restored. Paul revels in this fact when he notes the monumental effect the atoning work of Jesus has on our relationship with God.

> For if while we were enemies we were reconciled to God by
> the death of his Son, much more, now that we are reconciled,
> shall we be saved by his life. More than that, we also rejoice in

> God through our Lord Jesus Christ, through whom we have
> now received reconciliation. (Rom. 5:10–11)

We move from enemies of God to reconciled and saved. Later
Paul will speak of the "free gift of righteousness" (v. 17). He already
established earlier in the chapter that we have peace, love, hope, and
grace. These gifts from God should produce joy in us. Our situation has
indeed changed, from being God's enemy to receiving gifts from him as
our heavenly benefactor.

The restoration of the human-to-human relationship will be discussed shortly. To avoid redundancy, the relationship between humans and their environment will be discussed in chapter 11 on transformation.

The Practical Implications of Vertical Reconciliation

We can only experience reconciliation with God because of what
was objectively done on our behalf two thousand years ago. L. L.
Morris comments on the scope and sequence of Jesus' atoning work:
"Reconciliation in some sense was effected outside man before anything happened within man."[10] Hence, the by-product of a restored
relationship with God—what we call "vertical reconciliation"—should
be seen in our relationship with others, what we refer to as "horizontal
reconciliation." Both of these are seen in Paul's letter to the Ephesian
believers.

> For he himself is our peace, who has made us both one and
> has broken down in his flesh the dividing wall of hostility
> by abolishing the law of commandments expressed in
> ordinances, that he might create in himself one new man in
> place of the two, so making peace, and might reconcile us
> both to God in one body through the cross, thereby killing
> the hostility. (Eph. 2:14–16)

Note that twice Paul mentions "hostility" and "peace." The hostility
that existed between man and God, and between Jew and Gentile, has
been replaced by the peace that comes through the cross.

---

10. L. L. Morris, "Reconciliation" in *New Bible Dictionary*, 1003.

In evangelical circles, we rightly emphasize the grace of the gospel message, and it plays a key role in the biblical understanding of salvation. However, it is not the sole emphasis in the Christian message. Take a look at the opening verses of every New Testament epistle. Grace is almost always coupled with peace in the salutations. "Peace" appears nearly one hundred times in the New Testament and is a central theme of the Christian message.

The world craves peace. It is the desire of every United Nations diplomat and beauty pageant contestant. Yet, the world has rejected the Prince of Peace and thus will never experience the genuine peace God has offered through his Son.

Followers of Jesus should be peace-loving, peace-creating people. Citizens of the kingdom of God do not simply keep the peace, they make it. "Blessed are the peacemakers, for they shall be called sons of God" (Matt. 5:9). As God has reconciled Jew and Gentile in Jesus, Christians ought to be concerned with racial reconciliation and harmony.

In our relationship with others, followers of Jesus turn the other cheek when offended, they go the extra mile when taken advantage of, and they love their enemies and pray for them (Matt. 5:39–44). They repay evil with good; they leave vengeance to God (Rom 12:19–21).

Paul says, "If possible, so far as it depends on you, live peaceably with all" (Rom. 12:18), and the author of Hebrews concurs when he writes, "Strive for peace with everyone" (Heb. 12:14). Our relations with nonbelievers should communicate what it means to live reconciled to God.

Similarly, our relationship with our brothers must bear this out. Jesus commands,

> So if you are offering your gift at the altar and there remember that your brother has something against you, leave your gift there before the altar and go. First be reconciled[11] to your brother, and then come and offer your gift. (Matt. 5:23–24)

Unfortunately, many Christians are known as contentious and disagreeable. Rather than peacemakers they are troublemakers. This being the case, they imitate Satan more than Christ.

---

11. Here in Matthew 5:24 is the only time in the New Testament where the word *diallassō* appears.

All Believers Are Ambassadors

Not only do our relationships change, but our responsibilities do as well. Paul calls Christians ambassadors of the message of reconciliation (2 Cor. 5:20). Understanding what an ambassador did in the first century will help us better grasp why Paul chooses this word to describe the role of the person who has been reconciled to God.

The Roman Empire was divided into two types of provinces. One type was under the control of the Senate, the other under the direct control of the emperor, known as imperial provinces. The distinction was made purely on the basis of military matters. Those provinces that were dangerous and had troops stationed there were under the emperor. In the imperial provinces, the man sent to direct the administration of the province was the ambassador. He was the emperor's direct representative, commissioned expressly by him. This is the primary picture of a first-century ambassador.

However, it goes even further. When the Senate had determined to bring a conquered country or state into the empire and make it a province, an envoy of ambassadors was sent to draw up the terms of the new agreement, set the boundaries, and formulate a new constitution. In other words, these ambassadors were given the responsibility of bringing this new people into the empire.

These examples give us great insight into why Paul considered himself an ambassador of Christ. In the first place, an ambassador speaks for the party he represents. Much like the Roman ambassador was the direct representative of the emperor, Christians represent Jesus. Secondly, an ambassador has the responsibility of bringing people into the kingdom, in Paul's case, God's kingdom.

Consider an example from today. The United States has sent an ambassador to reside in South Africa. That ambassador represents the Obama administration. She does not speak for herself, but she speaks for the administration. The very honor of the country she represents is in her hands. Possibly the only American the South African president will ever personally meet is the ambassador from America. If she leaves a bad impression, President Zuma's opinion of America will be adversely affected. History is filled with examples of bad ambassadors and the negative consequences produced when they poorly represented their homeland.

Christians are ambassadors of Jesus, and we should wish that it were as easy as representing a country! We are the ambassadors of something far greater, the ministry of reconciliation. When others see us, they see Jesus. When we speak, it is not to be for our own cause but for the cause of Christ. How we act may have a direct impact on how others view the one we represent. Consequently, we are "ministers of a new covenant" (2 Cor. 3:6).

Paul makes this clear in 2 Corinthians 5:20: "Therefore, we are ambassadors for Christ, God making his appeal through us." God has already made his appeal to humankind through Jesus, but now he is making his appeal through believers. Why? Because Christ has entrusted us with his representation. What a privilege and solemn responsibility it is. It is one that should never be taken lightly.

However, we often do not take this duty seriously. We neglect the task of sharing the gospel with unbelievers, or we live unfaithful lives that call into question our ambassadorship. John Calvin comments on this duty as noted in Isaiah 2:3 and Matthew 16:19, respectively:

> [N]othing could be more inconsistent with the nature of faith than that deadness which would lead a man to disregard his brethren, and to keep the light of knowledge choked up within his own breast. . . .
>
> Christ therefore declares that, by the preaching of the Gospel, is revealed on the earth what will be the heavenly judgment of God, and that the certainty of life or death is not to be obtained from any other source.
> This is a great honor, that we are God's messengers to assure the world of its salvation.[12]

If we have truly been reconciled to God, how can we not faithfully serve as Christ's ambassadors?

12. John Calvin, *Commentary on the Prophet Isaiah*, vol. 1, comments on Isa. 2:3, accessed June 22, 2014, http://www.ccel.org/ccel/calvin/calcom13.ix.i.html; John Calvin, *Commentary on a Harmony of the Evangelists, Matthew, Mark, and Luke*, vol. 2, comments on Matt. 16:19, accessed December 22, 2014, http://www.ccel.org/ccel/calvin/calcom32.ii.lii.html.

Worship and the Language of Reconciliation

"What a Friend We Have in Jesus" has been a popular hymn for decades, and for good reason. It emphasizes the newfound relationship sinners have with their Creator. While elsewhere I bemoaned the "fluffy" style of worship prevalent in churches today and called for more solemnity toward God, this should not be at the expense of the reminder that Jesus considers his followers his friends.

Who Is Your Friend?

James notes that Abraham was called God's friend.[13] If we share the same faith in God that Abraham had, we will be reckoned as Abraham's children (Romans 4; Galatians 3). Two chapters later, James says something else about friendship, but this time in the negative.

> You adulterous people, don't you know that friendship with the world is hatred toward God? Anyone who chooses to be a friend of the world becomes an enemy of God. (James 4:4 NIV84)

A genuine faith that produces works of reconciliation is a sign of a relationship with our Creator. Jesus said, "You are my friends if you do what I command you" (John 15:14). Either you are a friend of God or you are a friend of the world and hence God's enemy.

What does it mean to be saved? It means having the barrier of hostility removed between yourself and God. It means becoming an ambassador of God's gracious reconciliation so that you may draw others to Christ. It means moving from being an enemy of God to becoming his friend.

For there is one God, and there is one mediator between God and men, the man Christ Jesus.

1 Timothy 2:5

---

13. James 2:23; also 2 Chron. 20:7 and Isa. 41:8.

Key Terms for Salvation Expressed in the Language of Diplomacy

reconciliation, mediator, ambassador, enmity, hostility, enemy, friend, peace, covenant, minister, ministry

---

Questions for Group Discussion

1. Who do you consider your enemies, and how, in light of Christ's reconciling work, should you behave toward them? Are there any areas in your life where you need to more properly live out the type of reconciliation believers enjoy through God's forgiving love? Explain.

2. Do you consider yourself an ambassador for Jesus? If so, how have you recently performed this role?

3. Consider the three relationships damaged by sin. How is your church working to help reconcile those relationships? What role can you personally play?

4. Discuss the differences between peacekeepers, peacemakers, and troublemakers. Which one are you?

8

The Language of Astronomy
From Darkness to Light

ILLUMINATION

**I pray also that the eyes of your heart may be *enlightened* in order
that you may know the hope to which he has called you,
the riches of his glorious inheritance in the saints, and his incomparably
great power for us who believe.**

Ephesians 1:18–19a NIV84

We noted earlier that certain theological terms seldom used in the Bible are helpful nonetheless for describing an array of biblical teaching. Illumination is such a term, appearing one time in English in the Bible (Rev. 18:1), but not in reference to the topic of salvation. So why utilize the word when speaking about this topic?

The Greek verb *phōtizō* (which is related to the noun *phōs* from which we get the English word "photo") appears numerous times in the New Testament. This verb is normally translated "to give light" or "to enlighten." Frequently *phōtizō* is used metaphorically to speak about what happens to people who have seen the light of the truth found in the gospel, and from this we get the theological term "illumination." In secular Greek, *phōtizō* (and the noun *phōs* meaning light) was employed in astronomy as a common word referring to the light of the sun and stars.[1]

Illumination is a helpful term when discussing the work of God's Spirit on believers. Biblically speaking, salvation is envisioned as taking a person from darkness to light, from ignorance to understanding. Investigating this theme, we will look at what was lost in the fall of Adam, and then see how it is regained through faith in Jesus. We will also investigate related terms including revelation, wisdom, and mystery.

Why the Need for Illumination?

Popular secular thinking maintains that humanity is basically good. The problem is not depravity or corruption of character, but rather a lack of education. As long as a person is properly educated, he will act in the best interest of the good.

The Christian understanding of human nature, though, is decidedly different. Humanity is corrupt and fallen, and not even the best education will fix the problem. It not only affects how individuals live their lives, but it affects something as elementary as their perception of God.

Humanity overwhelmingly believes in a reality outside this world, what could be called a supreme being. Atheism stands in the minority in the vast scope of human history, with the most primitive to the most sophisticated societies affirming a god or gods. This being the case, why has a steady tradition within Christian history maintained that humanity's perception of God is warped and corrupted?

The answer, once again, is sin. The effects of sin are not merely found in the actions of humans, but even in the way their minds operate. Sin is an insidious cancer that affects everything humans think, say, and do. This is particularly important when considering the idea of revelation and how we perceive God.

Foundational to Christian doctrine is the understanding that God cannot be comprehended unless he reveals himself. There have been few truths more important in my own theological training than this realization. We can only affirm those things about God that he chooses to reveal to us. Humanity's right perception of God comes from God alone. We refer to this as the self-revelation of God.

---

1. Kittel, *Theological Dictionary of the New Testament*, 9:310–12.

There are two categories of revelation. There is revelation that is equally revealed to all people, what we designate *general revelation*. Nature is an example of this revelation accessible to each human.

The other kind is *special revelation*, knowledge to which certain people are privy. If a particular piece of information is not expressly revealed, you cannot otherwise know it. The classic example of this form of revelation is the story of Jesus as Lord and Savior found in God's Word.

An example may be helpful in distinguishing the two kinds. As I walk around, my skin color is easy to see. It is a form of general revelation about me to the world. But what is my favorite food? This is a personal fact about me that is not generally plain. The only way others can realize it is if I specifically reveal it to them. This is an example of special revelation.

We speak the same way when discussing God and what can be known about him. There are general truths about God evident to all humanity, but there are also specific truths solely acquired via special revelation.

Suppose a boat with a family capsized at sea, and a baby was the lone survivor as it was washed ashore on a deserted island. A group of primates on the island raised the child, who grew to adulthood. One day, this human among apes looked around the island, contemplated the trees and the water, his compatriots and his own existence, and was naturally driven to the inference that these things did not come about by accident. He determined what virtually every civilization in human history has concluded, that there is a being who made the world. His own existence must find its source in this being.

But what does he know about this being? He may discern the being is powerful, perhaps very big and quite intelligent. If our shipwrecked human is philosophically inclined, he may understand that there can only be one such being as opposed to many, and he may further surmise that the being has a personality.

However, a question as simple as, "Does this being care for me or love me?" is not easy to answer. The man can look at the flowers and consider the rain, concluding that this being is a loving provider. However, once the man thinks about monsoons or ravaging storms that hit the island, the being appears more angry than loving. He can recognize some bald facts about the existence of this being, but he has no clue how to relate to it. Does the being hear and answer prayers? Should he sacrifice to this being, or make an idol in its image? None of these questions can be satisfactorily answered.

Whatever the case, one thing is assured. The man cannot wake up one day, look at the sky and the mountains and his own skin, and conclude, "Jesus died for my sins." Because our shipwrecked individual does not have any books to read, or other humans to tell him, he cannot know the gospel.

However, suppose another human were to shipwreck on this island. This new castaway teaches the man how to speak and he tells him about the God who sent Jesus. This is distinct information our original man could not have attained unless someone were to tell him. Now the man can discern how to have a relationship with God. He understands what it means to sin against him and how to be reconciled to him.

Via general revelation we can recognize that God is Creator, but only through special revelation can we grasp that he is also Savior. In fact, special revelation is required to properly interpret general revelation.[2]

Humans have an innate perception of God's existence. Scholars call it the *semen religionis*, a seed of religion or intuitional knowledge that drives humans to conclude that a supreme being exists. It is what the seventeenth-century mathematician Blaise Pascal dubbed a "God-shaped vacuum" in each human soul.

Furthermore, along with this basic awareness of God's existence inherent in humans, there is a vague understanding of right and wrong. This we label conscience, what many think of as an inner voice that often condemns us when we do something wrong, even if there is no specific law that prohibits us from doing it (Rom. 2:14–15).

Lastly, a comprehension of God is gained by rational reflection upon the data of creation. The psalmist can exclaim, "The heavens declare the glory of God; the skies proclaim the work of his hand" (Ps. 19:1 NIV), because God is revealed in his handiwork. Paul says that in the cosmos the "eternal power and divine nature" of God are revealed (Rom. 1:20),

---

2. Martin Luther describes this dependence of general revelation on special revelation: "There is a vast difference between knowing that there is a God and knowing who or what God is. Nature knows the former—it is inscribed in everybody's heart; the latter is taught only by the Holy Spirit" (*Lectures on the Minor Prophets: Part II: Jonah, Habakkuk*, comments on Jonah 1, in *Luther's Works*, 19:54–55, quoted in Demarest, *General Revelation*, 48).

so that by thoughtful contemplation on creation, humans can come to some understanding about God and his nature.

In short, within each human being there is enough data to know God exists. This being the case, why are there people who either question God's existence (agnostics) or outright reject it (atheists)? Additionally, why are there varying degrees of belief in God and his nature? If the knowledge of God is in every human heart, inscribed upon human conscience, and evident in the created order, why the disagreement about God's nature?

Paul makes plain reference to this matter and it is worth quoting in full:

> For the wrath of God is revealed from heaven against all ungodliness and unrighteousness of men, who by their unrighteousness suppress the truth. For what can be known about God is plain to them, because God has shown it to them. For his invisible attributes, namely, his eternal power and divine nature, have been clearly perceived, ever since the creation of the world, in the things that have been made. So they are without excuse. (Rom. 1:18–20)

Sinful humans suppress their innate understanding of God's existence. R. C. Sproul's comments on this passage get to the root of the problem: "The excuse that is banished, the excuse every pagan hopes in vain to use, the excuse that is exploded by God's self-revelation in nature is the pretended, vacuous, dishonest appeal to *ignorance*. . . . The problem is not a lack of evidence, nor a lack of knowledge, nor a lack of natural cognitive equipment—it is a *moral deficiency*."[3]

Note that the suppression of the innate knowledge of God and his existence is done "by their unrighteousness." The result is rejection of God's existence, but the cause is sin.

Out of the Darkness

Even though God has left himself numerous witnesses in general revelation, sinful humans reject him. This is why illumination is needed, but when we say illumination, we do not mean simple education. We

---

3. Sproul, Gerstner, and Lindsley, *Classical Apologetics*, 46.

mean spiritual enlightenment—a miraculous working of God's Spirit in the heart and mind of the sinner.

Worship and the Language of Illumination

The use of Scripture has become greatly diminished in many churches. Part of the problem is that a biblically illiterate Christendom is produced, where people read less and less of the Bible, often no longer bringing one to church. Our worship must be bathed in the Word of God, lest we become a church fed on baby's milk and not solid, spiritual food.

The eleventh-century Italian monk Anselm is famous for his premise, "I believe in order that I may understand." For Anselm, true knowledge of God could only flow from genuine faith. Six centuries earlier North African bishop Augustine said something similar: "If you will not believe, you will not understand." This formulation is preferable because it takes into consideration willful, insubordinate human nature. It is not a passive ignorance that Scripture recognizes, but an active, rebellious one driven by the sinful nature. That is why Paul can say, "The sinful mind is hostile to God. It does not submit to God's law, nor can it do so" (Rom. 8:7 NIV84). It is an inability that is triggered by a willful rebellion.

This theme of darkness in a moral sense is instrumental to our understanding of salvation as illumination or enlightenment. Consistently, Scripture depicts lost humanity as in a state of darkness. This darkness affects numerous aspects of human existence, but for each devastated element, there is a countermeasure to be found. We will investigate six areas.

1. The Heart

God's Word portrays the sinner's heart in stark terms. The prophet Jeremiah provides a powerful indictment: "The heart is deceitful above all things, and desperately sick." God says in Genesis, both before and after the flood, that every inclination of man's heart is continually evil. What is often depicted as the central element of a person, the heart, is seen to be entirely corrupt. For this reason Paul speaks of darkened hearts and hardened hearts that result in rejection of God.[4]

---

4. Jer. 17:9; Gen. 6:5; 8:21; Rom. 1:21; Eph. 4:18.

145

Proverbs 4:23 describes the heart as "the wellspring of life" (NIV 84), but it is a dirty well. Jesus noted that the reason he spoke in parables was because of the dullness of heart of his listeners (Matt. 13:15), and several times he spoke of the heart as the source of man's evil.

> But what comes out of the mouth proceeds from the heart, and this defiles a person. For out of the heart come evil thoughts, murder, adultery, sexual immorality, theft, false witness, slander. (Matt. 15:18–19)

It is from this "heart of darkness" that evil actions flow. Human corruption is not a superficial problem. It is one of nature and integral to humanity's composition.

However, salvation is seen as countering this darkness. In the Old Testament, God promised to give his people a new heart, replacing the heart of stone with one of flesh (Ezek. 36:26). Man's corrupt heart will be cleansed and inclined toward God, whereas before it was obsessed with evil. This is seen in the new covenant, predicted in the Old Testament and consummated in the age to come.

> This is the covenant that I will make with the house of Israel after those days, declares the LORD: I will put my law within them, and I will write it on their hearts. (Jer. 31:33; see also Heb. 8:10; 10:16)

Whereas the heart was the instrument of man's evil, it now becomes a fit parchment upon which God's law is written. This is why David can ask God to create a "clean heart" in him despite his wicked deeds (Ps. 51:10). In the innermost recesses of their being, sinners can have the light of God's truth illumine them. "For God, who said, 'Let light shine out of darkness,' has shone in our hearts to give the light of the knowledge of the glory of God in the face of Jesus Christ" (2 Cor. 4:6).

2. The Mind or Intellect

Scripture has much to say about darkened understanding and, conversely, the benefits of an enlightened mind.

Man's understanding, especially concerning spiritual matters, has been colored by sin. Paul can speak about the futility of the mind and darkened understanding that result from being separated from the life of God (Eph. 4:17–18). This works itself out in the inability to make reasoned judgments, particularly as it relates to living godly lives.

A major biblical theme involving foolishness and wisdom is seen in this matter. "The fool says in his heart, 'There is no God'" (Ps. 14:1). An individual can possess incredible intellect and yet be deemed foolish by biblical standards because he denies the one truth that governs all truths.

Paul constructs an elaborate argument along these lines in the opening chapters of his first epistle to Corinth. The gospel message, which is the very power of God, is seen as foolishness by unbelievers. There is a contrast between worldly wisdom and the wisdom that comes from God. Paul makes it apparent that godly wisdom is spiritually discerned, not naturally acquired.

> So also no one comprehends the thoughts of God except the Spirit of God. . . . The natural person does not accept the things of the Spirit of God, for they are folly to him, and he is not able to understand them because they are spiritually discerned. (1 Cor. 2:11b, 14)

If an individual does not possess God's Spirit, that person cannot discern spiritual wisdom. Thus, the message of hope and salvation in Jesus Christ appears foolish.

The practical implications of this truth are immense. Often we view successful evangelism as using the latest marketing tools. Success depends on appealing props. Yet, when unambiguous presentations are given, we can fully expect unbelievers to reject the message unless God's Spirit enlightens their minds to grasp its truth. We can never "argue people into heaven" or persuade them through natural means. Besides, when Jesus himself performed miracles some people did not believe. Why do we think that through clever gimmicks we can do better?

Witnessing and the Language of Illumination

Often, models of evangelism and apologetics concentrate on how to win arguments with unbelievers. While it is true that we should be prepared to give an answer for the hope we have (1 Peter 3:15), any encounter with non-Christians that does not wittingly rely on the Spirit's power to reveal our spiritually discerned gospel will be unfruitful. Prayer is more important in witnessing than winning a rational debate.

A spiritual message can only be understood by spiritual people. Flesh will simply continue to produce a fleshly response. A spiritual response to a spiritual message occurs solely in those people enlivened by God's Spirit. The natural mind, corrupted by sin, does not have the capacity to understand or accept the message of salvation in Jesus Christ.

Each and every conversion is a miraculous work of the Spirit. Since sinners have minds that are darkened, an act of God's Spirit is vital to lifting this darkness. Paul likens this darkness to a veil covering the minds and hearts of unbelievers, a veil that Christ takes away (2 Cor. 3:14b, 16).

A new covenant has come where the law of God is written on both the hearts and minds of God's people. Renewing of the mind (Rom. 12:2) counters the darkened understanding that previously characterized the individual. What used to be foolishness is now reasonable. An ability to discern spiritual truth has been granted.

This is portrayed throughout Scripture in the concepts of mystery and secret. For example, Jesus can speak to his disciples of the "secret of the kingdom of God" (Mark 4:11), a secret that has been given to them but hidden from others. Paul talks about the "secret and hidden wisdom of God" and the "secret things of God" (1 Cor. 2:7; 4:1 NIV84). The biblical understanding of mystery and secret connotes something that was formerly hidden but is now revealed. Spiritual illumination brings with it knowledge of that which was hitherto unknowable.

There are several mysteries in Christianity: the mystery of the incarnation, God becoming a man; the mystery of the atonement, that this God-man has died for the sins of humanity; the mystery of Jews and Gentiles being brought together in one body, the church; the mystery that all things will be brought under Christ; and the mystery of the bodily change that will take place at the resurrection of believers.[5] Talk of mystery permeates the New Testament.

These mysteries were formerly hidden. The Old Testament provides clues, but the mysteries are not fully revealed until the advent of God's Son. This being the case, the only people who can truly understand these mysteries "hidden for ages and generations but now revealed to his saints" (Col. 1:26) are those who have faith in Jesus, who have been illumined by his Spirit. They possess the "mind of Christ" (1 Cor. 2:16).

3. The Will

Human will is enslaved by sin and is unable and unwilling to obey God. In the will we can include motivations, intentions, and desires, for these drive the individual's subsequent choices. The unbeliever's will is corrupt, yet it is set free through faith in Jesus. We have already discussed this topic in chapter 4 on redemption.

4. Our Conscience

One way God is known is via conscience. The awareness that our actions are judged implies a Judge. If there are rules, there must be a Ruler. In this sense, Christian scholars throughout the centuries have argued that conscience reveals the existence of God.

However, we would be foolish to trust in the so-called voice of conscience alone, because its response in various moral situations is often muddled and confused. No human possesses a pure or uncorrupted conscience. The stain of sin affects even this aspect of humankind. Paul recognizes this when he says, "My conscience is clear, but that does not make me innocent. It is the Lord who judges me" (1 Cor. 4:4 NIV). The perception of an innocent conscience does not in itself prove that our actions are without sin. In the same letter, Paul mentions weak and defiled consciences (1 Cor. 8:7, 10, 12), so obviously we should not take our conscience as an infallible guide.

For example, through the practice of habitual sin, a person can have a "seared conscience" (1 Tim. 4:2). In time, the individual's conscience becomes numb to sinful behavior, because the sin has become accept-

---

5. 1 Tim. 3:16; 1 Cor. 2:1; Eph. 1:9; 3:3–6; 1 Cor. 15:51.

able. We can all relate experiences when we committed a sinful deed that, at first, caused our conscience to pang. But in time, with repeated infractions, we no longer felt the guilt or remorse that came with the original misstep. Given this fact, we acknowledge the weakness of conscience as a sure guide for our lives.

Titus 1:15 says unbelievers have minds and consciences that are "defiled." Their perception of truth becomes clouded and untrustworthy, and they are unable to judge between purity and impurity. The impure conscience resides in darkness and it must, along with each component of a sinner, be illumined in order to properly function.

This is precisely what happens via the gospel. Hebrews notes that the old sacrificial system was unable to effectively clear the conscience of the sinner. However, through the blood of Jesus our perfect High Priest, we can have a cleansed conscience (Heb. 9:9; 10:19–22). With the indwelling power of the Holy Spirit, believers are able to use their consciences as reliable guides, when coupled with submission to the revealed will of God found in his Word.

5. *The Eyes*

Both in popular as well as biblical understanding, the eyes are portrayed as the portal to the soul. Scripture regularly speaks about the eyes of sinners being shut. This is a metaphor for spiritual blindness that Jesus was fond of utilizing, notably when speaking to the religious leaders of his day. The Old Testament prophets were equally accustomed to speaking about eyes that could not see and ears that could not hear. In a New Testament passage that combines several elements of teaching from the Old Testament, we see this truth clearly:

> As it is written, "God gave them a spirit of stupor, eyes that would not see and ears that would not hear, down to this very day." And David says, "Let their table become a snare and a trap, a stumbling block and a retribution for them; let their eyes be darkened so that they cannot see, and bend their backs forever." (Rom. 11:8–10)

In Paul's discourse in Romans 3 concerning the universal plight of humanity under the power of sin, he identifies the root cause: "There is no fear of God before their eyes" (v. 18). Jesus similarly notes the importance of the eye:

> Your eye is the lamp of your body. When your eye is healthy, your whole body is full of light, but when it is bad, your body is full of darkness. (Luke 11:34; see also Matt. 6:22–23)

Interestingly, the lie the serpent used in the garden reversed this truth. He implied that as long as Adam and Eve obeyed God, their eyes would be closed. "For God knows that when you eat of it your eyes will be opened, and you will be like God, knowing good and evil" (Gen. 3:5). Of course, the exact opposite occurred. When our first parents ate the forbidden fruit, they fell into spiritual darkness.

Despite the universal, spiritual blindness that affects humanity, the revealing light of God's Word has the power to open darkened eyes. Through faith in God, the psalmist implores the Lord to "open my eyes, that I may behold wondrous things out of your law" (Ps. 119:18). God's Word is frequently portrayed as a light and lamp able to lead the sinner out of darkness.[6]

Paul's commission to the Gentiles given by the risen Lord was "to open their eyes, so that they may turn from darkness to light and from the power of Satan to God" (Acts 26:18). The children of God have received the capacity for spiritual light. "So we fix our eyes not on what is seen, but on what is unseen. For what is seen is temporary, but what is unseen is eternal" (2 Cor. 4:18 NIV84). A spiritual realm exists that can only be perceived by those whose eyes have been illumined to its truth.

6. Our Actions

We have already noted that the truth of God is suppressed by sinners because they love their evil deeds. Jesus likens these deeds to darkness, and Paul speaks of "unfruitful works of darkness" (Eph. 5:11). Since the entire being of a sinner is corrupted, it makes sense that his actions reflect a similar sickness. Like a tree with bad roots, we cannot expect the corrupt person to produce healthy fruit. If spiritually dead people can produce anything, their works will be spiritually deficient. We will look at this in greater detail in chapter 10 on fruitfulness.

---

6. Ps. 119:105, 130; Prov. 20:27; 2 Peter 1:19.

In these areas of a person's being—heart, mind, will, conscience, eyes, and actions—Scripture portrays salvation as a movement from darkness to light, an act of illumination by God's Spirit in the innermost being of the sinner.

Sources of Illumination

Jesus called himself the light of the world, and it is only in him that true illumination can be found. Those who do not have a living relationship with Christ still reside in the darkness, with all the consequences that residence entails. Defiled minds, darkened hearts, and depraved actions are the hallmarks of the denizens of darkness.

This may be hard to swallow, because we all know unbelievers who are decent, good people. They care for their families, pay their taxes, and are kind and honest citizens.[7] But Scripture leaves no room for a middle ground. Either you have a relationship with the Light, or you do not. A lamp is either plugged into the outlet or it remains disconnected.

Interestingly, believers are "children of the light" and appear to be considered a light source in the world as well. Much like the moon reflects the light of the sun, believers reflect the glory of God's Son.[8]

Another source of illumination is the Holy Spirit. Broadly speaking, the Spirit illumines everyone who has been regenerated, but in a narrower sense, the Spirit has the task of making Scripture understandable to the reader. This we similarly term illumination. The spiritual truths of Scripture only make sense to those who are illumined by God's Spirit.

God's Word is also a source of illumination. Although some scholars posit that the illuminating work of the Spirit can come apart from Scripture and can be found in non-Christian religions, traditional evan-

---

7. We briefly mentioned "common grace" in chapter 4 in the section "Bondage of Our Sinful Flesh." Common grace refers to the grace God gives to all humans in "common" or in general. It refers both to the kindness God shows to all that he has created, as well as his restraint of humanity's sin, corporately lessening its effects. Put another way, if God were to leave us to ourselves, humanity would quickly spiral into depravity on a grand scale. Think of humanity during the time of Noah for some idea of what this might entail. It is called "grace" because as rebellious sinners we do not deserve this kindness shown us by a holy God. Some biblical hints of this general grace shown to sinners are found in Psalm 145:9, Matthew 5:45, Luke 6:35, and Acts 14:17. Talk of common grace is usually coupled with the idea of "saving grace," which is the grace God gives to individuals who have faith in his Son.

8. Matt. 5:14; Eph. 5:8; Phil. 2:15.

gelicalism has taught that the Bible's special revelation is essential for saving knowledge of God. This knowledge can be taught via evangelistic enterprises, yet the truth of the missionary's message comes because God's Word first establishes its veracity.

The words of the prophets are characterized as "a light shining in a dark place" (2 Peter 1:19). True spiritual illumination comes from Scripture, which is "profitable for teaching, for reproof, for correction, and for training in righteousness, that the man of God may be complete, equipped for every good work" (2 Tim. 3:16–17). As the man of God is equipped for *every* good work, we see that Scripture is not only indispensable, but also sufficient. No other supposed sources of truth need be consulted to receive the spiritual illumination necessary for salvation.

The Benefits of Illumination

The benefits of illumination are numerous: possessing a heart and eyes that can perceive a spiritual reality that an unregenerate person cannot sense; understanding the deep mysteries of God, especially as they relate to having a saving and meaningful relationship with our Creator; and enjoying a desire and an ability to submit to God's law, with the capability for producing works of righteousness.

In Paul's prayer for the Ephesian believers cited at the opening of this chapter, he asks that the "eyes of [their] heart" will be enlightened. What an intriguing figure of speech. In this enlightenment, Paul envisions three benefits: the Ephesians will understand the hope they have in Christ Jesus, know that they already possess a "glorious inheritance" in him, and recognize that God's "incomparably great power" is available to them. What magnificent benefits!

What does it mean to be saved? It means seeing when you were formerly blind, acquiring wisdom when you were once a fool, and having a mind, conscience, and will that are illuminated with God's truth. It means stepping out from the darkness into the light.

I am the light of the world. Whoever follows me will not walk in darkness, but will have the light of life.

John 8:12

Key Terms for Salvation Expressed in the Language of Astronomy

illumination, enlightenment, mystery, secret, revelation, wisdom, foolishness, conscience, light, darkness

---

Questions for Group Discussion

1. Paul calls believers "children of light." In the past week, how have you shown yourself to be a child of light?

2. Conversely, in what areas of your life do you still reflect the "darkness" of your pre-conversion days?

3. What is the role of the Holy Spirit in the life of a believer when it comes to reading, studying, and understanding God's Word? Can an unbeliever understand the message of the Bible? Explain.

4. If all the wisdom of God is hidden in Christ, what can we conclude about the wisdom of the world? Must we determine that every good thing the world produces apart from Christ is worthless?

9

The Language of Industry

From Impurity to Purity

SANCTIFICATION

Now may the God of peace himself **sanctify** you completely,
and may your whole spirit and soul and body be kept blameless
at the coming of our Lord Jesus Christ.

1 Thessalonians 5:23

In the eight years following my graduation from college, I worked for a metallurgy company. I had earned a bachelor of science degree in chemical engineering, and for the remaining years of the decade of my twenties, I was a technical sales engineer in the Midwest. Among other things, I made sales calls on the steel mills of northwestern Indiana and the forging houses throughout the midwestern states, as well as visiting my employer's manufacturing mill along the Ohio River in West Virginia.

In order to purify a metal, you must melt it and remelt it. With one product we produced, the nickel content was over 99 percent. This meant removing as many impurities as possible through several remelting stages.

This is especially true of recycled metals. If you have been through a steel mill, you have seen the large pots known as crucibles that are used in steel production. The scrap metal is thrown into the crucible where it is heated until molten. The slag or dross—the waste material that is the impurity that you want to remove—floats to the top and is scooped off. The more times you remelt the metal, the more refined it becomes.

This is an excellent image of sanctification. In terms of their character and conduct in life, Christians are being melted and remelted, placed in the crucible so that dross in their lives can be removed. Scripture consistently speaks this way about the life of a believer. Sanctification is the removal of impurities as we become more and more holy in word, thought, and deed. With this chapter we will explore this language.

However, it should be noted that this chapter and the next are two sides of the same coin. On the one side, God scrubs you clean. On the other, he makes you productive. As such, the fruit of being sanctified will be discussed in chapter 10.

Sanctifying Language

Sanctification is the language of industry because it encompasses terms such as purify, refine, wash, and purge. The biblical authors regularly employ the language of the refinery to speak of the process through which believers are made holy. Two main categories of Greek words are used for this concept.

The first category includes the verbs *hagnizō* and *hagiazō*, which have the same root as *hagios*, meaning "holy." The earliest usage of *hagios* in ancient Greek refers to things not accessible to the public. They are set apart from the common. So when we see verbs translated "sanctify" or "purify," the primary meaning of the original Greek is "to be set apart."

However, when we see the word "holy" we usually think of sinlessness, but that is actually a secondary meaning. To make this clear, consider things that Scripture refers to as holy. There is holy ground, as when Moses approached the burning bush. A day could be considered holy. There is holy fruit and holy water. There are holy buildings such as the tabernacle and temple. Even rooms within these buildings are considered holier than others (e.g., the Holy of Holies). There are holy courts, chambers, furniture, and tools used in the tabernacle. Tithes and offerings are holy. Jerusalem is considered a holy city.[1]

---

1. Exod. 3:5; 16:23; Lev. 19:24; Num. 5:17; Exod. 40:9; 1 Chron. 29:3; Exod. 26:33–34; Isa. 62:9; Ezek. 42:13; 1 Chron. 9:29; Lev. 27:30; Neh. 11:1; Isa. 52:1.

None of these items have a moral quality to them. When speaking of ground as holy, this can hardly mean sinless. Rather, it means to be set apart for a special purpose. In this sense, it is the fundamental quality of God. God is set apart from all other beings. More will be said about holiness later.

The second category includes *katharizō*, the Greek word frequently translated "purify." From this Greek term we get our English word "catharsis," the act of purging emotional tension. This word was used in the Greek translation of the Old Testament, the Septuagint, for "purify" and "refine" as seen in Malachi 3:3:[2]

> He will sit as a refiner and purifier of silver, and he will purify the sons of Levi and refine them like gold and silver, and they will bring offerings in righteousness to the LORD.

In the New Testament, *katharizō* (and its derivatives) has a range of meanings. It can speak of making something clean such as a leper from disease, cleaning utensils, or even pruning trees.[3] The same root word is used metaphorically for clearing the threshing floor (Matt. 3:12) and purging a lump of leaven (1 Cor. 5:7). However, it is used primarily in the New Testament in a moral sense.

> Cleanse your hands, you sinners, and purify your hearts, you double-minded. (James 4:8b)

We will consider these moral uses later. Here is a passage where several Greek words of sanctification are used together (Within the brackets below and elsewhere I'm showing the root word for each Greek term).

> Husbands, love your wives, as Christ loved the church and gave himself up for her, that he might sanctify [*hagiozō*] her, having cleansed [*katharizō*] her by the washing of water with the word, so that he might present the church to himself in splendor, without spot or wrinkle or any such thing, that she might be holy [*hagios*] and without blemish. (Eph. 5:25–27)

---

2. *Katharizō* was also used for purging the land of idolatry (2 Chron. 34:3) and rebels (Ezek. 20:38).

3. Matt. 8:2–3; 23:25–26. The same Greek root (*kathairō*) is used for "pruning" (John 15:2), but we will deal with this in the next chapter.

This is what Christ does to the church. He makes believers holy, but to what end? So that he may "purify for himself a people for his own possession who are zealous for good works" (Titus 2:14). Believers are set apart for service to God.

A key biblical word for "church" brings out this idea. *Ekklēsia* is a combination of two Greek words literally meaning "called out." It is from this word that we get "ecclesiastical" and other cognates. As such, believers are regularly called "saints" (*hagioi*), literally "holy ones" (e.g., Rom. 1:7; Eph. 1:1).[4]

Witnessing and the Language of Sanctification

Our evangelistic enterprises are undermined by impure Christian living. "Do what I say, not what I do" is communicated to the world when out of one side of our mouths we confess Jesus as Lord, while from the other side we proclaim our allegiance to the world in living unholy lives. Hypocritical Christians should not be surprised when the world rejects our message.

The Roman Catholic Church teaches that *certain* Christians are saints. These people immediately go to heaven when they die because they have obtained enough merit. However, the New Testament does not call select believers "saints." It refers to everyone as a saint who has faith in Jesus. Every believer is part of the "called out ones."

How Justification and Sanctification Relate

Which one of the following statements is true concerning your salvation?

- "I was saved"
- "I am saved"
- "I am being saved"
- "I will be saved"

---

4. Believers are also referred to as a holy priesthood and a holy nation (1 Peter 2:5, 9).

Hopefully you realize this is a trick question. Depending on what aspect of salvation you choose to emphasize, each statement is true. What Jesus did two thousand years ago secured the salvation of everyone who has faith in him. Paul says that all our sins were nailed to the cross (Col. 2:13–14), not just the ones up to the time of our conversion, or only the ones cleansed by baptism or covered by communion as some churches teach. Every single sin we have ever committed and ever will commit was nailed to that cross. Believers were objectively saved long ago.

While the salvation of every Christian was objectively secured at the cross, it subjectively begins at the moment of conversion. Evangelicals often express salvation as a future reality—when we die and go to heaven we will be saved. It is true that our salvation is completed then, but if heaven exclusively is viewed as "being saved," this is a deficient view of salvation. Christian salvation is much more than a future reality; Christian salvation begins *now*. "I am saved" and "I will be saved" are both true.

Sanctification is best expressed in the third statement, "I am being saved." However, this declaration cannot be understood apart from the other three equally valid assertions.

Justification is the legal declaration that you are guiltless. Sanctification is the actual process by which you become sinless. Justification is an objective reality from the past. Sanctification is an ongoing, present progression in the life of the believer that culminates in the future. Justification is something God does on your behalf—believers do not effect it or add to it. Sanctification, on the other hand, is something that both God and humans do in cooperation. This tension has created certain problems throughout the church's history, to which we will turn shortly.

Justification and sanctification are frequently confused with each other. To illustrate this, here is a quote from well-known Christian author and speaker Joyce Meyer:

> Now whether you like it or not, whether you want to admit it
> or not, whether you want to operate on it or not, you are made
> the righteousness of God in Jesus Christ. Most people who go
> to denominational churches never ever hear that! They never
> hear it! Never! All I was ever taught to say was, "I'm a poor,

miserable sinner." I am not poor, I am not miserable and I am not a sinner. That is a lie from the pit of hell. That is what I were and if I still was, then Jesus died in vain. Amen? . . .

I'm going to tell you something folks, I didn't stop sinning until I finally got it through my thick head I wasn't a sinner anymore. And the religious world thinks that's heresy and they want to hang you for it. But the Bible says that I'm righteous and I can't be righteous and be a sinner at the same time.[5]

Regardless of whether or not Meyer stands by these statements today, when she said these things she muddied the waters between the judicial declaration of righteousness all believers receive, and the sanctification that justified sinners presently undergo. There is a half-truth in this quotation. Yes, I am "made the righteousness of God in Jesus Christ" (justification). Yet, I am still a sinner in need of sanctification.

We are saved from the bad effects of our sin (e.g., eternal condemnation, God's wrath). Yet, we are also being sanctified and made holy. God saves us from something, but he also makes us into something.

In this sense, sanctification is not merely the by-product of being saved; it is salvation. The only people being made holy are those who have genuine faith in Jesus Christ. Unbelievers remain in their contaminated, polluted state. There are two kinds of people, those who are set apart for God, and those who are not.

Present-Future Tensions

A pendulum has swung throughout Christian history between two views of salvation that have unfortunately been played against each other. This tension is between "heaven is the sole goal of Christianity" and "making the world a better place *now* is the Christian's goal."

This is a false dichotomy. It plays one aspect of genuine biblical salvation against another. We will consider two ways this clash exists.

---

5. Joyce Meyer, "From the Cross to the Throne" (sermon, Life Christian Center, St. Louis, MO, n.d.), cassette tape audio clip accessed December 29, 2014, https://craig brownsreformedtheology.files.wordpress.com/2011/09/clip-9-joycemeyer.mp3. Online transcripts have the paragraphs in reverse order, but the quotation follows the audio clip, which does not include the entire quotation.

1. Perfectionism (Legalism) versus Antinomianism

Antinomianism is a fancy word that simply means living without the law (the Greek for "law" is *nomos*). Some Christians have argued that because salvation is by grace, works become unimportant, thus juxtaposing faith and good works.

The argument follows a simple path. The law was put in place to condemn me, convince me of my sinfulness, and drive me to God's grace. However, now that I have become a believer, the law has done its job and is of no more importance to me. I can basically live my life as a forgiven sinner the way I want to live it. This position is an emphasis on justification to the exclusion of sanctification. Liberal Lutheranism as it can be found in Germany, Scandinavia, the United States, and southern Africa has suffered from this imbalance.

This attitude is nothing new. Christians in first-century Corinth reveled in their freedom in Christ, so much so that a fellow believer was having sexual relations with his father's wife and the church appeared to be quite comfortable with it. After all, in Christ we are set free from the law.

Paul's command to the Corinthians was that they "purge" the offending brother from the church (1 Cor. 5:13). In other words, sanctify the church. Refine it. Purify it.

In reaction to this tendency to abuse the grace of God as a "license for immorality" (Jude 4 NIV), the pendulum has swung too far the other way. A perfectionism or legalism has cropped up in Christendom that stresses living a holy life to such a degree that it appears a person is saved by his good works.

There is a long history of these sentiments. Both the Novatianists of the third century and the Donatists of the fourth called themselves the "pure ones" because they saw in other Christians an intolerable willingness to coddle sin. Certain pietistic groups like the Moravians and Mennonites, along with churches that have been affected by John Wesley's teaching on "perfect love," and twentieth-century Pentecostalism have all leaned toward this side of the debate. Theirs is an emphasis on sanctification at the neglect of justification.

I am reminded of a story my uncle told about a woman who stood up in his church one Sunday evening during a time for giving testimonies and thanked the Lord that she had not sinned in the previous seven years. Forget for the moment that this woman's understanding of sin was rather narrow, limited to overt, conscious choices she could number and recall. Sin is much more than external actions. The real problem was she actually believed she was sinless. This was a product of her Wesleyan background.

Believers sit between these two tendencies. We are commanded to not use our freedom as an excuse to indulge the flesh (antinomianism). However, to guard against this possibility, many Christians create a series of human-based stipulations (legalism) that are meant to yield a perfect adherence to God's commands.

Admittedly, it is difficult to keep these two tendencies in balance. As an evangelical, at times it may be easy to make a conscious choice to sin and, with a shrug of the shoulders, count on the forgiveness of God. Others may struggle with the self-righteous attitude that they among all Christians are the ones who are pure and undefiled.

2. Fundamentalism versus Liberalism

Some Christians view salvation as two points on a line. The first point is conversion, the second heaven. Everything in between is fairly negligible. Getting into heaven is the sole aim of salvation according to these Christians, and that was assured at conversion. This I am calling the fundamentalist view of salvation.

Fundamentalist Christianity tends to fixate on the doctrinal purity of the faith, while good works appear minor. What this yields is a "holy huddle" mentality, caring very little about this fallen world. All that matters is getting to the next life. This attitude can be expressed in the adage, "Some people are so heavenly minded that they are no earthly good."

"When you die, do you want to go to heaven?" is certainly an apt question, but there is an equally relevant question to ask. "Do you want your life *now* to count for something of eternal value?" Theologically speaking, fundamentalists fixate on justification at the expense of sanctification.

This is also seen in missions endeavors where the sole purpose is to reach the unreached. While spreading the gospel is a paramount obligation for all believers, we are commanded to make disciples, not converts. Often these movements are more concerned with counting heads and moving on to the next unreached area.

Picture a train screaming through the countryside of an unreached territory. Two men stand near an open window on the train. One holds a pen and pad, while the other commands a stack of Bibles. As the train passes through the land, the man with the Bibles throws them out at people. Wham! The Bibles hit the people square in the chest, and with each impact, the man with the pen makes a checkmark. "Another person reached for Jesus," he says with a smile.

This caricature of evangelistic enterprises solely worried about "getting people into heaven" is not far from the truth. Without proper discipleship, I daresay the majority of the people initially reached will be lost. For the fundamentalist who cares little about this present world, all that matters is getting a person converted.

However, an equal yet opposite problem exists. Normally found in liberal Christian circles, there is such a concentration on this life that the next is forgotten. Liberals envision "salvation" in wholly earthly terms, repackaged to mean being saved from poverty or friendlessness or purposelessness. Talk about sin and eternal salvation are virtually eliminated, replaced by more immediate considerations. Theologically speaking, liberals fixate on sanctification at the expense of justification.

To the idea that as Christians we are commanded to make this world a better place, a fundamentalist might say that this world will burn in the coming judgment, so there is little point in worrying about it. To the idea that as Christians we are told that an eternal afterlife with God awaits us, a liberal Christian might say that such thinking makes a person unfit for doing what needs to be done at present in this world, things like caring for the poor, feeding the hungry, clothing the naked, and so on.

For the fundamentalist, talk of "saving the world" is entirely misplaced, emphasizing the temporal over the eternal. For the liberal, talk of "getting to heaven" makes Christians uncaring and unconcerned with the plight of the suffering in the here and now, emphasizing an eternal blissful existence at the exclusion of a present reality of being "Christ in the world."

Both sides of the dichotomy are right, and both are wrong. Of course, one could argue that eternal matters trump temporal ones. There is no point in feeding a beggar a meal a day, only to have him spend an eternity in hell. Sharing the gospel with him and bringing him to a saving knowledge of Christ is far more important than filling his empty belly. Yet, supplying his physical needs is not unimportant. The fault of liberal Christians is that they make the minor aspect the complete picture, while the fundamentalist makes the major aspect the whole story. In this sense, the fundamentalist commits a slighter error, but it is an error nonetheless.

An example might help. Suppose you want to run a soup kitchen to help street children. This is undoubtedly a noble cause for a Christian, but if there is no eternal angle to the endeavor—no sharing of the gospel or a daily Bible story to go along with the food—this is a wasted opportunity to address both the physical and spiritual needs of the children. James and John speak about our faith being seen in how we treat others.[6] The liberal has works without faith, while the fundamentalist has faith without works.

The fundamentalist must learn that the goal of the Christian life is not heaven, it is becoming like Jesus. Heaven is the icing on the cake. When Paul writes, "If only for this life we have hope in Christ" (1 Cor. 15:19 NIV), he implies that there is a hope not only for the age to come but also for this present reality, just not exclusively for the here and now.

On the other hand, the liberal Christian must stop pretending this life is all that matters. Feeding the poor is indeed worthwhile, but only when the eternal consequences of this life are also addressed.

A proper view of Christian salvation encompasses both this life as well as the next. Certainly we can speak in terms of justification—having our sins forgiven and having the hope of eternal life—but our salvation does not begin when we die. It begins at the moment new life in Christ begins. Salvation should be lived out. As James declares, "Faith apart from works is dead" (2:26).

> But now that you have been set free from sin and have become slaves of God, the fruit you get leads to sanctification and its end, eternal life. (Rom. 6:22)

I am occasionally asked why Africa has so many problems when the majority of the continent is Christian. However, it wasn't long ago that Europe waged two world wars, in large part between so-called Christian

---

6. James 2:15–16; 1 John 3:17.

nations. Much of church history for the past several centuries has been characterized by Christians killing Christians. Perhaps it is because we have a lopsided view of salvation, with too much emphasis on justification and too little on sanctification. Thus, we tend to minimize our own contribution to the sanctifying process.

Who Does the Sanctifying?

The primary agent of sanctification is God. This makes good sense. An imperfect creature cannot make itself perfect. It must be perfected by a perfect Being. In this sense, sanctification is a passive activity. Note the passive verbs in the following verse:

> But you were washed, you were sanctified, you were justified
> in the name of the Lord Jesus Christ and by the Spirit of our
> God. (1 Cor. 6:11)

In the opening verses of Ephesians, Paul writes that believers were predestined by God before the foundation of the world, to make them "holy and blameless before him" (Eph. 1:4). God does this through two primary means, the Holy Spirit and the Holy Scriptures. This is why it is irresponsible for people to downplay the role of the Bible in our lives, or to place the work of God's Spirit at odds with God's Word. The Holy Spirit never contradicts the Word he inspired.[7] A sure guide for understanding how the Spirit works is to know the Spirit's Word.[8]

In his high priestly prayer, Jesus emphasizes the sanctifying power of Scripture:

> They are not of the world, just as I am not of the world. Sanctify
> [hagiozō] them in the truth; your word is truth. As you sent me
> into the world, so I have sent them into the world. And for
> their sake I consecrate [hagiozō] myself, that they also may be
> sanctified [hagiozō] in truth. (John 17:16–19)

This echoes the Old Testament declaration about God's Word, again couched in the language of industry.

---

7. For this reason, the Bible is called "the sword of the Spirit" (Eph. 6:17).
8. For passages that speak of the Spirit's role in sanctifying believers, see Rom. 15:16; 2 Thess. 2:13; 1 Peter 1:2.

> The words of the Lord are pure words,
> like silver refined in a furnace on the ground,
> purified seven times. (Ps. 12:6)

Many Christians look for quick fixes or gimmicks meant to effect immediate sanctification, but the time-honored method of reading, memorizing, and meditating upon God's Word is a sure means to godliness. As we expose ourselves to Scripture, we are made holy by God's Spirit.[9]

However, sanctification is also an active participation by the believer. The imperfect creature can be involved in its own sanctification by submitting to the work of the perfect Being. Both Old Testament Israelites and New Testament Christians are commanded to be holy (Lev. 11:44; 1 Peter 1:15–16). God's people should set themselves apart; they do this by refraining from sin.

For example, because this present world will be destroyed, Peter commands believers to live holy, godly lives (2 Peter 3:11). Paul commands saints to "cleanse ourselves from every defilement" (2 Cor. 7:1). In his epistle to the Thessalonians, Paul makes an intimate connection between the indwelling Spirit and our responsibilities as believers to live holy lives. Believers should walk pleasing to God. By disregarding the Holy Spirit we absent ourselves from God's sanctifying power (1 Thess. 4:1–8).

Perhaps the most powerful argument, though, is found in Paul's temple analogy. Because God's Spirit lives in believers, how can they not sanctify themselves?

> Do you not know that you are God's temple and that God's Spirit dwells in you? If anyone destroys God's temple, God will destroy him. For God's temple is holy, and you are that temple. (1 Cor. 3:16–17)

As the physical temple in Jerusalem was the special place where God met his people, so God meets us through his Spirit in our bodies. Therefore, we should live lives that reflect that spiritual communion.[10]

---

9. The blood of Jesus also "cleanses [*katharizō*] us from all sin" (1 John 1:7).

10. Paul speaks similarly elsewhere when he couples this idea of our bodies as temples with the prohibition against frequenting prostitutes (1 Cor. 6:12–20) and being "unequally yoked with unbelievers" (2 Cor. 6:14–16).

In one sense, Christians are already holy in God's sight. In another sense, they are being made holy. Sanctification is both an active and a passive process. The following passage from Paul wonderfully expresses this twofold nature of sanctification:

> Work out your own salvation with fear and trembling, for it is God who works in you, both to will and to work for his good pleasure. (Phil. 2:12–13)

Further Industrial Language

There is a wide array of biblical words conveying related sentiments of sanctification such as burning, purging, testing, wiping, and filtering. We will briefly consider a few of these as we conclude this chapter.

God expects certain behavior from his people, and when he does not find it, he resorts to refining them. For example, God told the prophet Ezekiel that he was displeased with Israel for breaking his covenant.

> Son of man, the house of Israel has become dross to me; all of them are bronze and tin and iron and lead in the furnace; they are dross of silver. (Ezek. 22:18)

Almost always when a metal is mined from the earth, it comes with impurities. Silver can be mixed with metals like iron or lead. God looked to his chosen people to find pure metal, but what he found was silver contaminated with dross.[11] Therefore, he will refine his people. One way God does this is through suffering.

> Behold, I have refined you, but not as silver; I have tried you in the furnace of affliction. (Isa. 48:10)

This is analogous to the idea of discipline we saw in chapter 3 on adoption. As our heavenly Father, God disciplines his children to correct us. As the author of Hebrews makes clear, suffering is an effective means of separating unwanted dross from the believer's life (Heb. 12:7).

In both the Old and New Testaments, certain words are consistently used to convey this idea of refining or separation. To test and to burn are two such concepts. For example, the psalmist writes that Joseph was "tested" through his suffering (Ps. 105:19). Both the Hebrew here

---

11. Also Ps. 119:119; Isa. 1:25.

and the Greek used to translate it in the Septuagint have the idea of burning as with fire.

We often think that being sold into slavery by his jealous brothers and falsely accused by Potiphar's wife were simply "bad luck" on the part of Jacob's favorite son. However, these events were means by which God tested Joseph's faith. Having been tested and proved trustworthy, he was used by God to preserve Jacob's household in Egypt.[12]

> And I will put this third into the fire,
>> and refine them as one refines silver,
>> and test them as gold is tested. (Zech. 13:9)

Christians can expect a similar burning. Peter tells believers that God uses suffering "so that the tested genuineness of your faith—more precious than gold that perishes though it is tested by fire—may be found to result in praise and glory and honor at the revelation of Jesus Christ" (1 Peter 1:7).

This testing by fire does not happen solely in this life. Paul tells the Corinthians that, upon building their faith on the foundation of Christ, in the last day their work will be tested with fire. "If the work that anyone has built on the foundation survives, he will receive a reward. If anyone's work is burned up, he will suffer loss, though he himself will be saved, but only as through fire" (1 Cor. 3:14–15).

Worship and the Language of Sanctification

When Isaiah had his vision of the Lord on his throne, the prophet cried out that he was a man of unclean lips (Isa. 6:5). Our acts of worship in the context of a two-hour Sunday service will avail little if the rest of the week our lives are unclean.

In light of this present and future testing, believers should be motivated to produce the fruit of sanctification. We will look more closely at that fruit in the next chapter.

---

12. A similar concept is found when Gideon was preparing to fight the Midianites. God "tested" the fighting men before winnowing down their number from ten thousand to three hundred soldiers (Judg. 8:4–8).

However, despite these biblical warnings, Christians sin. The progress of sanctification is a bumpy road for the vast majority of believers. Knowing that our sanctification is regularly impeded by our own behavior, we need to constantly seek the Lord in repentance.

King David knew this all too well. After his sin with Bathsheba, he came to the Lord and sought purification. This should be the heartfelt cry of every believer.

> Have mercy on me, O God,
>   according to your steadfast love;
> according to your abundant mercy
>   blot out my transgressions.
> Wash me thoroughly from my iniquity,
>   and cleanse me from my sin! (Ps. 51:1–2)

Holy, Holy, Holy

Scripture repeatedly speaks about holy things. Every major player of the biblical story is referred to as holy. God, Jesus, the Spirit, Israel, the church, angels, and believers are all "set apart." The Lord's Prayer begins with this language: "Our Father in heaven, hallowed [*hagiozō*] be your name" (Matt. 6:9). Holiness is a key concept throughout the Bible.

> Without holiness no one will see the Lord. (Heb. 12:14 NIV)

The sanctification of every believer is to be expected. God does not merely justify us and leave us to ourselves. He looks to make us holy, and he gives us the means to participate in that process.

What does it mean to be saved? It means being set apart for service to God. It means being refined and purged of sin in your life as you submit to God's Spirit in obedience to God's Word. It means being declared a saint. It means moving from impurity to purity.

Since we have these promises, beloved, let us cleanse ourselves from every defilement of body and spirit, bringing holiness to completion in the fear of God.

2 Corinthians 7:1

Key Terms for Salvation Expressed in the Language of Industry

sanctification, sanctify, purify, refine, burn, purge, holy, holiness, saints, temple, Holy Spirit, washing, cleansing, testing, dross

---

Questions for Group Discussion

1. As you look back at your Christian walk, can you see clear evidence of sins that have been purged? What dross in your life has been refined by God?

2. Are you uncomfortable being called a saint? If so, why? If not, why not?

3. If you were forced to choose one of the following labels to describe yourself, which would it be: fundamentalist, legalist, perfectionist, or liberal? Explain your selection.

4. Is the holiness of God something you regularly contemplate? Is it a deterrence against sin in your life as it should be?

10

The Language of Agriculture
From Barrenness to Productivity

FRUITFULNESS

Likewise, my brothers, you also have died to the law through the body of Christ, so that you may belong to another, to him who has been raised from the dead, in order that we may *bear fruit* for God.

Romans 7:4

Our first two years in Namibia, my wife and I lived in the farming town of Grootfontein. Namibia is a desert country and even in the agricultural triangle in which we lived, the prospect of rain was dodgy at best. Whereas the place where I grew up in America, "the Garden State" (New Jersey), is characterized by lush greenery, Namibia is arid and brown.

The lack of water had an effect on plant life, and something that immediately stood out upon arrival was the lack of grass. Homeowners used a rubber rake to comb their dirt yards. It looked quite nice when the job was done, resembling the pregame paths on a baseball diamond. Still, it was just dirt.

If you wanted grass, you had to plant it. Mind you, this was not sod that you laid out like a carpet. I had to go to the sewage plant and cut up runners of grass in the open field, the only place in the area where grass

171

grew freely. I cleaned up a section of my yard about four by six meters and I planted the runners. Every day I doused them with a considerable amount of water. Few people did this because water was expensive and it made little sense to waste money in this way, but I wanted a patch of green in my yard.

The grass grew wonderfully but with it came a lot of weeds. Every day I went out and pulled the unwanted plants. After several weeks of care, I had a solid patch of grass in my front yard that even needed mowing. I nursed the twenty-four square meters of green for half a year, until wintertime. By then, Namibia was so dry that it was virtually impossible to keep the grass alive.

If I am honest about it, the time and cost associated with keeping that grass alive was not worth it. After all, it produced nothing of value. It was simply nice to look at. However, in an entire location of dust and dirt, it was a place your bare feet could feel something alive. It reminded me a bit of home as well.

The New Testament borrows liberally from the language of agriculture to speak about the life of a believer. Sow, plant, reap, harvest, prune, water, and grow are consistently used in this way.[1] That little patch of green got me thinking about God caring for and nurturing us. God takes a piece of dirt and plants grass on it. What formerly was barren is now vibrant and alive. It becomes something of value that can eventually produce fruit.

Some may object that with this chapter I am muddying the waters between justification and sanctification, with fruitfulness typically understood as coming after a person has been justified. While I do not dispute that distinction, the point I want to make is that if you are not saved, you can produce nothing of value. However, if you are saved, you are productive and fruitful. One's salvation can indeed be characterized as the difference between being productive versus unproductive, just as much as it can be characterized as being alive versus dead, or acquitted versus guilty.

Bearing fruit is not something that is tacked on to salvation. As much as salvation means being forgiven of your sins, or being set free from

---

1. Had we broadened the scope of this chapter from language of agriculture to farming, we could include biblical material on shepherds and sheep.

the slavery of Satan and death, salvation is also being able to produce good works acceptable to God. Only Christians can yield spiritually commendable works of eternal significance. Forgiveness, freedom, and fruitfulness are all ways of expressing biblical salvation.

You may have noticed that each model of salvation features the pattern of a problem with an accompanying solution. However, there is also the pattern of the result being produced once the hindrance has been removed. For example, with adoption we noted that we are outside the family of God but then are brought into it as sons. The result is that we must perform the proper duties of God's household.

The same can be said for redemption. Our freedom from sin, death, and the devil was bought at a price, but not so we could go our carefree way. Rather, as free men and women we have duties as "slaves of righteousness" (Rom. 6:18). We have been ransomed to produce works pleasing to God.

The difficulty with a chapter on fruitfulness is that there is too much to say. As I heard at a Bible conference, Christians have minds through which Christ thinks, hearts through which Christ feels, hands through which Christ works, and voices through which Christ speaks. All of this is the fruit God expects from followers of his Son. A whole book could cover just this aspect.

However, as my goal throughout these chapters has been to contrast the believer with the unbeliever, I will do the same here. I do not intend to speak about those general things that anybody can do, the "be nice to everyone, even the neighbor's dog" kind of ethic.

For example, I recently heard a preacher speak about how Christians need to show others the love of Christ. He shared an experience at the grocery store. While he stood at the checkout counter, the cashier emptied his basket, moving each item past the scanner. Their eyes never met and no word was spoken. The pastor noted how impersonal the encounter was. He determined to make more of it, so as he was about to leave, he looked the young lady in the eyes and told her to have a nice day. She smiled.

As I listened to this story, I must admit I expected more. In a message devoted to showing others the love of Christ, I anticipated something would actually be said about Jesus. I suppose I was envisaging evangelism, not sentimentalism.

I want to concentrate on those works that set believers apart from the unregenerate, what John refers to as the "righteous deeds of the saints" (Rev. 19:8). Anybody can smile at the cashier. We will look in what follows at the fruit that followers of Jesus exclusively can yield.

One or the Other

The book of Psalms opens with a contrast between two men, one godless, the other godly. The psalmist associates the two people to things found in agriculture. The righteous man is like a healthy, productive tree. The tree is planted near water, its leaf does not wither, and it produces fruit in the right season. He prospers in all that he does.

The wicked man is compared to chaff. Chaff is the debris that is discarded after the harvest has been winnowed. In ancient times winnowing involved repeatedly throwing the produce from the harvest up in the air. The good materials fell back to earth, while the chaff was blown away. The psalmist equates a wicked man to agricultural waste that "the wind drives away" (Ps. 1:4).

The contrast is stark. The man approved by God does well no matter what he does, while the man rejected by God does nothing of any value. "The LORD knows the way of the righteous, but the way of the wicked will perish" (v. 6).

When we come to the New Testament, that teaching fundamentally remains. Scripture portrays two options. There are righteous people and there are wicked people. There are no neutral people. This has been obvious in the previous chapters. Either you are dead or you are alive. There is no such thing as half-dead or half-alive. You are either pardoned or you are guilty. You are either controlled by the Holy Spirit or by the sinful flesh. You are either a friend of God or his enemy. You are either set free or still in bondage.

Jesus routinely speaks this way in his parables. There is a separation that takes place. He speaks of wheat and weeds, good fish and bad fish, sheep and goats, and two roads and two gates with two eternal destinations.[2] Like the psalmist, Jesus used trees as an analogy of the faith to show that people are recognized by the fruits their lives produce.

---

2. Matt. 13:37–43; 13:47–50; 25:32–33; 7:13–14.

> Are grapes gathered from thornbushes, or figs from thistles? So, every healthy tree bears good fruit, but the diseased tree bears bad fruit. A healthy tree cannot bear bad fruit, nor can a diseased tree bear good fruit. Every tree that does not bear good fruit is cut down and thrown into the fire. Thus you will recognize them by their fruits. (Matt. 7:16–20)

You cannot look at a fruit tree that bears no fruit and say that it is a good fruit tree. It is declared a good fruit tree because it bears fruit. Barren fruit trees are worthless and only useful for burning. Jesus says a bad tree cannot produce good fruit. The righteous man is a productive tree, the wicked man a barren one.

There are many Christians today who rail against this notion. They say this teaching creates an "us versus them" mentality. Jesus came to unite, not to separate and divide. However, it truly is an either-or world, and Jesus made that crystal clear.

> Do not think that I have come to bring peace to the earth. I have not come to bring peace, but a sword. For I have come to set a man against his father, and a daughter against her mother, and a daughter-in-law against her mother-in-law. And a person's enemies will be those of his own household. (Matt. 10:34–36)

Jesus knows that a divine divide with eternal consequences has been created through his advent. In fact, this is what good farmers have to do. They separate the wheat from the weeds. Skilled fishermen divide the good fish from the bad ones. Competent arborists separate productive trees from unproductive ones. As the "good shepherd," our Lord is no different. Good shepherds separate the sheep from the goats.[3]

---

3. Middle Eastern sheep and goats at the time of Jesus looked surprisingly alike, so it took a keen eye to separate them. Several reasons have been suggested for why the two needed to be separated. Goats tend to be cantankerous beasts while sheep are docile. The two have grazing habits which can be counterproductive (sheep graze from the bottom up, goats from the top down). Lastly, there may be some reason why the animals needed to be separated based on Mosaic law. The law prohibited the intermingling of herds and the wearing of garments with mixed fibers (Deut. 22:11; Lev. 19:19). There appears to be a very practical reason for both prohibitions. If the grazing habits of sheep and goats are counterproductive to each other, then it makes good sense to prohibit the mixing of fibers in clothing. The concern for mixing the fibers would encourage the Israelites to keep the animals apart, thus producing better grazing practices.

When the Bible speaks of good works, these are not things any old person can do. Scripture calls them the "fruit of righteousness" and as such, only the righteous can perform them. Spiritually dead people do not produce anything spiritually worthwhile. Paul speaks similarly about the fruit of the light and the "fruitless deeds of darkness."[4]

> Every plant that my heavenly Father has not planted will be rooted up. (Matt. 15:13)

Attached to the Vine

How can the wicked move from their unproductive life? Here we must consider the elementary concepts of repentance and confession. This is the "firstfruits" of the Christian's life.

Repentance was the message of John the Baptist; it was the message of Jesus; it was the message of Peter to the Jews and Paul to the Gentiles.[5] Repentance involves turning from your old ways to God's ways. Your outlook and purpose in life are transformed. This is the sole way that godly, spiritual fruit can be produced by a sinner. True repentance requires a change of heart wherein one's perspective on sin is altered. In fact, hatred of sin is the hallmark of genuine repentance, with the subsequent endeavor to live a holy life.

This is why Paul could say that his message to the Gentiles was that "they should repent and turn to God, performing deeds in keeping with their repentance" (Acts 26:20). This, then, is where we begin. If we are ever to become fruitful, we must repent.

Of course, repentance is not a one-off activity. The life of a believer entails consistent repentance, since we realize that we regularly fall short of the holiness we are called to emulate. Daily we admit we are not what we should be; God cleanses us (1 John 1:9) so we may serve him as we ought. In this sense, then, we become connected to Jesus.

> Jesus answered them, "This is the work of God, that you believe in him whom he has sent." (John 6:29)

---

4. Phil. 1:11; Heb. 12:11; Eph. 5:9–11 NIV.
5. Matt. 3:2; 4:17; Acts 3:19; 17:30.

Closely related to repentance is confession. The Greek for "confession" presents connections to the subjects of two previous chapters. It is a public declaration, either of one's guilt in a court of law (chapter 2 on justification), or of allegiance to a king's covenant (chapter 5 on citizenship). Spiritually speaking, when we confess, we declare our personal relationship with Jesus and our open commitment to obey him. Therefore, confession is indispensable to one's salvation.

> If you confess with your mouth that Jesus is Lord and believe in your heart that God raised him from the dead, you will be saved. (Rom. 10:9)

Unbelievers do not do these things. Thus, they cannot produce fruit pleasing to God. Jesus makes this compelling point when he speaks about his disciples abiding in him.

> I am the true vine, and my Father is the vinedresser. Every branch in me that does not bear fruit he takes away, and every branch that does bear fruit he prunes, that it may bear more fruit. . . . As the branch cannot bear fruit by itself, unless it abides in the vine, neither can you, unless you abide in me. I am the vine; you are the branches. Whoever abides in me and I in him, he it is that bears much fruit, for apart from me you can do nothing. If anyone does not abide in me he is thrown away like a branch and withers; and the branches are gathered, thrown into the fire, and burned. . . . By this my Father is glorified, that you bear much fruit and so prove to be my disciples. . . . If you keep my commandments, you will abide in my love, just as I have kept my Father's commandments and abide in his love. (John 15:1–2, 4b–6, 8, 10)

Note that even disciples of Jesus cannot produce any fruit unless they remain in him.[6] Apart from Jesus Christ, we can do nothing of any spiritual or eternal significance. Branches that have become detached from the vine are fit for burning. What, then, must we conclude about branches that were never attached to the vine in the first place?

---

6. This passage hints at what it means to participate with Jesus, something we will discuss in chapter 12.

> For it is time for judgment to begin at the household of God;
> and if it begins with us, what will be the outcome for those
> who do not obey the gospel of God? (1 Peter 4:17)

Abiding in Christ is essential for the fruitful Christian life. Jesus hints at this in the Great Commission, where he declares, "Behold, I am with you always, to the end of the age" (Matt. 28:20). This is not said to simply comfort us, although it certainly does that. Jesus says this because, functionally, we cannot perform the tasks Jesus commands us to do without his presence.

Witnessing and the Language of Fruitfulness

Apart from Jesus we can do nothing. This truth gives us boldness in our evangelism, as the fruit of every endeavor exclusively comes from Christ. Our responsibility is not to change the sinner's heart, it is simply to share the gospel. God through his Spirit provides the growth.

Obeying the Vine

When you love someone, you might show your devotion by baking a cake, or going out to a movie, or buying a fancy gift. Of course, with God such displays of affection are not possible. It is for this reason that Jesus says if we love him, we will obey his commands. Obedience is a sign of adoration for our divine Lover.

> And this is love, that we walk according to his commandments.
> (2 John 6; see also 1 John 2:5–6)

However, the sinner's default mode is autonomy. From the Greek meaning "self law," autonomy refers to our desire to be self-governing. As sinners, we do not appreciate God looking over our shoulders telling us what to do. We prefer to be answerable only to ourselves.

The Christian life, on the other hand, is one of submission to the will of Christ. If we call him Lord, then we must obey him, otherwise our words are empty declarations of allegiance.[7]

> If you love me, you will keep my commandments. (John 14:15; see also vv. 21, 23–24)

The entire law, Jesus says, is summed up in two commands involving love (Mark 12:28–31). Even our witness to the world, our supreme apologetic, is portrayed in the language of love.

> By this all people will know that you are my disciples, if you have love for one another. (John 13:35)

If we want to bear fruit, we must exude love, as biblically defined. The world habitually equates love with infatuation or tolerance or lust. However, Jesus tells us that the love he expects is the type that motivates a person to lay down his life for another (John 15:13). This teaching comes shortly after the verses cited above about Jesus and the vine.

Paul speaks at length about godly love in 1 Corinthians 13. There he provides sixteen characteristics of the love believers ought to exude (vv. 4–8).[8] However, elsewhere Paul makes a direct connection between love and being fruitful.

> And it is my prayer that your love may abound more and more, with knowledge and all discernment, so that you may approve what is excellent, and so be pure and blameless for the day of Christ, filled with the fruit of righteousness that comes through Jesus Christ, to the glory and praise of God. (Phil. 1:9–11)

Without love, we cannot produce fruit of righteousness.

---

7. This is the hard truth of the "Lord, Lord" passage at the end of the Sermon on the Mount. Only those who do the will of the heavenly Father have the right to call Jesus "Lord" (Matt. 7:21–23).

8. Most English translations of these verses describe love with adjectives (e.g., patient, kind), but the Greek actually uses sixteen verbs (e.g., love is being kind, love is not being irritable). Genuine, godly love is seen in action.

Fruit of the Spirit

Usually we think of the "fruit of the Spirit" as those nine attributes given by Paul in Galatians 5:22–23. His list in fact begins with love. However, we can think more broadly of the fruit of the Spirit as anything done by believers that is commendable to God. Put another way, the only works that are pleasing to God are those that have been empowered by his Spirit.

> Not by might, nor by power, but by my Spirit, says the LORD of hosts. (Zech. 4:6)

Consider two adjacent fields. Both enjoy the same amount of sunlight and rainwater. When the time for harvesting comes, I go out into my field with a rather dull handheld sickle. I whack away at the stalks with my feeble arm. Not much is harvested.

My neighbor, however, goes out in his gas-powered combine and harvests his field. What takes me all day to reap by hand he completes in less than half an hour. This is the difference between doing works in our own strength versus through the power of the Spirit. Many Christians work hard and accomplish good things, but they rely more on their own talents and abilities than on the Spirit. Consequently, they produce a fraction of the fruit they could produce.

> For the one who sows to his own flesh will from the flesh reap corruption, but the one who sows to the Spirit will from the Spirit reap eternal life. (Gal. 6:8)

Unbelievers only reap the fleshly seed they have sown. However, believers often sow with perishable seed. This is why Jesus reminds his disciples:

> The Spirit gives life; the flesh counts for nothing. (John 6:63 NIV)

Along with the fruit of the Spirit come spiritual disciplines. These include activities such as prayer, fasting, meditating upon God's Word, regular worship and Christian fellowship, and generously giving of our money and time. It is through these activities that believers become productive. Taking one of these as an example, here is what Paul says about Christian generosity:

> Whoever sows sparingly will also reap sparingly, and whoever sows bountifully will also reap bountifully. (2 Cor. 9:6)

Spiritual disciplines produce a spiritual crop that is harvested by those empowered by God's Spirit.

Other fruit of the Spirit includes spiritual gifts that are given to everyone who has the indwelling Spirit. There are over twenty spiritual gifts listed in the New Testament, and each believer has at least one.[9] It is here that confusion exists when comparing Christians with non-Christians.

So far I have belabored the dissimilarity between believers and non-believers. Our knee-jerk reaction is to fight against this stark distinction, mainly because we know numerous non-Christians who are gifted, hardworking, morally upright individuals. Surely they do works pleasing to God, don't they?

However, we must maintain the distinction between "good" things and spiritually commendable ones. Many unbelievers are quite talented and skillful, but they still produce nothing of spiritual or eternal significance.

Likewise, unbelievers can be loving and patient and kind. However, there is a qualitative difference between fruit that is sown in the flesh and fruit sown in the Spirit. As we have already seen, biblical love is embodied in obeying Jesus, something unbelievers do not do.

The sole way to produce spiritual fruit is to yield to the Spirit. Believers are commanded to walk by the Spirit, be led by the Spirit, live by the Spirit, keep in step with the Spirit, and be filled with the Spirit.[10] Bearing godly fruit is a Trinitarian activity. As we abide in the Son, through the power of the Spirit, we produce pleasing fruit for the Father.

---

9. The main lists are found in Rom. 12:3–8, 1 Cor. 12:8–10; 28–30; and Eph. 4:11.
10. Gal. 5:16, 18, 25; Eph. 5:18.

Worship and the Language of Fruitfulness

All of Christian life is worship. Sometimes believers are more concerned with what kind of music is sung Sunday morning at church than how they live. Our lives should be a twenty-four-hour declaration of worship.

Fruit of Sanctification

As noted in chapter 9, sanctification and fruitfulness are two sides of the same coin. God does not simply clean us up (sanctification); he also makes us productive workers for his kingdom (fruitfulness).

Sanctification is like watching a tree grow. You can sit there for several days and not recognize any change in the tree. However, if you see it a year later, there is obvious growth. As believers, we should see an increasing holiness in our lives the longer we walk with Christ.

We can speak of sin in two categories. One is what we most often envision: those things we do that are wrong—"sins of commission." However, sin is also not doing what we are supposed to be doing, known as "sins of omission." We tend to congratulate ourselves on the really bad things we have avoided. However, we neglect the many good things we ought to be doing that we fail to do.

It would be easy to create a list of the vices Christians are supposed to shun. I did a simple word search in the New Testament on "do not" and it yielded 366 hits. "Do not steal," "do not be anxious," "do not be arrogant," "do not lose heart," "do not be ashamed," and "do not repay evil for evil" are just a few of them. All of this has something to do with God purifying us from the sinful habits and actions to which we were accustomed before our conversion.

However, there are things we should be doing as well. In the parable of the sower (Mark 4:3–8), Jesus speaks of four types of soil. The first three represent various degrees of unproductivity; the fourth soil alone produces a crop. Jesus does not merely want a cleaned-up field, where all the weeds and brush and undesirable materials are swept away. He wants a field that produces a crop, and not any old crop. He expects a solid return on his investment—a crop that produces thirty-, sixty-, or a hundredfold. Jesus expects a "harvest of righteousness" (James 3:18).

As we are purged of our sinful tendencies, we become more willing and able to do the good things expected of followers of Jesus. Part of becoming a productive plant is to be pruned of your unproductive parts.

Living in Namibia I tried my hand at growing fruit trees, and I must say I was less than successful. Namibia is a harsh environment, and we could easily go for half a year without rain. There were nine dams built around the capital city, reservoirs meant to collect water during the rainy season to guard against those times in the year when there was no rainfall. It was not uncommon to hear about the percentage of capacity the dams had as a sign of whether or not we were okay with water availability that year.

Hence, trees in Namibia tend to be gnarly, bent over, and short. The contrast was immediately evident whenever we traveled down to South Africa, where water is abundant and the trees grow tall and strong.

One thing I tried to learn was how to prune a fruit tree. Frequently it involved cutting away good branches so that other branches could grow properly. Occasionally a particular branch required pruning because it bore too much fruit, starving the other branches of sap. Of course, pruning also entailed cutting away dead branches, much like Jesus speaks about in his vine and branches talk.

> Every branch in me that does not bear fruit he takes away,
> and every branch that does bear fruit he prunes [*kathairō*],
> that it may bear more fruit. (John 15:2)

Whereas I was pretty much a failure when it came to pruning trees, Jesus is a master at it. Undoubtedly, this cutting away can be difficult for believers to endure. This echoes what has previously been touched upon with the giving and receiving of discipline.

> For the moment all discipline seems painful rather than
> pleasant, but later it yields the peaceful fruit of righteousness
> to those who have been trained by it. (Heb. 12:11)

Being pruned by God can be painful, but he does this so we can "grow in the grace and knowledge of our Lord and Savior Jesus Christ" (2 Peter 3:18).[11]

---

11. Further horticultural language includes Paul's discussion about Jews and Gentiles being "grafted" into the same olive tree (Rom. 11:17–24).

Often we view the "great Christians" as the prominent speakers, evangelists, and television personalities with large ministries. However, *how* we do the Lord's work is just as important as what we do for him. As such, there are numerous exhortations in the New Testament in this regard.

For example, Scripture speaks of seeking God's kingdom and his righteousness, serving wholeheartedly, patiently enduring difficulties, and working hard.[12] In terms of the last item, Paul compares the Christian life to being a hardworking farmer (2 Tim. 2:6). James does the same.

> Be patient, therefore, brothers, until the coming of the Lord. See how the farmer waits for the precious fruit of the earth, being patient about it, until it receives the early and the late rains. (James 5:7)

In a definitive passage about the kind of worker Jesus requires, he uses agricultural language:

> No one who puts his hand to the plow and looks back is fit for the kingdom of God. (Luke 9:62)

Jesus demands absolute commitment from his disciples. As we will see shortly, God is the one responsible for the growth. Thus, the humble housewife who faithfully raises her children in the nurture and admonition of the Lord is as much a fruitful laborer in God's field as the high-profile evangelist or pastor.

White Fields and Vineyards

If these are operative in our lives—repentance and confession, remaining in the vine, being led by the Spirit, and endeavoring to be patient, hardworking laborers—we will produce righteous fruit for God. That will involve abstaining from the corruption that has overtaken the world, but it will also encompass doing the things God expects us to do. Paul says that we were "created in Christ Jesus for good works," works that God "prepared beforehand" for us to do (Eph. 2:10).

How we live and what we proclaim are equally important. Paul told Timothy, "Watch your life and doctrine closely" (1 Tim. 4:16 NIV).

---

12. Matt. 6:33; Eph. 6:7 NIV; 2 Thess. 1:4; 3:6–10; 1 Thess. 4:11.

However, at times one of these can be emphasized at the expense of the other.

For example, I have heard Christians misappropriate a famous quotation attributed to Francis of Assisi (1181–1226), "Preach the gospel at all times; when necessary, use words." In essence, as long as you are living the Christian life, you do not need to explicitly declare your faith in Jesus.[13]

This is nonsense, as if there exists a dichotomy between living the Christian life and verbally proclaiming salvation in Jesus. Both are demanded by our Lord. I get the sense that some people are fond of this saying because it absolves them of the uncomfortable obligation of overtly broaching the topic of salvation with unbelievers. Frequently ours is a passive evangelism that waits for non-Christians to ask us about Christ, as opposed to being proactive in proclaiming our faith. This is the product of a regrettable lack of urgency in the church today.

If you saw someone dying of thirst in the desert and you stumbled upon an oasis that could save him from certain death, would you be embarrassed or hesitant in pointing the dying man to water? Warning people of the coming judgment was a favorite method of Jesus. Telling unbelievers that salvation is in Christ alone should be a favorite practice of ours as well.

Lots of people dislike Christians for this very reason. "Why can't you allow us to live our lives the way we choose to live them? Why do Christians always have to keep trying to get others to believe what they believe?" However, the last words Jesus shared with his disciples before he left this earth had to do with making more disciples (Matt. 28:18–20; Acts 1:8). The "non-witnessing Christian" is an oxymoron. A Christian who does not share his faith is like a fish that does not swim, or an airplane that does not fly. Witnessing is not an optional activity for the believer. It should be vocational, not recreational.

In the parable of the wicked tenants (Matt. 21:33–46), Jesus speaks about a vineyard that was supposed to produce fruit for the owner, but the tenants consistently frustrated him from getting any of its produce. Eventually the wicked tenants were killed and the vineyard was "given to

---

13. There is considerable debate on whether Francis even said this. I have heard it humorously noted that this statement is akin to saying, "Feed the hungry; when necessary, use food."

a people producing its fruits" (v. 43). The Jewish religious leaders knew that Jesus was speaking about them.

This idea of an unfruitful vineyard is not unique to Jesus. God speaks similarly about Israel (Isa. 5:1–7). His chosen people were supposed to be a model of righteousness for the pagan nations around her, but instead of finding justice, God found bloodshed (v. 7).[14]

The people who now proclaim the righteousness of God are Christians. For this reason, Peter describes believers as "a royal priesthood, a holy nation" meant to "proclaim the excellencies of him who called you out of darkness into his marvelous light" (1 Peter 2:9). Unfortunately, we often shy away from this responsibility.

If as a Christian you are not involved in evangelism and missions in some way—be it actively sharing your faith, or financially supporting missionaries, or praying for unbelievers or those Christians who are in this ministry—then you are sinning. Proselytizing is a fundamental obligation of all followers of Jesus. It was the last command Jesus gave his disciples before he ascended into heaven. It should be the first thing in which believers are engaged today.

> Look, I tell you, lift up your eyes, and see that the fields are white for harvest. Already the one who reaps is receiving wages and gathering fruit for eternal life, so that sower and reaper may rejoice together. (John 4:35–36)

The God of Growth

Every believer has a responsibility to tend the field of God's kingdom, but the actual growth is something that comes from God.

> I planted, Apollos watered, but God gave the growth. So neither he who plants nor he who waters is anything, but only God who gives the growth. He who plants and he who waters are one, and each will receive his wages according to his labor. For we are God's fellow workers. You are God's field. (1 Cor. 3:6–9a)

---

14. Jesus cursing the fig tree appears to be an acted out parable with the same message of unfruitfulness (Matt. 21:18–22).

God expects fruit from his children, and he gives us every tool necessary to plant and water and sow in his vineyard. He continually prunes us so we can produce an abundant crop, the fruit of righteousness.

What does it mean to be saved? It means repenting of your former empty life and confessing faith in Jesus. It means being attached to Jesus and walking by the Spirit so that you can produce works that are pleasing to God. It means moving from barrenness to productivity.

> He who supplies seed to the sower and bread for food
> will supply and multiply your seed for sowing and
> increase the harvest of your righteousness.
>
> *2 Corinthians 9:10*

Key Terms for Salvation Expressed in the Language of Agriculture

fruit, produce, Jesus the true vine, branches, reap, sow, harvest, crop, pruning, growing, grafting, vineyard, trees, fruit of the Spirit, fruit of righteousness

Questions for Group Discussion

1. List all the ways this past week you were "Christ in the world." Separate the list between those things you did and those times you verbally shared the gospel with unbelievers. Is one list larger than the other? Do you need more balance between the two?
2. Discuss how believers can be attached to Jesus the vine. Are there spiritual disciplines that are easier for you than others? Are there some you entirely omit in your Christian walk?
3. Are you able to identify the spiritual gifts God has given you for service in his kingdom? Are you regularly exercising them? If no, why?
4. Besides witnessing, what other fruit do you think believers should produce? Think here of the things Christians must do, not the things they ought to avoid.

11

The Language of Science
From Deformity to Glorification

TRANSFORMATION

And we all, with unveiled face, beholding the glory of the Lord, are being _transformed_ into the same image from one degree of glory to another.

2 Corinthians 3:18a

When I was growing up, I frequently saw a particular magazine advertisement for bodybuilding. It featured the well-chiseled figure of Charles Atlas, his muscular physique flexed to the max. With this ad came a promise: You too can look like Charles Atlas. "No longer do you have to be embarrassed by your body or picked on by bullies bigger than you." For a skinny, preteen boy like me, it was a powerful promise.

With the advertisement was a testimonial from a satisfied client, and the all-too-familiar before and after pictures. "Previously, I was skinny and frail, unable to even pick up a gallon of milk without straining. Now, I bench press three hundred pounds, and all the women adore me." And all this in only eight weeks!

We see similar pictures today, especially with the fetish many have for dieting. Lose all the weight you want simply by drinking chocolate shakes. Nutrasize your body. Weight Watchers—"losing weight never tasted so good." And always we are shown the before and after pictures.

Or consider the modern craze for "extreme makeovers." Many of us love the comparisons between an average-looking woman and one all dolled up like a movie star. We even have extreme makeovers for homes and automobiles and household pets.

Scripture has its own before and after account, but it involves a far greater transformation. In it we see individuals previously unfit for any godly purpose being made into the likeness of the perfect Son of God. With this chapter, we will look at what it means to be made in the image of God, how that image was marred by sin, and the positive effects of being transformed into the image of Christ.

It's All Greek to Me

Have you ever been in a conversation where you struggled to find the right word to express a thought or meaning? Authors often wrestle with this, as several synonyms convey the same basic idea, but only one of them hits the contextual nail on the head.

Throughout this book, we have presented key words from the biblical Greek that help us understand important Christian doctrines. I am sure that for readers who do not know Greek, this can be somewhat tedious. However, an understanding of these terms is crucial for grasping why the biblical authors selected these specific words to convey Christian salvation. With the model of transformation, precise word selection is vital. An illustration might help.

The Greek word *morphē*, translated "form" in English, was used in a variety of ways in the ancient world. In botany it referred to the different types of plants (where we get the word "morphology"). It was used in reference to various animal forms, to compare anatomy of veins and skin, and in philosophical descriptions of form and matter. For these reasons, our chapter is titled "The Language of Science" because *morphē* was employed across numerous disciplines.

The word has a different form, *metamorphoō*, which is related to the noun from which we get the English "metamorphosis." It depicts a genuine change from the inside out. The metamorphoses of a caterpillar to a butterfly or a tadpole to a frog are perfect examples of this change. In Greek, metamorphosis often carried a distinct religious connotation, dealing with a supernatural change empowered by the gods.

The New Testament uses metamorphosis four times. Twice it describes the transfiguration of Jesus (Matt. 17:2; Mark 9:2). We are told that his features were metamorphosed, such that his face shone like the sun and his clothing became "dazzling white" (Luke 9:29). Mark makes the somewhat humorous observation that not even human bleach could make his clothing this white (Mark 9:3). I am sure modern detergent manufacturers might disagree!

Paul uses the word when speaking about a change that occurs in Christians, either in having their minds transformed (Rom. 12:2) or their very being (2 Cor. 3:18). This is a decidedly different way of using the term than was typical in ancient Greek. There, the gods were usually the ones being transformed in order to take on an appearance capable of communicating with humans. For Paul, though, it is sinners who are transformed in order to become more like Christ.

There are other Greek words that can be translated "transform." *Metaschēmatizō* is one of them. Even if you do not know Greek, you can see that it combines *meta-* with *schēmatizō*, which is related to the noun from which we get our English "scheme." "To change schemes" is the literal translation of the Greek verb. Here is a passage where *metaschēmatizō* appears three times:

> For such are false apostles, deceitful workers, *transforming* themselves into the apostles of Christ. And no marvel; for Satan himself *is transformed* into an angel of light. Therefore it is no great thing if his ministers also *be transformed* as the ministers of righteousness. (2 Cor. 11:13–15a KJV)

Metaschēmatizō in this context refers to the deceptive practices of Satan and his minions. They are not genuinely changed from the inside out (metamorphosis), but merely appear to be changed. They change schemes.[1]

I prefer the New International Version here since it uses "masquerade" to describe what Satan and his ministers do. Everyone understands what happens at a masquerade party. You go dressed up pretending to be somebody else. Jesus conveys the idea figuratively when he says that

---

1. The Greek word in the passage translated "deceitful" (*dolios*) has the sense of setting a trap or snare, like one might do to catch a bird.

false prophets are ravenous wolves "in sheep's clothing" (Matt. 7:15). On the outside they look like believers, but on the inside, they are beasts looking to devour.

Christians are involved in a metamorphosis, a process of change from a worthless sinner to a glorious child of God. The change is dramatic and will eventually be complete the other side of glory. Understanding what happens in this process will help us see how wondrous this transformation is. Therefore, we need to return to the original creation of mankind, to follow the simple path of where we were, what went wrong, and how we return to a better place.

Imago Dei

In what appears to be an Old Testament hint at the Trinitarian nature of God, Genesis records God's words at the creation of humanity, "Let us make man in our image, in our likeness" (Gen. 1:26 NIV84).[2] This image of God (Latin, *imago Dei*) sets apart humanity—both male and female (v. 27)—from the rest of creation. The Creator, in speaking within the Godhead, verbalizes the supreme distinction between humans and all other creatures. Humans are the pinnacle of God's creative energy, made like him. But what precisely does this mean, and what effect does sin have on that image?

Scholars through the centuries have debated what exactly this image entails, but there is broad agreement that it involves several characteristics that humans share with God. One way to discern these traits is to compare humans to animals, as the latter are not made in God's image. These similarities between God and man are:

- *Spiritual Traits*: Every human has a soul and is capable of spiritually communing and relating with God, who is spirit.
- *Moral Traits*: If a feral dog wanders around the neighborhood killing other dogs, we may call that animal a nuisance, but the killing is not immoral. However, if a man behaves similarly, slaying other people with malice aforethought, he would be

---

2. Throughout Christian history there has been debate about the difference, if any, between "image" and "likeness." However, there is enough biblical evidence to suggest that these terms are synonymous and are used interchangeably (compare Gen. 1:26–27 with Gen. 5:1 and 5:3).

wicked because humans made in God's image should not act that way. As God in his holiness has a moral nature, humans possess a conscience, making them capable of moral choices. Animals do not make moral decisions, but humans are held accountable by their Maker for every choice they make.

- *Rational Traits*: As God said "I am," humans are sentient beings capable of rational thought and discourse. We are creative. We are self-aware. While animals exhibit some level of intellect, it is nowhere near the capabilities of humans. Animals are not cognizant of their purpose in this universe. They are not self-aware.

- *Relational Traits*: God exists in an eternal relatedness in the Trinity. As such, he made humans as relational beings. Solitary confinement is one of the worst forms of punishment that can be inflicted on humans. When Adam was created, despite living in a paradise with direct communication with God, he still was alone and God made him a partner suited to his humanness, a woman. Male and female gender is what makes marriage possible, and human friendship and fellowship more broadly is rooted in the being of the triune God. As humans made in God's image, we can relate both with God and with others bearing his image.

- *Emotional Traits*: While animals possess emotional attributes at a certain level, they are not expressed to the degree humans articulate them. Further, some emotions like vengeance or wrath are not present in animals at all. Humans have bodies that are fit vessels for expressing these emotional and communicative characteristics, traits that God also possesses.

- *Volitional Traits*: Humans were given a will to make decisions, an obvious necessity given the choice presented to Adam and Eve concerning the tree of the knowledge of good and evil. Animals make choices, but these can never be spiritual or moral in nature. In the garden, Adam possessed genuine freedom of will to either obey or disobey his Maker, and with the exercise of that will came moral and spiritual consequences.

- *Rulership Traits*: God made man and placed him in the garden. With the responsibility of tending the environment, he was given dominion over the creation. Man would "rule" over the birds of the air, creatures of the sea, land animals, and vegetation. In the foundational "image of God" passage of Genesis 1:26–27, dominion is the first responsibility mentioned. As God is sovereign over all things, he granted humans a "derived authority" over his creation.

In these seven ways, human beings reflect the nature of God. Unfortunately, something happened that deformed the *imago Dei* and resulted in humans becoming less than they should be. That, of course, was the fall of Adam and Eve into sin.

Before and After

After God made humans, he declared his creation "very good" (Gen. 1:31). God looked at his handiwork and it was precisely the way he wanted it to be. However, soon thereafter, Genesis 3 records the fall of humanity. With it came a distortion of that goodness.

There are several passages in the New Testament that paint a before-and-after picture of conversion, and we will briefly highlight two of them, Ephesians 2:1–10 and Titus 3:3–8. Both follow a similar track and assume the prior events in Eden.

Paul speaks of fallen humanity as being dead in trespasses and sins (Eph. 2:1). While this is clearly a spiritual depiction, this deadness affects all that humans do. Similarly in Titus, Paul describes our pre-conversion state as foolish, disobedient, and enslaved to destructive emotions like malice, envy, and hatred (Titus 3:3).

However, a change takes place in the situation of sinners. God breaks into their lives and, through his kindness and mercy, shines his love into their hearts. The emphasis is noticeably on grace in both Ephesians and Titus. The gift of salvation is undeserved. It comes through faith in Jesus via the renewing of God's Spirit. "Sons of disobedience" (Eph. 2:2) become "heirs according to the hope of eternal life" (Titus 3:7).

Sinners move from a position of utter spiritual emptiness, by nature objects of God's wrath, to people who genuinely perform works pleasing to God. This is most remarkable. Earlier Paul told Titus that unbelievers were unfit for "doing anything good" (1:16 NIV). Now he writes that as believers they can "devote themselves to doing what is good" (3:8 NIV). A similar passage appears in Ephesians:

> For we are his workmanship, created in Christ Jesus for good
> works, which God prepared beforehand, that we should walk
> in them. (Eph. 2:10)

Paul refers to believers as God's "workmanship." This word has the sense of a work of art, what the New Living Translation calls a "masterpiece." Everything in believers is transformed. The way they think, talk, dream, plan, work, live, and even die is all changed. What they commit themselves to, what they most value, and what they hope for are wrapped up in this metamorphosis.

Transformed sinners are "sealed" by God's Spirit and become his "possession" (Eph. 1:13–14). This is why Paul regarded his life before his conversion to Christ as "rubbish" (Phil. 3:8). The Greek for this word is indeed earthy, almost vulgar in the sense of describing something of no value whatsoever, thus the King James Version's translation "dung." "From dung to glory" could very well have been the title for this chapter!

Witnessing and the Language of Transformation

Everyone wants to feel valued, to have real meaning and purpose in life. Our evangelism must point people to the eternal value of following Jesus, while pointing out the temporary, fading nature of everything else that is subject to decay and destruction.

Of note is that *all* Christians participate in this metamorphosis. Certain churches teach that only some are truly transformed. There are inferior believers and super believers. This false dichotomy usually encourages an emphasis in particular spiritual gifts that are claimed to demarcate mature Christians from the immature ones. Much like the medieval Catholic Church's delineation between clergy and laity, these modern churches write off Christians who do not exhibit these "super spiritual" gifts.

However, the transformation the Bible portrays is one in which all believers participate. We are all being made into the image and likeness of Christ, by the same Spirit, through the same Word. There are no Christians who have more of the Holy Spirit, or an "extra portion," or a "special anointing," in contrast to other believers. We all have the same Spirit indwelling us to the same proportion.

Yet, while no believer can claim more access to or greater influence from God's Spirit than any other believer, there are Christians who are led more readily or walk more closely with the Holy Spirit than others do. While some Christians quench or grieve the Spirit, others are filled by him.[3]

Similarly, while all believers may have comparable access to God's Word, this does not mean we all avail ourselves of it equally. While some Christians read the Bible daily, others barely read it at all. Therefore, we can expect that believers who consistently feed on the Word of God will grow into stronger, more mature Christians than those who do not.

The same principle is true when it comes to the transformation that comes through the work of the Spirit. Christians who stubbornly live in unrepentant sin, for example, will not experience the vibrancy of faith that others do who habitually yield to the Spirit's leading.[4]

Elsewhere Paul speaks of moving from the "old self" to the "new self" (Col. 3:9–10). The old self is "corrupt through deceitful desires" (Eph. 4:22). The Greek for "corrupt" can have the meaning of being destroyed or decaying or perverting. In English, to pervert something means to thoroughly turn it to a wrong purpose or end. Is this not precisely what has happened to mankind through sin? What was created good and in God's image has become corrupted, twisted toward evil purposes, and thus perverted.

Complete Transformation

However, the *imago Dei* still exists in all humans, albeit in a deformed state. For example, after the flood in Noah's day, God declared capital punishment a fitting judgment upon those who dare to take human life. The reason is that "God made man in his own image." James deplores

---

3. 1 Thess. 5:19; Eph. 4:30; 5:18.

4. In the context of Ephesians 5:18–21 and what it means to be "filled with the Spirit," submission to each other is one way Paul envisions this filling taking place. He also speaks of a life characterized by gratitude and praise as another way to be filled. Some churches claim that in order to be filled with God's Spirit, a person must exhibit some of the spiritual gifts like prophecy or speaking in tongues. But this is not what Paul says in this passage. Again, all Christians can be filled with the Spirit.

the foul use of the tongue in cursing others, because they are made in the likeness of God. Paul calls humans the "offspring" of God in the sense that we are his creatures, akin to likeness and image terminology.[5]

In turning to Christ, the image of God is restored. Believers are being "conformed to the image of his Son" (Rom. 8:29). The new self is being remade "after the likeness of God" and "after the image of its creator."[6] We will consider four specific ways that in Christ the *imago Dei* is renewed.

1. Transformation of the Soul

As we learned in our chapter on justification, we do not simply become somewhat like Jesus; we become exactly like him. The very righteousness that Jesus earned in his perfect life he confers to all who believe in him. In granting us his perfect righteousness, Jesus makes us his image bearers.

> And we all, with unveiled face, beholding the glory of the Lord, are being transformed into the same image from one degree of glory to another. For this comes from the Lord who is the Spirit. (2 Cor. 3:18)

Note two things from this verse. First, we are "*being* transformed." It is a passive verb, something that is done to us.[7] We are not making ourselves into the image of God's Son. God is doing it to us. Therefore, we have nothing to brag about, as if we are better than others. Again, we are reminded that a gospel of grace excludes all boasting.

Second, we are being made into the "same image" of Jesus. This image will be perfected when we meet the Lord, but even now it is being morally renewed. We are called to imitate Jesus in our actions, to be humble as Jesus was humble, to forgive as he forgave us. Husbands should love their wives as Christ loves the church. We must love others with an *agapē* kind of love, one that causes the believer to lay down his life for others.[8]

---

5. Gen. 9:6; James 3:9; Acts 17:28–29.

6. Eph. 4:23–24; Col. 3:10.

7. The verb is *metamorphoō* and is similarly passive in Romans 12:2.

8. Phil. 2:5, Eph. 5:2; Col. 3:13; Eph. 5:25; 1 John 3:16.

This transformation necessarily involves suffering. You cannot take sinners and make them into the image of the perfect Son of God without it involving a painful process. Since Jesus, who is our model of holiness, was perfected through suffering, it stands to reason that repentant sinners require a similar process.[9] When Jesus calls us to suffer for his name, he does not ask us to do anything he was not first willing to do for us. Jesus redeemed suffering; he gave it value and purpose. For unbelievers, suffering is simply suffering. There is nothing that ultimately comes from it of any eternal value. But for Christians, suffering produces fruit.[10]

It is here that we begin to see a difference between being made in the image of God versus the image of Christ. God has something greater in store for us than returning to Eden. There is a qualitative difference between the image of God as originally given to Adam, and the image of Christ found in all believers. Our glorification does not take us back to the garden but to heaven.

As we saw in chapter 5 on citizenship, believers are presently seated in the "heavenly realms" (NIV). However, a time is coming when heaven will be our permanent residence and we will be changed into something greater than Adam experienced in Eden. Adam was capable of sinning, but in Christ, believers will ultimately lose this ability (Rev. 21:4). We will genuinely be free to serve God for eternity.

2. Transformation of the Body

As Christ's resurrection is the guarantee that believers will also be resurrected (1 Cor. 15:20, 23), Christians will receive resurrection bodies. What does a resurrection body look like? Much like Jesus' resurrection body during the forty days he walked on earth before his ascension into heaven.

Often Christians wrongly think that we will be given an entirely new body. However, if that were the case, then the idea of "resurrection" becomes nonsensical. It would be a different body, not the same one brought back to life. The former idea is more akin to reincarnation, the latter to what happened to Jesus. He had a body that still had nail prints

---

9. Heb. 2:10; 5:8; Rom. 8:17; 1 Thess. 1:6; 1 Peter 2:21.
10. Rom. 5:3; James 1:2–4; 1 Peter 3:14.

from the crucifixion. Jesus could invite "doubting Thomas" to place his hand in his side where the Roman soldier's spear had penetrated (John 20:27). There was a continuity between the body Jesus had before his resurrection and the one after.[11]

Nor was Jesus a disembodied spirit. He could be recognized and touched (Matt. 28:9). Jesus points out that a spirit does not have flesh and bones, and then he eats broiled fish to prove his point, because his disciples thought they were seeing a ghost (Luke 24:36–43).

Yet, his resurrected body appears to have some supernatural qualities as well. John points out that despite the doors being locked, Jesus appeared in the room with the disciples. He was not initially recognizable to Mary at the tomb nor to the disciples on the road to Emmaus, yet later he became recognizable. Then Jesus vanished from their sight.[12]

It appears that the body Jesus has post-resurrection is not subject to time and space as our bodies presently are. This suggests a most incredible transformation, and this is one reason why Paul can say, "For I consider that the sufferings of this present time are not worth comparing with the glory that is to be revealed to us" (Rom. 8:18). Paul knew that something ineffably wondrous was going to happen to believers at the resurrection.

Paul attempts a description of this transformation. It appears he is answering a question, perhaps from believers in Corinth. "But someone will ask, 'How are the dead raised? With what kind of body do they come?'" (1 Cor. 15:35). Paul then provides an extensive contrast between the believer's natural body and the supernatural one yet to be received.

> What is sown is perishable; what is raised is imperishable. It is sown in dishonor; it is raised in glory. It is sown in weakness; it is raised in power. It is sown a natural body; it is raised a spiritual body. (1 Cor. 15:42–44)

It is fitting that Paul differentiates between the first Adam and the last, as only in Christ do we receive this resurrection body.

---

11. However, it is probably best to regard the nail prints as an exception here, that Jesus maintained these marks as an eternal reminder for us of his crucifixion. In other words, Christians should not worry that every scar they have will be visible in their resurrection body! See further discussion below.

12. John 20:15, 19, 26; Luke 24:31. Interestingly, here is an example where *morphē* describes "another form" Jesus adopts (Mark 16:12).

> The first man was from the earth, a man of dust; the second
> man is from heaven. As was the man of dust, so also are those
> who are of the dust, and as is the man of heaven, so also are
> those who are of heaven. Just as we have borne the image of
> the man of dust, we shall also bear the image of the man of
> heaven. (1 Cor. 15:47–49)

The glorification of our bodies is something that occurs through Christ's Spirit who alone makes us into the "image of the man of heaven." As Jesus told Nicodemus, flesh only gives birth to flesh. However, God's Spirit can both produce spirit and give life to our mortal bodies. In the "twinkling of an eye," the metamorphosis will take place, and our resurrection bodies will become imperishable and immortal. This only happens through Jesus, who is the "resurrection and the life," the one "who will transform our lowly body to be like his glorious body."[13]

In this respect, Christianity is distinct. It is not that the soul escapes the prison house of the body, as many religions teach. Rather than discarding the body, the Spirit will give life to it. Rather than throw away a physical shell subject to corruption and decay, the Spirit will renew it and transform it into an imperishable body.

This truth should affect the way we live. There is an intimate connection between our sins and Christ's resurrection (1 Cor. 15:17). It is in this light that Peter commands believers to be holy (1 Peter 1:15–21).

Paul ends his discussion on the resurrection with a practical imperative.

> Therefore, my beloved brothers, be steadfast, immovable,
> always abounding in the work of the Lord, knowing that in
> the Lord your labor is not in vain. (1 Cor. 15:58)

In light of the glorification we will receive, Christians ought to persevere in their service to God. Believers are presently able to put to death the misdeeds of the body, through the enabling of God's Spirit (Rom. 8:13), a topic we already dealt with in chapter 4 on redemption.

---

13. John 3:6; Rom. 8:11; 1 Cor. 15:52–53; John 11:25; Phil. 3:21.

3. Transformation of the Mind

Paul writes to believers in Rome:

> Do not be conformed to this world, but be transformed by the renewal of your mind, that by testing you may discern what is the will of God, what is good and acceptable and perfect. (Rom. 12:2)

Paul uses two Greek words we have already seen. Believers must not "be conformed" (*syschēmatizō*) to the world but must instead "be transformed" (*metamorphoō*). As Paul utilizes "conform" here, the word "refers to the external conformity . . . and indicates the adoption or imitation of a pose."[14] The one other time this word is employed in the New Testament is when Peter writes, "As obedient children, do not be conformed to the passions of your former ignorance" (1 Peter 1:14). In both cases, Christians should not adopt the pattern or posture of the fallen world.

There is a difference between transformation and information. Christianity is not merely information-driven, as if all that happens is we learn something new and are saved by this knowledge. It involves being transformed, not just in our minds (something that information does), but in our entire being. It is this kind of transformation that makes it possible for us to love God as we ought, with all our heart, soul, mind, and strength.[15]

In chapter 8 on illumination we went into considerable detail about Christians possessing minds and consciences that have been enlightened by God's Spirit, so we will not repeat things here. However, we do see that in this sense, the rational characteristics of the image of God are renewed in believers. As transformed sinners, Christians have minds capable of discerning God's will, something they could not do in their former state of corruption and depravity.

We again see how the various facets of biblical salvation are interrelated. Our will, formerly hostile to God and of no spiritual value, has been renewed so we may faithfully serve him (chapter 4 on

---

14. Rogers and Rogers, *New Linguistic and Exegetical Key to the Greek New Testament*, 339.

15. Mark 12:30; Luke 10:27.

redemption). Our relationship with God and with others is transformed (chapter 7 on reconciliation). Being transformed, we can make moral choices that are pleasing to our Lord, bearing godly fruit. Even our emotions are transformed, bearing the fruit of the Spirit as opposed to the fruit of the fallen nature (chapter 10 on fruitfulness).

4. Transformation of the Creation

Paul speaks of a transformation of creation as it "waits with eager longing," "was subjected to futility," "groaning . . . in the pains of childbirth," and "will be set free from its bondage to corruption" (Rom. 8:19–22). As we saw in chapter 7 on reconciliation, when Adam sinned his relationship with the environment was damaged. The image of God involving his dominion over the creation was compromised. Both Adam and the cosmos under his care began the process of corruption and decay.

While we do not worship "Mother Earth" or pretend that this planet is our permanent home, Christians should earnestly embrace the responsibility God gave us in caring for his creation. Often our knee-jerk reaction against this neo-pagan idolatry is to trash the place. "It will all burn in the end anyway, so who cares how we treat the earth now?" This is wrongheaded and does not take seriously our mandate to be stewards of God's wonderful creation. We ought to care for it properly. Tend it. Repair, maintain, and keep it.[16]

Suppose you gave me a home to live in, but told me that in the future, you would tear that house down and build me a new one. Yet, when you later returned, you found the house to be run into the ground, with little care given to maintaining it. What would that say about my attitude toward your generosity? The way we care for God's creation implies something about the way we honor God himself.

Still, we noted in chapter 5, this earth is not our permanent home. Believers are strangers and aliens in it. Through Christ there will be a new heaven and a new earth. The implication of this biblical truth

---

16. I am not opposed to the idea that a reconstituted or reformed earth, as part of the "new heaven and new earth," becomes the new home of believers after the consummation of all things (2 Peter 3:13; Rev. 21:1). However, I strongly believe that the new earth will only come about after this present one is judged and destroyed by fire: "the earth and everything in it will be laid bare" (2 Peter 3:10 NIV84).

is clear. The current created order needs renewal and restoration, and while we can play a small part in preserving our planet, it will require a new creative power from God himself to remake it.

> The heavens will pass away with a roar, and the heavenly bodies will be burned up and dissolved. . . .
>> The heavens will be set on fire and dissolved, and the heavenly bodies will melt as they burn! (2 Peter 3:10, 12)

This destruction of the present order will necessitate a new heaven and new earth and will ultimately bring about a renewal of humanity's mandate of dominion over creation. Consider what David writes about man's authority over God's handiwork.

> When I look at your heavens, the work of your fingers,
>> the moon and the stars, which you have set in place,
> what is man that you are mindful of him,
>> and the son of man that you care for him?
> Yet you have made him a little lower than the heavenly beings
>> and crowned him with glory and honor.
> You have given him dominion over the works of your hands;
>> you have put all things under his feet,
> all sheep and oxen,
>> and also the beasts of the field,
> the birds of the heavens, and the fish of the sea,
>> whatever passes along the paths of the seas. (Ps. 8:3–8)

The psalmist is amazed God subjected his extraordinary creation to human beings. Even though we were made a little lower than the angels, our responsibility is supremely higher.

Post-fall, that responsibility and privilege was relinquished to the prince of the kingdom of the air (Eph. 2:2). Jesus, however, has come to reverse that. We are told that the Son of Man came to destroy the works of the devil (1 John 3:8). One way is to renew the image of God with respect to humanity's dominion over creation.

This is why Psalm 8 is repeated by the author of Hebrews in reference to Jesus (Heb. 2:5–8). There is a very practical benefit to the incarnation. Jesus came as the quintessential man to regain what Adam lost: the dominion of humanity over the created order. This will finally be accomplished when Jesus brings "many sons to glory" (Heb. 2:10). Then believers will reign with Christ.[17]

In all of these ways, the image of God marred by sin is regained. The spiritual traits of the image are transformed as believers receive the perfect righteousness of Christ. The rational and volitional traits are restored in Christians who now can discern God's perfect will and can exercise a free will to turn away from sin and follow Jesus. The moral traits are renewed in Christians who produce good works pleasing to God. The emotional traits are seen in the fruit of the Spirit, whereas previously only godless fruit was produced. Relationally, believers are reconciled to God and to others. Lastly, the rulership traits of the image are recovered in believers who will be given dominion again over God's creation. As such, Christians possess an "imperishable, undefiled, and unfading" inheritance (1 Peter 1:4).

Reflecting God's Glory

Related to the idea of transformation is the biblical teaching on glory. As Christ is the "exact imprint" of God's nature (Heb. 1:3), believers should similarly reflect his glory. Paul writes that believers "shine as lights in the world" (Phil. 2:15).

There are many things in Scripture that bring God glory. The creation, the Israelite nation, miracles including the raising of Lazarus from the dead, answered prayer, and believers who produce good works and serve others are all means by which God is glorified.[18]

Related to this, Paul makes an incredible argument when he contrasts the glory of the old covenant with that of the new. Paul says that the glory that accompanied the giving of the law of Moses is not worth comparing to the glory believers experience now in the church (2 Cor. 3:7–11). I find that remarkable because when I read the Old Testament accounts of Moses, these events must have been awesome to witness.

For example, the glory of the Lord fell upon Mount Sinai with a display of fire, lightning, and smoke that terrified the Israelites. The priests were unable to perform their duties as the glory of the Lord filled the temple. Likewise, after Moses entered the tabernacle to speak with

---

17. 1 Cor. 6:3; 2 Tim. 2:12; Rev. 20:6.
18. Ps. 19:1; Isa. 43:6b–7; John 11:4; 14:13; John 15:8; Matt. 5:16; 1 Peter 4:11b.

God, he had to put a veil over his face in order to shield the glowing glory, his face bright with light.[19]

Perhaps you are like me, thinking that if I were there, surely I would not have forgotten these spectacular events. When Paul says the glory of the new covenant is greater, I stand dumbfounded. Believers become part of the body of Christ, the church, which is meant to radiate with the glory of God. I certainly would have liked to see Moses' glowing face, but what we have today is far greater and far more glorious.

Worship and the Language of Transformation

God has provided corporate worship to transform his children into the likeness of his Son. We should never fashion worship as something done for unbelievers or "seekers." The primary focus of worship is Godward. Only God-focused worship can genuinely transform sinners.

But how, you might ask? Wouldn't it be more glorious to see pillars of fire and smoke, to hear the voice of God booming out of the sky, or to see the prophet's face glowing like the sun? However, those spectacular displays were necessary because God had to treat the Israelites like infants who constantly desired reaffirmation from him.

Consider a baby. He sees his mother, but as soon as his mother leaves the room, he begins to cry. That is what the Israelites were like. Lacking real faith, they required constant signs and wonders from God. However, we are not meant to be like that. We have the indwelling Holy Spirit and the complete Word of God to guide us. We do not need signs and wonders. We do not need God to treat us like infants. We live by faith, not by sight.

Something more glorious than anything in the Old Testament has come, and we are part of it. As Paul writes, "What once had glory has come to have no glory at all, because of the glory that surpasses it" (2 Cor. 3:10). The church proclaims the "manifold wisdom of God" and brings him glory (Eph. 3:10, 21). For the Christian, Paul summarizes our responsibility: "So, whether you eat or drink, or whatever you do, do all to the glory of God" (1 Cor. 10:31).

---

19. Exod. 19:19; 20:18; 40:35; 34:29–35; 1 Kings 8:11.

The Christian you sit next to in church is more glorious than a pillar of fire that might appear in the church's parking lot Sunday morning. The believer brings as much glory to God as the expansive cosmos. For in that person, God is crafting a work of art, transforming a corrupt sinner into the image of his perfect Son. As Jesus prayed to the Father, "The glory that you have given me I have given to them, that they may be one even as we are one" (John 17:22).

Christ Formed in You

In his letter to the Galatians, Paul hopes they will resist the empty instruction of false teachers and turn back to the gospel they initially embraced through his ministry. The apostle looks forward to a time when "Christ is formed [*morphoō*] in you" (Gal. 4:19).

Until that time, the young church in Galatia will struggle. The false teachers want them to turn back to the law, to become legalists once again, but Paul knows there is no power in the law to overcome sin. The law could never transform a sinner; it could never conform a person to the likeness of Jesus. Rather, Paul wants the Galatians to walk by the Spirit, who alone is capable of turning those young believers from the desires of the flesh to following Christ (Gal. 5:16–17). Only through God's Holy Spirit can sinners be remade into the image of Christ.

Next come verses in Paul's letter that are quite familiar to us. They paint a similar before-and-after picture that we have seen elsewhere, as Paul contrasts the life given over to the desires of the sinful flesh with the life led by the Spirit.

> Now the works of the flesh are evident: sexual immorality, impurity, sensuality, idolatry, sorcery, enmity, strife, jealousy, fits of anger, rivalries, dissensions, divisions, envy, drunkenness, orgies, and things like these. I warn you, as I warned you before, that those who do such things will not inherit the kingdom of God. But the fruit of the Spirit is love, joy, peace, patience, kindness, goodness, faithfulness, gentleness, self-control; against such things there is no law. (Gal. 5:19–23)

What does it mean to be saved? It means turning from a life characterized by corruption and decay, to the living God who through his Spirit gives purpose and significance. It means being changed from a person who is of no use to God and his kingdom, to one who is capable of serving and glorifying him. It means the renewal of the *imago Dei* as believers are remade in the likeness of Christ. It means moving from deformity to glorification.

> But our citizenship is in heaven, and from it we await a Savior,
> the Lord Jesus Christ, who will transform our lowly body
> to be like his glorious body, by the power that enables him
> even to subject all things to himself.
>
> *Philippians 3:20–21*

Key Terms for Salvation Expressed in the Language of Science

transform, conform, seal, corruption, decay, image of God (*imago Dei*), image of Christ (*imago Christi*), likeness, glory, ascension, glorification, resurrection

Questions for Group Discussion

1. Would some in the group be willing to share their "before and after" testimonies, highlighting in what ways their lives are different now that they have turned to Jesus?
2. How can Christians campaign for proper care of the environment without becoming earth worshippers or falling for the pseudoscience of global warming fanatics?
3. In what specific ways can a Christian presently participate in the transformation of his body and mind for service to Christ?
4. In what ways have you brought glory to God this week?

12

The Language of Community

From Separation to Union

PARTICIPATION

By which he has granted to us his precious and very
great promises, so that through them you may become *partakers*
of the divine nature, having escaped from the corruption
that is in the world because of sinful desire.

2 Peter 1:4

Eastern Orthodoxy is one of the three branches of Christendom and by far the smallest. Russian Orthodoxy, Greek Orthodoxy, and the Ethiopian Orthodox Church are examples of this historically rich form of Christianity. Eastern Orthodoxy became a branch in its own right when in 1054 a major schism occurred, splitting the universal church into halves roughly mirroring the eastern and western portions of the Roman Empire. The western half eventually became Roman Catholicism, while the eastern half—centered at the time in Constantinople (modern Istanbul, Turkey)—became the Orthodox Church.

Evangelicals would be remiss to reject Orthodoxy out of hand. Its history is nearly one and a half millennia older than Protestantism's. Early church fathers Irenaeus, Athanasius, Basil the Great, and John Chrysostom have decidedly Orthodox theology, yet are frequently cited by Protestant scholars in important doctrinal debates. Much of what Protestants believe relating to the Trinity and the person and nature of Christ has been heavily influenced by Orthodox scholars. We owe a great debt to these important witnesses in the early centuries of Christianity.

In this chapter, we will concentrate on one element of Orthodoxy's understanding of salvation that has unfortunately been ignored by many Protestant formulations. That aspect involves the idea of participation (what some scholars prefer to call "union").

A variety of English words including fellowship, companion, communion, partaker, partner, and partnership, come from the Greek word *koinōnia*. In secular Greek, *koinōnia* and its derivatives were used to describe common enterprises, business partners or associates, legal partnerships, and communal sharing of possessions. It was also employed in discussing friendship, marriage, and fellowship of citizenship. It was the quintessential connotation of community. However, its religious usage was made prevalent by the biblical authors.[1]

This Greek word is seen in the verse from 2 Peter cited at the head of this chapter. The phrase "partakers of the divine nature" is indeed intriguing. Eastern Orthodoxy has built its understanding of salvation here, a salvation that has a different emphasis than traditionally found in Protestantism, but one that is biblical nonetheless.

An Incarnational Emphasis

God did something more than declare us forgiven. He became a man. He participated in our human nature through the incarnation of the Son. This model of salvation is not a declaration of innocence but rather the participation of humanity with the divine nature.

Athanasius, the fourth-century Egyptian bishop of Alexandria, made this understanding of the incarnation his central argument against the heresy of Arianism. Arius taught that the preexistent Son of God, the Logos, was a creature. The Logos was the first of God's creations and through him everything else was made. Athanasius discerned that this understanding of the Logos entirely undercut Christian salvation.

A synod of Libyan and Egyptian bishops was convened to debate Arius's views, and along with several other men he was declared a

---

1. Kittel, *Theological Dictionary of the New Testament*, 3:797–99.

heretic. Undeterred, Arius moved to Palestine and began to promulgate his views further, garnering a fair following. Constantine, the first Christian emperor of the Roman Empire, saw the disunity these debates were causing in his empire and summoned a council to settle the matter. This first ecumenical (Greek meaning "worldwide") council was held in 325 in the city of Nicaea.

Athanasius' arguments against Arianism were instrumental in exposing its weaknesses and validating its condemnation in the earlier synod. His primary contention was deeply soteriological: "If we do not have a savior who is one in nature with God, then we do not have God as our savior."

When teaching a course on the doctrine of God, I write fifteen words on the board and ask students to categorize them. The list contains some of the following: lion, God, man, book, apple, angel, river, woman, tree, Satan. I have the students group the items as they see fit. Occasionally, students put animate and inanimate objects together. Others see a spiritual connection between God and angels, but are hesitant to place Satan (another spirit being) in that same category. Still others are so confused that they almost have as many categories as items!

Rarely, though, do I have a student place God in a category by himself. Yet, in a fundamental sense, every item in the list is finite except for God. God is uncreated and infinite.

Athanasius saw a problem with Arianism, in that it placed the Logos in the finite category. His argument was related to another Christian doctrine that has bearing on this discussion. That is the understanding of the creation as *ex nihilo*, Latin for "out of nothing."

Out of Nothing

As Christians, we do not believe everything is God (known as pantheism, a belief found in Hinduism, Buddhism, and various religions influenced by Eastern mysticism). Nor do we believe that the creation is part of God (panentheism), or that it is coexistent with God (dualism). Rather, the creation has an existence that is substantially separate from God yet dependent upon him for its continuation.

Made out of nothing, the creation has no existence in itself. The creation solely exists because at each and every moment, God sustains it through his providential word (Heb. 1:3). If for one moment God were to withdraw his sustaining hand from creation, it would immediately slip back to nothing. *Ex nihilo* is a foundational understanding of the cosmos, one that separates the Christian faith from virtually all other religions.

If the Logos is part of the *ex nihilo* creation, the Logos would not have life in himself and could not give life to the rest of fallen creation. Only a Logos who is one in substance with God (the Greek *homoousios* is the traditional theological term used to describe this) could give life to an *ex nihilo* creation. As Athanasius powerfully argued, the Logos must be one in nature with God, or the Logos could not save humanity.

Someone may ask, "Can't God just declare fallen humanity forgiven?" This is where I think we have allowed the justification model of salvation to dominate our evangelicalism, losing sight of other valid explanations. The predominant evangelical portrait of salvation envisions God sitting in the judge's seat, declaring the guilty sinner innocent. In the justification model, sin is the sole problem of humanity.

In the participatory model, mortality is the problem, the constant threat of returning to a state of *ex nihilo*. The only solution for this problem is God becoming a human. This is why Eastern Orthodoxy is labeled "incarnational," yet it is a pity that evangelicalism is not equally reckoned. Surely the incarnation is as important to evangelicals as to any other Christians.

Picture sinners hooked up to blood transfusion machines, as the blood of fallen humanity is replaced with the blood of the perfect man, Jesus. We are not saved simply because we have been forgiven. We are saved because we actually participate in the incarnate God-man. His blood is coursing through our veins. As scholar P. D. Steeves succinctly puts it:

> Orthodox theology viewed man as called to know God and share his life, to be saved, not by God's external activity or by one's understanding of propositional truths, but by being himself deified.[2]

In this perspective, God is more the giver of life than of forgiveness, and salvation is more victory over mortality than over sin.

---

2. P. D. Steeves, "The Orthodox Tradition," *Evangelical Dictionary of Theology*, 874. By "deified" Orthodox theologians mean humans become like God, not that humans actually become gods. The technical term for this is "theosis."

"This Is My Body"

However, evangelicals do have an idea of this participation when we speak about the indwelling Holy Spirit. We partake of the divine power of God through his Spirit, and yet, rarely do we verbalize salvation in this fashion.

As noted in our first chapter, this indwelling does not begin after we confess faith in Christ. Rather, we cannot confess faith in Jesus without the Spirit's indwelling. Regeneration, then, is intimately linked to the participatory model of salvation. The reason why we are made alive is because God's Spirit lives in us, giving us life, granting us freedom from the corruption of Adam's fall. If we did not participate with the divine nature, we would have no hope of salvation.

Why have evangelicals often failed to emphasize this incarnational aspect of salvation? Perhaps it is because of the perceived abuses we fear. For example, sacramentalism runs strongly through Eastern Orthodoxy. When participation in the divine energy is emphasized, this can have a dramatic effect on one's view of communion. It becomes a short leap to the understanding that the bread changes into the flesh of Jesus and the wine into his blood. Communion becomes a feeding on Jesus, another opportunity to participate in the divine energy.

However, we need not take this participatory model of salvation that far. As a Protestant, I have extreme objections to this view of communion. It makes little sense of the last supper shared by Jesus and his disciples. That piece of bread was just a piece of bread, and if the original communion meal did not involve bread actually becoming the flesh of Jesus, why should we believe that every subsequent communion does?

Yet, in negatively reacting to what is also the Catholic view of communion, Protestants have moved too far in the opposite direction.[3] In communion there *is* participation with Christ, just not in a physical manner. In the Lord's Table believers become participants (*koinōnos*) with Christ and have communion (*koinōnia*) with him through the Holy Spirit.

Some Protestants have made communion more of a memorial service. Certainly, "do this in remembrance of me" is part of the

---

3. Both Roman Catholicism and Eastern Orthodoxy believe that the bread and wine become the flesh and blood of Jesus during communion. However, they differ as to when exactly that occurs during the meal.

ceremony, but it is not the only part. More happens at communion than an exercise of the mind. When we divorce communion from any activity of God's Spirit, we have inadvertently robbed it of its true power.

Participating with Demons

Paul recognizes more is happening in communion than simply remembering what Jesus did for us. When evangelicals celebrate the Lord's Table, we usually read the familiar passage from 1 Corinthians 11 that deals with the communion ceremony. However, in the preceding chapter, Paul says something of great importance for our understanding of what takes place during this sacrament.

> The cup of blessing that we bless, is it not a participation in the blood of Christ? The bread that we break, is it not a participation in the body of Christ? Because there is one bread, we who are many are one body, for we all partake of the one bread. Consider the people of Israel: are not those who eat the sacrifices participants in the altar? What do I imply then? That food offered to idols is anything, or that an idol is anything? No, I imply that what pagans sacrifice they offer to demons and not to God. I do not want you to be participants with demons. You cannot drink the cup of the Lord and the cup of demons. You cannot partake of the table of the Lord and the table of demons. (1 Cor. 10:16–21)

Paul makes a shocking connection between idol worship and participation with demons. To be sure, idols are nothing more than blocks of wood or fashioned metal. However, when participants sacrifice to these idols, demons take the opportunity to commune and have fellowship with them. When Paul warns the Corinthian believers to not be "participants with demons," he is not suggesting that when they sacrifice to demons, they are remembering what demons do. He means that they *participate* with the demons. Something greater is implied here than merely an exercise of the mind.

When Christians partake of communion, they are participating with Christ. Although the exact nature of this participation is not spelled out, we ought not jump to the conclusion that the elements of the communion physically become the flesh and blood of Jesus. However, we can argue from other biblical principles that this participation is spiritual in nature. In a mysterious way, believers who partake of communion participate in Christ through the Spirit.

Worship and the Language of Participation

Historically, it has been a small minority of Christians who believe that communion is nothing more than a mental exercise of remembrance. The vast majority of believers throughout church history have viewed communion as an actual participation in Christ. Do you ever sense a strengthening of your faith upon observing the Lord's Supper? God has intended it to fortify us not merely in mind but also in spirit.

This is why Paul finds it abominable that Christians could participate with both demons and Christ. If the communion meal or the sacrifices to idols were meat and drink with no other spiritual significance attached, then eating both would not necessarily cause difficulty. However, because there is spiritual participation with demons in pagan sacrifices, and spiritual participation with Christ in the communion, the two cannot possibly be maintained simultaneously.

In fact, if we take this spiritual participation seriously, we can begin to understand why some of the Corinthian believers were becoming ill and even dying when they abused communion (1 Cor. 11:30). If the bread and wine in the communion service imbue nothing of greater significance than their physical characteristics, why would they have such drastic consequences upon those who ingest them?

Understanding the Lord's Table in this spiritual manner makes better sense of the Last Supper as well. When Jesus held the bread and cup and said, "This is my body" and "This . . . is . . . my blood," he was not speaking in physical terms; he was revealing a spiritual reality. Believers spiritually participate in Christ's crucifixion. If we do not, we would have no hope of salvation.

Paul makes a similar argument about baptism. It is not simply the intermingling of water and the body that occurs. There is a spiritual participation with Christ. This is why Paul can say,

> Do you not know that all of us who have been baptized into
> Christ Jesus were baptized into his death? We were buried
> therefore with him by baptism into death, in order that, just
> as Christ was raised from the dead by the glory of the Father,
> we too might walk in newness of life. (Rom. 6:3–4)

Obviously Paul does not envision a physical dying of believers here. Believers spiritually participate in Christ's death through the sacrament of baptism.

Protestant Reformer John Calvin defined communion as "a spiritual banquet, wherein Christ attests himself to be the life-giving bread, upon which our souls feed unto true and blessed immortality."[4] Calling it "food of our soul," Calvin perceived a spiritual participation between Christ and the believer through communion. In referring to the words of Jesus in John 6:53—"Truly, truly, I say to you, unless you eat the flesh of the Son of Man and drink his blood, you have no life in you"—Calvin saw a participation in the spiritual life of Christ through the sacrament.

> As it is not the seeing but the eating of bread that suffices
> to feed the body, so the soul must truly and deeply become
> partaker of Christ that it may be quickened to spiritual life
> by his power.[5]

One final quotation from Calvin's commentary on the significance of the Lord's Table combines numerous aspects of Christian salvation as seen in previous chapters, but also recognizes this participation in the divine nature.

> This is the wonderful exchange which, out of his measureless
> benevolence, he has made with us; that, becoming Son of
> man with us, he has made us sons of God with him; that,
> by his descent to earth, he has prepared an ascent to heaven
> for us; that, by taking on our mortality, he has conferred his
> immortality upon us; that, accepting our weakness, he has
> strengthened us by his power; that, receiving our poverty
> unto himself, he has transferred his wealth to us; that, taking

---

4. Calvin, *Institutes*, 4.17.1.
5. Ibid., 4.17.5.

the weight of our iniquity upon himself (which oppressed us), he has clothed us with his righteousness.[6]

Of special note is Calvin's comment that Jesus took on our mortality so that we might be given immortality. This is precisely the Orthodox understanding of participation with the divine energy.

Union with Christ

Certain Christian scholars speak of union with Christ. I have preferred the term "participation" in this chapter because it is the more direct English equivalent of the Greek words expressing this idea. However, there are other biblical phrases that similarly express the idea of being united with Christ.

1. "In Christ"

This phrase is seen dozens of times throughout Paul's epistles, crystallizing the abundant advantages believers experience through their faith in Jesus. To be "in Christ" means that we benefit from everything Christ did on our behalf.

Consider a prison break. Jesus breaks the cell bars and you escape with him. His freedom is your freedom. His success is your success. This is the idea of union with Christ. Whatever Jesus accomplishes is as if you have accomplished it.

Because this New Testament concept is too widespread to cover in detail here, we will limit our discussion to one portion of Paul's opening chapter to the Ephesians. There he uses the phrases "in Christ" and "in him" ten times in the first fourteen verses. We learn that believers were chosen in Christ before the foundation of the world. Christians have every spiritual blessing in Christ; they have redemption and forgiveness of sins in Christ. In him they also have been sealed by the Holy Spirit and have obtained an inheritance.

> For we have come to share in Christ, if indeed we hold our original confidence firm to the end. (Heb. 3:14)

---

6. Ibid., 4.17.2. Calvin speaks at length elsewhere in the *Institutes* about what it means to participate with Christ (see 3.1.1 and following).

2. "With Christ"

There are several things Christians experience "with Christ." They have died with Christ, were buried with Christ, they live with Christ, they have been raised with Christ, have been crucified with Christ, and when they depart this world they will be with Christ and reign with Christ.[7]

> For you have died, and your life is hidden with Christ in God. (Col. 3:3)

3. "Put on Christ"

Paul uses the language of clothing to speak of the believer's union with Christ. The New International Version captures the literal sense of "putting on Christ" when it translates the following:

> For all of you who were baptized into Christ have clothed yourselves with Christ. (Gal. 3:27 NIV)

The same Greek term is seen in Ephesians 6 when Paul tells believers to put on the whole armor of God, and a similar term is used when Peter speaks of everyone clothing themselves with humility. Christians likewise clothe themselves with compassion, kindness, gentleness, and patience.[8]

> But put on the Lord Jesus Christ, and make no provision for the flesh, to gratify its desires. (Rom. 13:14)

Christians participate in everything Jesus did in his earthly life. They participate in his sinless life, his atoning crucifixion, his death-defeating resurrection, his glorification, and his ascension to heaven where Christians are "seated . . . with [Christ] in the heavenly realms" (Eph. 2:6 NIV). As our sins were imputed to Jesus, his righteousness was

---

7. Rom. 6:4, 8; Col. 3:1; Gal. 2:20; Phil. 1:23; Rev. 20:4.

8. Eph. 6:11; 1 Peter 5:5; Col. 3:12. Those who believe themselves to be righteous in the eyes of God via their own works are like people who clothe themselves with filthy rags (Isa. 64:6). In Hebrew, Isaiah is literally speaking of the rags a woman used during her menstruation, something the Jews considered supremely unclean. As believers, we go from filthy rags to a white robe from Christ (Rev. 3:18; 6:11).

imputed to us by reason of this spiritual union with him. Yet, this union is not only in what Jesus did in the past. Even now in the Christian's walk of faith, he is clothed with Christ. In this sense, Christians were united with Christ before the foundation of the world and will remain united with him throughout eternity. As New Testament scholar Edmund Clowney notes, "The status of Christians depends upon the status of Christ, for they are joined to him."[9]

Referring back to our opening verse for this chapter from 2 Peter, we are told that this participation affects the believer's escape from "the corruption that is in the world because of sinful desire" (1:4). This corruption echoes the previous chapter concerning the loss of the image of God. Fallen humanity no longer has the life that it was created to have. Overcome by mortality, humanity can only return to that pristine existence by participating in the life of God. This happens through the incarnation.

How Does This Relate to Regeneration?

The shrewd observer will note that in both regeneration and participation, believers are taken from death to life. This being the case, are we not talking about the same thing when using the two terms?

Yes and no. There *is* similarity between the idea of participation and regeneration. Being born from above and having bodies that are the temple of the Holy Spirit reflect the sentiment of "partakers of the divine nature." What was dead is given life. Amazingly, the same Spirit who was present at creation and who raised Jesus from the dead is now living in us.[10]

However, there is a change in emphasis in Orthodoxy's understanding of participation, and it is one reason why I hesitate to fully applaud it. Regeneration is the work of the Holy Spirit mediated through God's Word (James 1:18; 1 Peter 1:23), but Orthodoxy emphasizes the incarnation as the sole means by which fallen humanity participates in new life. This may appear to be splitting hairs, but the emphasis is dramatic, the differences becoming apparent in that all-too-important matter of sin.

---

9. Clowney, *The Message of 1 Peter*, 83.
10. Gen. 1:2; Rom. 8:11.

Orthodoxy teaches that in the incarnation, humanity has *already* participated in new life.

> Orthodoxy rejects original sin; man is born mortal and therefore sins, instead of the other way around, as the West commonly states the matter.[11]

Sin appears almost an afterthought in Orthodoxy. The reason why Orthodoxy emphasizes the incarnation is because mortality is the problem, and this is addressed when finite and mortal humans participate in the life of the infinite and immortal Christ. Union with Christ is the key to everything in Orthodoxy.

Why spend an entire chapter on the Orthodox understanding of participation, only to disagree with its main emphasis? Because, as with the issue of communion, we need not go as far as Orthodoxy has gone. We can still maintain the basic point without falling into sacramentalism or a faulty view of sin and its effects on humanity. In Christ, fallen humanity has indeed participated with the divine nature, but that participation does not come via the sacraments, nor has it already been affected for all humanity in the incarnation alone. Rather, it comes through faith and is experienced through the indwelling of God's Spirit. In Orthodoxy, there is a sense in which the incarnation has already obtained salvation for humanity, an implicit universalism that is unacceptable given the biblical teaching that not everyone is saved.

However, this problem need not compel us to jettison all Orthodox understanding of Christian salvation. Paul says this concerning the effect of the incarnation:

1. The incarnation was necessary to break the power of sin.
   "For God has done what the law, weakened by the flesh, could not do. By sending his own Son in the likeness of sinful flesh and for sin, he condemned sin in the flesh. . . ." (Rom. 8:3)
2. The incarnation was necessary to fulfill the law's requirements.
   ". . . in order that the righteous requirement of the law might be fulfilled in us, who walk not according to the flesh but according to the Spirit." (Rom. 8:4)

---

11. P. D. Steeves, "The Orthodox Tradition," *Evangelical Dictionary of Theology*, 875.

3. The incarnation was necessary to conquer death.
   "For as by a man came death, by a man has come also the resurrection of the dead." (1 Cor. 15:21)

Biblically speaking, *both* sin and death are problems that must be overcome, and both the indwelling Spirit and the incarnation are means by which humanity is redeemed from corruption. As evangelicals, we can reclaim the participatory model of salvation, without wandering into the avoidable errors of Orthodoxy.

Witnessing and the Language of Participation

Everyone fears death. The finality of it, the universal scope of its reach, and its inescapability strike terror in us all. While our Christian evangelism is not a "scare them into heaven" methodology, to not address the inevitability of death and the coming judgment of God in our witnessing to unbelievers is to excise an important aspect of the message of Jesus. In Christ alone mortality is defeated.

The distinction between Western and Eastern Christianity should be apparent. Western Christianity emphasizes the individual, with sin the main problem. The key question in Catholicism and Protestantism is, How can *I* be saved? There is a strong accent on the individual. For evangelicals, the answer is participation with the Holy Spirit by becoming born again. Present profession of faith is the key.

For Eastern Orthodoxy, the question is best expressed: How can *humanity* attain life? The emphasis is more corporate than individual. The solution is all of humanity participating in the life-giving Christ. Union with Christ is the goal and this happened in the incarnation. The past event of the incarnation is the key.

There is much to appreciate in the Orthodox view, as long as it is properly balanced with the Western perspective on sin and individual salvation. We should not play the two against each other. However, since most readers of this book will be evangelicals, we need to learn from Eastern Orthodoxy's view of salvation in order to gain a greater appreciation for why the incarnation is important for our understanding of salvation.

Both Eastern and Western emphases are valid expressions of Christian salvation, expressing different sides of the same coin. Consider these verses from Paul:

> When the perishable puts on the imperishable, and the mortal puts on immortality, then shall come to pass the saying that is written:
>
> > "Death is swallowed up in victory."
> > "O death, where is your victory?
> > O death, where is your sting?"
>
> The sting of death is sin, and the power of sin is the law. But thanks be to God, who gives us the victory through our Lord Jesus Christ. (1 Cor. 15:54–57)

Both sin and death are problems that are overcome by Christ. It is for this reason that Paul can remind the young pastor, Timothy, that Jesus has "destroyed death and has brought life and immortality to light through the gospel" (2 Tim. 1:10 NIV).

We can speak of individual and community, indwelling Spirit and incarnation, when verbalizing Christian salvation. However, placing greater emphasis on one to the total exclusion of the other is detrimental to our biblical understanding of salvation.

Further Benefits of Participation

Believers enjoy several benefits in this participatory model of salvation. We participate in Christ's glory, but not without participating in his suffering, a theme we noted in chapter 11. Many Christians do not perceive the benefits of sharing in Christ's suffering, but each New Testament author boldly proclaims that believers are privileged to share with Jesus in this way. It is the quintessential mark of mature believers when they can claim that suffering is a mandatory element of true Christian discipleship. Out of his love for us, suffering is employed by God, even in discipline that he initiates for our good, as a means of transforming his children, in order to bring them into full fellowship with his holiness.[12]

---

12. 1 Peter 5:1, 4:13; Phil. 3:10; Rom. 8:17; Heb. 12:10.

However, this participation with Christ and his sufferings is not experienced in isolation, since we participate with other believers as well. This is not limited to eternal participation, although that is certainly an aspect of it. It also involves sharing in blessings here and now.[13] In every aspect of the Christian walk, believers have communion with the body of Christ, both in this life and the one to come. In recognition of this participation the apostle John, when writing to other believers, referred to himself as "your brother and partner in the tribulation and the kingdom and the patient endurance that are in Jesus" (Rev. 1:9).

Lastly, Christians can participate in the plans and purposes of God through prayer. Jesus promises his disciples that where two or more are gathered in his name, there he will be with them. He further promises that prayers offered in his name will be granted.[14]

These blessings would not be possible if it were not for Jesus participating in our humanity. Through his incarnation Christ overcame our mortality.

> Since therefore the children share in flesh and blood, he himself likewise partook of the same things, that through death he might destroy the one who has the power of death, that is, the devil, and deliver all those who through fear of death were subject to lifelong slavery. (Heb. 2:14–15)

Community Language

Evangelicals can learn from the Orthodox understanding of salvation, with its emphasis on the incarnation and community. Second Peter 1:4 is not the whole story of salvation, but it forms one of the chapters. A humble acknowledgment that at times we in the West have been one-dimensional in our approach to salvation may help us recognize that Orthodoxy's understanding can provide needed balance and a fresh perspective. Every believer is called into "the fellowship of [God's] Son" (1 Cor. 1:9).

What does it mean to be saved? It means moving from an isolated existence where self is the center of meaning, to one where there is fellowship with the eternal God. It means living in a community

---

13. Col. 1:12; Rom. 15:27; 2 Cor. 1:7; 1 John 1:6–7.
14. Matt. 18:20; John 14:13–14; 15:16; 16:23; also 1 John 5:14.

of regenerated people who participate in the life of God's Spirit. It means being partakers of the divine nature, moving from mortality to immortality. It means moving from separation to union.

That which we have seen and heard we proclaim also to you,
so that you too may have fellowship with us; and indeed our fellowship
is with the Father and with his Son Jesus Christ.

1 John 1:3

Key Terms for Salvation Expressed in the Language of Community

participation, union, fellowship, partners, community, communion, divine energy, indwelling, *ex nihilo*, incarnation, mortality, immortality

---

Questions for Group Discussion

1. Why is it important that God not only overcome the effects of sin by declaring us forgiven, but also by becoming human?
2. How does a community-oriented view of salvation, as opposed to an individualistic one, help us when it comes to a proper view of the local church and how we should become involved?
3. Does an incarnational view of salvation affect your view of the sacraments or ordinances of baptism and communion? Explain.

13

The Language of the Military

From Defeat to Victory

SALVATION

Salvation belongs to our God who sits on the throne, and to the Lamb!

Revelation 7:10

As we consider our last model of biblical salvation, I want to reiterate what was said in the preface. These various ways of verbalizing Christian salvation do not stand in conflict with each other. Nor is one more important than another. Rather, they are facets of the same reality, different angles of viewing the salvation accomplished by Jesus Christ. Each emphasizes an aspect of the mess into which humanity has fallen, and how Christ has come to deliver us from it.

The term "salvation" encompasses the discussions from previous chapters, but it also has its own precise meaning from everyday language of the first century. For this reason, it warrants its own chapter.

To Heal, to Rescue, to Save

The Greek verb *sōzō* and the noun *sōtēria*[1] have the primary sense of "snatch[ing] others by force from serious peril." This was especially seen in the dangers of battle and sailing, or in the context of the gods

---

1. From this we get soteriology, the official term for the study of the doctrine of salvation. The same root is found for savior, *sōtēr*.

saving someone from peril. However, the words were also employed with reference to being saved from illness or general threats, or to speak of judicial pardoning by a king.[2]

While *sōzō* has multiple meanings, evangelicals have been conditioned to think of "saved" in spiritual, eternal, or eschatological terms. "God will save you" means something akin to "God will give you eternal life in heaven." However, the Greek does not always have this meaning.

For example, the word is seen in passages with Jesus healing someone: "Your faith has made you well."[3] However, in the episode with the woman who anoints Jesus' feet with ointment, upon telling the woman that her sins are forgiven, Jesus says, "Your faith has saved you; go in peace" (Luke 7:50). It is the identical Greek word *sōzō*, but in this case the ESV translators chose "save" instead of "to make well." Why?

The translators have made a judgment call based on context. If I were to tell you that I save money each week, this doesn't mean that I rescue it from eternal damnation. You understand the context, even though it is the same word we use to speak of being eternally saved. Similarly, the Greek word can have a wide range of connotations.

Other examples include the disciples asking Jesus to save them from the storm, or Peter sinking as he walked on the water, calling out to Jesus to save him. The equivalent Greek verb speaks of saving the sailors on the boat with Paul before they are shipwrecked on Malta.[4]

However, the noun for salvation, *soteria*, as employed in the New Testament "has to do solely with man's relationship to God."[5] Though "to save" in the New Testament might not mean eternal salvation, each time the word "salvation" appears, that is precisely what it means. This salvation is consistently couched in the language of warfare and the military.

---

2. Kittel, *Theological Dictionary of the New Testament*, 7:965–69.

3. Mark 5:34; 10:52; Luke 17:19.

4. Matt. 8:25; 14:30; Acts 27:20. The enigmatic statement by Paul, women "will be saved through childbearing" (1 Tim. 2:15), causes evangelicals difficulty as it seems to imply that women will be given eternal life if they bear children. However, this can hardly be the point Paul is making, and we do well to consider another possible meaning for the Greek. Moyer Hubbard covers this very issue in his article "Kept Safe Through Childbearing: Maternal Mortality, Justification by Faith, and the Social Setting of 1 Timothy 2:15," *Journal of the Evangelical Theological Society* 55, no. 4, 743–62. Hubbard lists thirty-seven instances where *sōzō* is used in a non-salvific sense in the New Testament (see p. 744, n. 7).

5. Kittel, *Theological Dictionary of the New Testament*, 7:1002.

Three Fronts of Spiritual Warfare

All Christians are involved in a bitter conflict that appears on three fronts: the world, the flesh, and the devil. James speaks of this threefold confrontation in the fourth chapter of his epistle. There he notes passions that are at war within believers (v. 1), a world that is at enmity with God (v. 4), and how believers can resist the devil (v. 7). Paul provides a more concise summary in Ephesians 2:1–3:

> And you were dead in the trespasses and sins in which you once walked, following the course of this world, following the prince of the power of the air, the spirit that is now at work in the sons of disobedience —among whom we all once lived in the passions of our flesh, carrying out the desires of the body and the mind, and were by nature children of wrath, like the rest of mankind.

However, there is a possible problem in viewing our spiritual difficulties through the lens of these three fronts. It is the potential of overemphasizing one front to the exclusion of the others.

For example, the monasticism so prevalent in Christian history thrived on the notion that a person could be a better Christian if he removed himself from the world. In dealing with Lawrence Taylor's problem of drug addiction noted in chapter 4 on redemption, the monks might have told him to move into the wilderness, away from the world's temptations and pitfalls—a sort of ancient rehab. The problem is that the monks took with them their biggest obstacle, their sinful hearts. And moving to the desert is not going to trick Satan.

Conversely, so-called deliverance ministries appear to place all the blame for our spiritual shortcomings on demons. In counseling Taylor, these ministries would argue that if his demons of addiction were identified and exorcised, he could be delivered from them. This ignores the other two fronts of the spiritual battle.[6]

---

6. The related practices of prayer walks and spiritual mapping suffer from the same misconception—as if all we need do is walk through a city, pray against the strongholds of sin such as taverns, gambling houses, and brothels, and the city's problems will disappear. This ignores the depravity in our hearts, placing the blame for our sins solely at the devil's feet, not our own.

Fundamentalist Christians tend to overemphasize the flesh. Similar to the Pharisees, they legalistically create rules and regulations meant to curb the body's appetites. However, the demonic front is frequently ignored. Often fundamentalists concentrate on sinful passions or confuse them with the world's temptations, and they entirely ignore Satan's involvement. Maybe they are afraid of "the devil made me do it" mentality that appears to skirt personal responsibility. Or they do not believe in an individual, spirit being known as Satan.

> For though we walk in the flesh, we are not waging war according to the flesh. For the weapons of our warfare are not of the flesh but have divine power to destroy strongholds. (2 Cor. 10:3–4)

Christians are in a spiritual war with monumental consequences. Regrettably, this struggle is often downplayed in our churches. However, we must never lose sight of the behind-the-scenes spiritual battle being waged.

> For we do not wrestle against flesh and blood, but against the rulers, against the authorities, against the cosmic powers over this present darkness, against the spiritual forces of evil in the heavenly places. (Eph. 6:12)

Yet this battle against cosmic powers expresses itself in flesh-and-blood struggle. We live in a world under the control of Satan. We wrestle with our own sinful desires. On all sides we are assailed.

Them's Fightin' Words!

There is a large amount of warfare language in the Bible, but we will limit our present discussion to four categories of words in the New Testament dealing with Christians.

1. Struggle and Fight

Non-Christians do not participate in spiritual warfare. To be sure, they have difficulties in life like the rest of us. However, they are citizens of the kingdom of Satan. They are quite at home in the world under his rule. They are slaves to sin and death.

On the other hand, every believer is engaged in battle. This fight is not optional. If you do not perceive this spiritual combat, perhaps you are not walking the Christian life as you should. Previously, Satan was quite content with us as unbelievers. We were in his camp, and the ideals of his world were our ideals. However, the presence of the Holy Spirit in our lives initiated the confrontation. We have made an open declaration to the heavenly realms that we oppose Satan and everything that is ungodly about his kingdom and ourselves. Believers "struggle against sin" (Heb. 12:4) each day. For this reason, Paul commands Timothy to "fight the good fight of the faith" (1 Tim. 6:12).

We tend to be surprised when professing Christians fall into sin, but why does this shock us? As a believer, the passions of the flesh "wage war against your soul" (1 Peter 2:11). People wrongly expect that once they are saved, things will get easier. However, the struggle has just begun. The hope of every believer is that we can say as Paul did at the end of his life, "I have fought the good fight . . . I have kept the faith" (2 Tim. 4:7).

2. Soldier

Scripture uses the metaphor of a soldier to speak of the Christian life, but this talk is not well liked in various churches today. It implies that Christians love violence. Gone are the days when "Onward Christian Soldiers" was a popular hymn sung regularly in our congregations.

However, God's Word does not shy from speaking about believers in this manner. Paul calls both Epaphroditus and Archippus "fellow soldier[s]" (Phil. 2:25; Philem. 2). The metaphor is employed wonderfully elsewhere by Paul when he writes to Timothy:

> Share in suffering as a good soldier of Christ Jesus. No soldier
> gets entangled in civilian pursuits, since his aim is to please
> the one who enlisted him. (2 Tim. 2:3–4)

The imagery is rich. Picture a warrior armed for battle, but his eyes wander. His commander barks out an order but the fighter is oblivious. His attention is elsewhere. Such a soldier is unfit to fight. Unfortunately, this describes many Christians who have become involved in "civilian pursuits" and have forgotten the spiritual battle that engages them. When real testing comes, they fail. Therefore, we must be prepared to "wage the good warfare" (1 Tim. 1:18).

3. *Weapons*

A soldier is only as good as the weapons he is given. Earlier we saw Paul refer to "weapons of our warfare . . . to destroy strongholds" (2 Cor.10:4). In that same letter he speaks of "weapons of righteousness" (2 Cor. 6:7). What is this armament?

Paul spent three years ministering in Ephesus during his third missionary journey. Ephesus was a major center for pagan worship. It had the temple of the goddess Artemis, one of the seven wonders of the ancient world. Minted on its coins was the phrase "servant of the great goddess," and a major economic enterprise was the making of miniature temples out of silver so worshippers could take them home or on their travels.

We read in Acts 19 that due to the evangelistic enterprises of Paul and the number of conversions to Christ, the replica temple business took such a hit that a riot resulted in the city. This was shortly after converts to the faith publically burned paraphernalia associated with exorcisms, witchcraft, and the magic arts. Ephesus was the chief seat of necromancy—communicating with the dead—for all of Asia Minor. The pagan trinkets of the new converts were valued at 137 years of wages, thus precipitating the riot (v. 19).

In light of this pagan context, Paul commands believers in Ephesus to put on the whole armor of God (Eph. 6:11). You don't wear armor to a picnic. A spiritual battle requires spiritual weapons.

Paul wrote the book of Ephesians years later while in prison. High-profile prisoners were often chained to soldiers, making their escape nearly impossible. Perhaps as Paul began to think about the spiritual battle that believers in Ephesus encountered, he looked at the guard to whom he was chained and saw his armor. What a perfect illustration for the young Christians in Ephesus. Everyone was well aware of the Roman soldier and his apparel.

Paul lists six pieces of this armor and with each, I provide a simple understanding of what that piece represents (Eph. 6:14–17):

- *the belt of truth*: integrity, single-minded devotion
- *the breastplate of righteousness*: living holy and righteous lives
- *feet fitted with readiness*: a willingness to share the gospel
- *the shield of faith*: fighting off the flaming arrows of Satan

- *the helmet of salvation*: confidence in our status as children of God
- *the sword of the Spirit*: knowing and effectively using the Word of God

Putting on this armor is akin to our discussion in chapter 12 about being clothed with Christ, but it also reflects much of what has been said concerning every model of salvation.

Worship and the Language of Salvation

Worship that does not honor the Son does not honor the Father. If Jesus alone has the words of life, then our worship must be bathed in Scripture. Preaching that is not from God's Word is not God-honoring.

After listing the pieces of armor, Paul spends the next three verses on the topic of prayer. It is no mistake. In a battle against unseen, spiritual forces, there is no better weapon than prayer. And there may be no more neglected weapon. "Arm yourself for battle!" is Paul's cry. "But don't forget an unseen piece of your armor, the one piece that holds the other pieces together."

In prayer we declare our utter dependence upon God to win this battle. For this reason, Paul notes that the goal of believers is not to storm the gates of hell or challenge the forces of evil in hand-to-hand combat. Rather, it is to stand our ground—ground that Jesus Christ alone is able to win (Eph. 6:13).

> So then let us cast off the works of darkness and put on the armor of light. (Rom. 13:12)

4. Conquer

The book of Revelation is a picture of warfare between Christ and the forces of evil. If I could summarize Revelation it would be "Jesus wins." Seventeen times the verb "conquer" appears. However, the majority of those times it speaks of believers conquering. In the letters to the seven churches in Asia Minor recorded in the first three chapters, the phrase "to the one who conquers" is used in each letter, referring to believers.

Of course, the victory believers enjoy is made possible solely by Christ's conquest. He came to crush the serpent's head. Jesus overcomes the world, and he destroys the power of sin and death.[7] Believers participate in the victory won by Christ over the principalities and powers. Nonbelievers continue in their defeat to these forces.

Obviously, there will be some overlap between the military language of salvation and other terms dealing with rescue and deliverance. For example, consider these verses from Paul, quoting the prophet Isaiah:

> The deliverer will come from Zion;
>> he will turn godlessness away from Jacob.
> And this is my covenant with them
>> when I take away their sins. (Rom. 11:26–27 NIV)

Here we have three models of salvation: the idea of a deliverer (redemption), turning godlessness away (sanctification), and forgiveness of sins (justification). Yet they are all related to the umbrella concept of salvation. You do not need a "savior" if you can save yourself, any more than you require a "deliverer" if you can set yourself free from captivity. It is impossible for sinners to turn away godlessness; only someone who is sinless can do that. In every way that biblical salvation is expressed, it is inconceivable that fallen humans could do it themselves. Salvation must come from elsewhere.

God Is Not Passive

We occasionally picture God in heaven, wringing his hands, hoping that sinners will buy into his salvation plan. But this is hardly the biblical picture. Jesus says he came "to seek and to save the lost" (Luke 19:10), not to seek and to offer salvation, as if he passively sits and waits for people to respond. He saves everyone he intends to save. He loses none that his Father gives to him (John 6:39).

Everything about biblical salvation is active on the part of God. He elects before the foundation of the world.[8] He decides to forgive sins and then sends his Son to become the atoning sacrifice. Adoption is left to the decision of the adopting parent, not the adoptee. Christ comes

---

7. Gen. 3:15; John 16:33; 1 Cor. 15:54–57.
8. Eph. 1:4; 2 Thess. 2:13; 2 Tim. 1:9; 1 Peter 1:20.

to break the power of sin and death and the devil, forces that humans otherwise willingly submit themselves to. God turns away his own wrath and creates the means by which he can become propitious toward sinners. While we were yet God's enemies, he provided reconciliation. There is nothing in the entire process of salvation that pictures God as passive. Salvation from beginning to end is a dynamic process of the active will of God who alone saves.[9]

The choosing of the twelve disciples is an image of this active will. In the time of Jesus, it was customary for disciples to choose the rabbi they wanted to follow. However, in the case of Jesus, the selection process was exactly backward. Jesus tells his disciples, "You did not choose me, but I chose you" (John 15:16). This is a microcosm of the selection of any follower of Jesus.

For this reason Jesus says, "All that the Father gives me will come to me, and whoever comes to me I will never cast out" (John 6:37). The Father is the one who gives disciples to Jesus. If he did not, rebellious sinners would never come to Christ. This is why Jesus says that no one can come to him unless the Father draws him and enables him (John 6:44, 65).

Nothing in creation can separate believers from God's love (Rom. 8:38–39). Why? Because God is the active will behind salvation. This makes the salvation of God's elect certain. God does not change, and because he has loved his children since before the foundation of the world, there can be no sense that he will change his mind. The salvation of the followers of Jesus—everyone who has been given God's Spirit as a deposit—is secured.

I always cringe when I see a movie where the protagonist tells someone, "I'll never let anything bad happen to you." Naturally, we have come to expect hyperbole from our cinematic heroes. However, people in the real world make similar empty promises. How dare a father give this guarantee to his child? He does not have the wherewithal to assure that commitment.

While Jesus has all authority in heaven and on earth, he never makes such a promise. What he does promise is that he will never leave us or forsake us. He assures us that all things will work for good for those who

---

9. Clowney notes, "The scriptural teaching of God's choosing is sometimes questioned because it is not understood, and sometimes hated because it *is* understood" (*Message of 1 Peter*, 91).

love God. He declares that in this world believers will experience difficulty and persecution and tribulation, but we should take heart because Christ has overcome the world.[10] Believers participate in this victory.

> For everyone who has been born of God overcomes the world. And this is the victory that has overcome the world— our faith. Who is it that overcomes the world except the one who believes that Jesus is the Son of God? (1 John 5:4–5)

Final Victory Is Assured

While living in Namibia, I occasionally had a friend mail a video of Dallas Cowboys games against key rivals. By the time I received the recording, it was several weeks after the game had finished and I already knew the outcome. However, despite knowing the final score, I still found the games exciting. At times, the Cowboys would be losing and I could not imagine how they were going to win, but I knew they were going to. The anxiety that normally comes with fear of losing was not entirely absent, but the excitement of an anticipated win was certainly present.

This is the same when it comes to the second coming and Christ's ultimate conquest. Presently, we are in a back-and-forth struggle with Satan and sin, and often it looks as if we will not succeed. Yet, the outcome is certain, the triumph already secured. We ought not to have the anxiety that comes with the fear of losing. Rather, we should possess the hope of an anticipated victory.

The second coming of Christ is a doctrine that tends to be either overemphasized or forgotten. It seems that weekly there is somebody making a prediction about Jesus' return, usually coupled with creative mathematics that make a specific date "certain." The prediction of a radio personality a few years ago that Jesus would rapture believers on May 21, 2011 was determined through rather convoluted calculations that included biblical numerology, with the number 5 standing for atonement, 10 equaling completeness, and 17 for heaven. By multiplying and squaring the numbers, the exact day of Christ's return was determined.

This would be funny if it weren't so sad. Tens of millions of dollars were spent by this radio ministry imploring people to turn to Jesus

---

10. Heb. 13:5; Rom. 8:28; John 15:20; 16:33.

before it was too late. False predictions like this make all Christians look foolish.[11]

In light of these shenanigans, many Christians deemphasize the Lord's return to the point where it functions little in their day-to-day walk with Christ. However, references to the second coming of Jesus are in virtually every New Testament book, providing hope for those who are suffering under persecution, spurring believers on to righteous living and preparedness, and warning those who scoff at the idea that there is a future judgment.[12] Clearly we should not overlook this important doctrine.

God's determination to not provide us with a specific date for Christ's return is a wise omission by the one who understands human nature perfectly. If God declared that on November 11, 2027, the end of the world was coming, assuming this was a genuine word from God you knew to be absolutely true, what would your reaction be? Given human nature, I think we might become lax in our vigilance. That date is sufficiently far off to not feel a sense of urgency.

I think Christians who set dates for the Lord's return, or appear fixated on figuring it out, reveal a deficiency in their discipleship. The long, uncertain grind that the Christian life entails, with the requisite attentiveness in not knowing precisely when the Lord will return, is too difficult for them. They must know! A firm date is necessary so, in essence, they can let their guard down with no real danger.

However, when Jesus tells us that the master is returning and we do not know exactly when, we are required to constantly be attentive and alert. This pressure is excessive for some Christians. Therefore, they seek an easier path. Rather than uncertainty with the date, they want certitude. The irony is that all their talk about being concerned about the Lord's return is just a cover for procrastination and laziness.

Nevertheless, there are things we are told in Scripture about the Lord's return. In a familiar second coming passage, we see the rich warfare imagery.

---

11. This tendency toward gullibility can be exploited. One person started a pet care service for the animals "left behind" from Christian owners taken up in the rapture. AftertheRapturePetCare.com charged $10 per pet and made a fair amount of money. Who will take care of your pet after the rapture, you may ask? Well-meaning atheists and agnostics, that's who.

12. 2 Thess. 1:6–8; 2 Peter 3:3–4, 11–12.

> For the Lord himself will descend from heaven with a cry
> of command, with the voice of an archangel, and with the
> sound of the trumpet of God. And the dead in Christ will
> rise first. Then we who are alive, who are left, will be caught
> up together with them in the clouds to meet the Lord in the
> air, and so we will always be with the Lord. (1 Thess. 4:16–17)

The "voice of an archangel" and the "sound of the trumpet of God" are both phrases that speak of warfare. The trumpet is blared, warning the soldiers to ready for battle, and the leader of the armies of the Lord shouts to be prepared. This battle language is unmistakable. However, there is further battle imagery in this passage that is often missed.

Paul says that believers will be caught up in the air with Jesus. This is the classic passage used for the doctrine of the rapture, a widespread belief that Christians still living will be taken away before the wrath of God (the "tribulation") is poured out on the planet. This is not the second coming in this theological system. Jesus comes on the clouds, believers meet him in the air, and together they proceed to heaven. Only later does Jesus return to earth.

The problem with this belief is that it misinterprets this passage. The language here is one of a triumphal return by a conquering king, not of someone who comes halfway and leaves. In ancient days, when the victorious king reappeared from battle, he rode into his kingdom, bringing with him spoils of conquest like captured slaves or precious materials seized in battle. These plundered possessions were paraded out before the king's citizens in what was called a "train" or "procession." This language is utilized elsewhere by Paul when he writes:

> But thanks be to God, who in Christ always leads us in
> triumphal procession, and through us spreads the fragrance
> of the knowledge of him everywhere. (2 Cor. 2:14)

This "triumphal procession" is military language of a returning king. Elsewhere Paul writes of Jesus: "having disarmed the powers and authorities, he made a public spectacle of them, triumphing over them by the cross" (Col. 2:15 NIV; also Eph. 4:8).

The imagery is clear. Jesus defeated the forces of evil, and he returns leading a train of vanquished foes. His people run out of the city to meet him on the road, and in celebratory procession they accompany him back to his kingdom. When Jesus comes again with great power and glory in the clouds, this is what Paul envisions happening to believers who are still living.[13] We meet him in the air (the Greek literally means to be seized or snatched up), and then we come down to earth triumphantly, where we reign with him forever.

Jesus speaks of his own return in similar language, co-opting the prophet Daniel's image of a glorious "son of man" who comes on the clouds (Dan. 7:13). Before his crucifixion, Jesus said to the high priest, "But I tell you, from now on you will see the Son of Man seated at the right hand of power and coming on the clouds of heaven" (Matt. 26:64). This return of our conquering Lord should be foremost in the minds of every believer.

> Christ was sacrificed once to take away the sins of many; and he will appear a second time, not to bear sin, but to bring salvation to those who are waiting for him. (Heb. 9:28 NIV)

One Way

We would be remiss if we did not emphasize that everything said in these thirteen chapters about biblical salvation only comes through faith in Jesus Christ.

> Jesus said to him, "I am the way, and the truth, and the life. No one comes to the Father except through me." (John 14:6)

There are two roads. One leads to destruction, the other to eternal life. As such, there are two gates leading to these two paths. Many enter through the gate proceeding to eternal condemnation; few go through the life-granting gate (Matt. 7:13–14).

Jesus is that gate. He tells his disciples there are false shepherds but he is the "good shepherd" (John 10:7, 11, 14). He knows his sheep and calls them by name, and his sheep recognize his voice. In our world today, there is a plethora of voices declaring the path to life. Do you hear the voice of Jesus our Savior?

---

13. Matt. 24:30; Mark 13:26; Luke 21:27.

> And there is salvation in no one else, for there is no other
> name under heaven given among men by which we must be
> saved. (Acts 4:12)

If you do not have faith in Jesus Christ, Satan is your shepherd. If Jesus is not your Lord, sin is your master. Apart from the resurrection and the life (John 11:25), your destiny is eternal death. There is one God and therefore one mediator. The teaching of Mohammed will not save you. Taking the way of Buddha or following the path of Confucius will lead you along the road to hell. All other supposed mediators, gurus, avatars, channelers, and messiahs are false shepherds who mislead the sheep and ultimately destroy the flock.

Witnessing and the Language of Salvation

We should never tire of pointing a lost world to its only Savior, and the best way to do that is to quote him. If our evangelism is not bathed in the teaching of Christ, the one who alone has the words of life, our efforts will remain misguided. Often our evangelism worries more about gimmicks, "felt needs," and contextualization than the actual words from our Savior and Lord. Point people to Jesus. Apart from him, there is no salvation.

Talk like this and you will be vilified by the world and probably by not too few "professing" Christians as well. The exclusive path of salvation in Jesus and him alone does not sell well in a world feeding at the smorgasbord of religious pluralism. "All ways lead to God" is a vacuous statement as empty as the serpent's lie in Eden that promised "salvation" if Adam and Eve turned from God's way. Disbelief in the promises of God led to the fall of mankind; continued disbelief in the promises of God's Son will leave us to spiritual death.

What does it mean to be saved? It means being plucked out of danger by God and rescued from harm. It means being given the weapons of righteousness necessary to wage war against every ungodly force as we patiently wait for the return of our triumphant Lord. It means moving from defeat to victory.

Behold, my servant whom I have chosen,
my beloved with whom my soul is well pleased.
I will put my Spirit upon him,
and he will proclaim justice to the Gentiles.
He will not quarrel or cry aloud,
nor will anyone hear his voice in the streets;
a bruised reed he will not break,
and a smoldering wick he will not quench,
until he brings justice to victory;
and in his name the Gentiles will hope.

Matthew 12:18–21

Key Terms for Salvation Expressed in the Language of the Military

salvation, saved, Savior, Son of Man, rescue, victory,
second coming, conquer, defeat, warfare, battle, struggle,
fight, armor, soldier

Questions for Group Discussion

1. With which front of spiritual warfare—the world, the flesh, or the devil—do you most struggle? Do you perceive any to be insignificant in your life? Explain.

2. Go through the six pieces of armor listed in Ephesians 6 and analyze your walk with the Lord. Which piece of armor do you frequently fail to put on each day? Are you adept at wielding the sword of the Spirit? What kind of flaming arrows does Satan shoot your way? Is your life characterized by single-minded devotion to Jesus?

3. Is the hope of the return of Jesus operative in your life? Do you err in either fixating on the second coming or completely neglecting it?

4. If salvation is only in Jesus, what are you doing presently to declare this truth to a perishing world? Are you afraid or embarrassed at times in sharing your faith? Or are your feet ready to take you here and there to share the gospel of peace?

14

The Non-Negotiables
of Biblical Salvation

*And this is the record, that God hath given to us eternal life, and this life
is in his Son. He that hath the Son hath life; and he that hath not
the Son of God hath not life.*

1 John 5:11–12 KJV

Christian salvation is multifaceted. There are many ways to express what happens when a person is saved, such that no single explanation fully does justice to the biblical data. All of the models must be combined into a comprehensive whole. Much like a mosaic, only when we step back and look at the big picture do the various pieces truly fit together.

Often we stand too close, seeing one or two portions and pretending that this is the complete picture. We have a tendency to emphasize one aspect to the exclusion of others. However, biblical salvation is more wide-ranging than it frequently is made to appear.

> You are in Christ Jesus, who became to us wisdom from God,
> righteousness and sanctification and redemption. (1 Cor. 1:30)

Each culture has its reasons for concentrating on one feature of salvation. For Africans, safety from the spirits is seen as encompassing Christian salvation. During colonialism in South America, liberation was the dominant view. In the Middle Ages, satisfying the honor of the feudal lord was central. In the Patristic period, paying a ransom to Satan was the key expression of salvation. For evangelicals, forgiveness of sins is the reigning paradigm. Each is true, but none entirely embodies the vast biblical imagery. To isolate one and make it the whole story of salvation yields an anemic picture of God's plan for saving humanity.

However, you may have noticed that there are certain themes that consistently run through all the models. These I call the "non-negotiables" of the Christian doctrine of salvation. Augustine famously said, "In essentials, unity; in nonessentials, liberty; in all things, charity." There are essentials of the Christian faith that, once removed, seriously jeopardize the gospel and could easily lead to a false or heretical notion of salvation. With these essentials evangelicals must be unified. We will briefly discuss four such themes as we conclude.

1. The Bible is our sole authority.

We cannot say anything true about God that he did not first reveal about himself. Scripture is our sole authority when it comes to matters of the faith. Who God is and how to have a relationship with him are only revealed in the Bible. We do not have to conjecture or speculate about what God is like or what he may or may not do. He has told us everything we need to know in his Word.

Scholars refer to this as the sufficiency of Scripture. There is no information lacking in the Bible that is necessary for salvation. This is why the apostle Paul can write:

> All Scripture is breathed out by God and profitable for teaching, for reproof, for correction, and for training in righteousness, that the man of God may be complete, equipped for every good work. (2 Tim. 3:16–17)

In certain Christian circles there is a constant pull away from the Bible and to more immediate forms of revelation. Christian speakers and television evangelists with this attitude are ubiquitous, claiming direct revelation from God. We are told that if we do not listen to their insights from God's special communication to them, we cannot live an effective Christian life. This almost always comes with a video series—at a price of course.

Recently a student in one of my classes said a guest speaker in his church shared his experience of being "slain in the Spirit." The speaker then said, "Unless you have a supernatural encounter with God, you cannot be saved." My student wanted to know what I thought.

Of course, the speaker is correct. Unless we have a "supernatural encounter" with God, we cannot be saved. However, I have a hunch he did not mean what I mean by that phrase. I held up my Bible and told the class, "This is a supernatural encounter with God. In Scripture, God speaks directly to each one of us." That is the beauty of God's revelation in his Word. He speaks to all of us equally through it. We need not be subject to the whims of conniving charlatans. As Peter writes, "In their greed these teachers will exploit you with stories they have made up" (2 Peter 2:3 NIV84).

The movie *Heaven Is for Real* recently came out in cinemas. It is the story of a four-year-old son of a Nebraska pastor who allegedly experienced heaven during an operation. The movie was a surprise hit, raking in over $100 million in domestic and overseas ticket sales in its first three months. Inevitably questions come up about such experiences.

While I believe God can do whatever he wants to do, we do not require a four-year-old boy to tell us about heaven. Jesus Christ, who alone came from heaven, has told us everything we need to know (John 6:33, 38, 46; 2 Peter 1:3). As Jesus said, "No one has ascended into heaven except he who descended from heaven, the Son of Man" (John 3:13).

Countless Christians run here or there looking for a word from the Lord while their Bibles sit on the shelf collecting dust. The reason why we have so many scrawny, malnourished Christians is because they are not being properly fed on God's Word. Give me one man who publicly and correctly exposits the Scriptures rather than one thousand babblers who speak of their private, untestable revelations. God's Word has always been the means by which God has fed and guided and sustained his people.

2. Sin is the problem.

There is a strong attraction away from the biblical portrayal of humanity's sin, and it pulls many people from the gospel. Every religious explanation for the plight of humanity and "salvation" is couched in the false terms of self-made religion. Only the evangelical message found in Jesus Christ gets the story straight, because in the gospel sin is rightly identified as our predicament. You can peruse the religions of the world and you will not find this emphasis in anything other than the Judeo-Christian religious tradition.

In Islam, talk of sin is virtually nonexistent. In neo-paganism, the ultimate evil is destroying Mother Earth. In Buddhism, suffering is the dilemma; sin does not have a real category. The world's self-made religions are littered with superstition and trinkets and gimmicks, like the New Age Movement with its crystals and amulets meant to get us in touch with the god inside us. Even within Christian circles the problem of sin is regularly downplayed, as noted in previous chapters concerning the prosperity gospel and the emergent church movement.

After the creation account of the opening two chapters of Genesis, the very next scene is the fall of Adam and Eve into sin. The entire sweep of the Bible can be summed up in creation and re-creation, or fall and redemption. Sin is the problem from cover to cover. The reason why there are countless false religions is because humanity has never liked looking in the mirror and truly admitting its flaw: the love of self and the sin that is its fruit.

Looking at the Old Testament, sin (or those overcome by it) is portrayed in a variety of ways: as a beast looking to devour (Gen. 4:7); as a wayward adulteress or prostitute (Prov. 6:20–29; Ezek. 16:15; 23:3, 5, 14); as a wasting disease (Ps. 32:3–5); as a useless vine (Ezekiel 15); as a barren woman (Isa. 54:1); as a rebellious house (Ezek. 2:5; 3:9; 17:12; 24:3); as chaff (Ps. 1:4; 35:5); as the constant inclination of the human heart both pre- and post-flood (Gen. 6:5; 8:21; Jer. 17:9); as willful and active rebellion against God's declared law (Zech. 7:12); as an unwanted child (Ezek. 16:1–5); or as the reason for specific acts of judgment by God (e.g., the flood, death of the lovechild of David and Bathsheba, or the Babylonian exile).

The Bible is unique among holy texts in its honest, forthright, blunt portrayal of humanity under the curse of sin, even when speaking about its "saints." Cataloging the numerous sins depicted in the Old Testament reads like a "Who's Who" of both the godly and godless: arrogance (Nebuchadnezzar), insubordination (Korah), presumptuousness (Saul), rage (Moses), adultery (David), greed (Balaam), trickery (Jacob), murder (Cain), jealousy (Leah), fornication (Samson), violence (Lamech), grumbling (Dathan), defiance (Jonah), lust (Solomon), impertinence (Jezebel and Ahab), covetousness (Achan), mockery (Job's wife), slander (Job's friends), deception (Rebekah), irreverence in worship (Aaron's sons Nadab and Abihu), faithlessness (Sarah), fearfulness (Abraham), carelessness (Esau), stubbornness (Lot's wife), blasphemy (Sennacherib), self-centeredness (Elijah), rashness (Jephthah), drunkenness (Noah), disrespect (Ham), gullibility (Eve), nepotism (Eli), foolishness (Josiah), hard-heartedness (Pharaoh), fraud (Haman), prostitution (Tamar). Sin permeates the whole fabric of the Old Testament, as does God's patient yet stern dealings with it.

Sin is the reason why we are spiritually dead. Sin is the reason why the wrath of God is upon us. Sin is the reason why we stand guilty before a holy God. Sin is the reason why we love the world and are under the sway of the prince of this world. Sin is the reason why our will and emotions are unable to produce anything of spiritual value. Sin is the reason why we have blind eyes and seared consciences. Our impurity, our alienation from God, and our inability to produce any worthy fruit are all the product of sin. In every model of salvation, sin is the fundamental problem that must be rectified.

3. Salvation is 100 percent by grace.

Salvation is not a cooperative effort. Sinners can never improve upon the perfect atoning work of the perfect Son of God. We do not add to it; we do not help it along; we do not perfect it or complete it. Jesus is the "author and finisher" of our faith (Heb. 12:2 KJV).

Even the act of believing the gospel must come from God, otherwise we could state that "our" faith is what has merited salvation.

> For by grace you have been saved through faith. And this
> is not your own doing; it is the gift of God, not a result of
> works, so that no one may boast. (Eph. 2:8–9)

It is "grace through faith" that is the gift from God. It is not God's grace coupled with our faith, as if salvation were a collaborative effort. A salvation that is 99 percent from God and 1 percent from us is not biblical salvation. That means we could boast about our 1 percent contribution that others did not make.

4. God became man in Jesus.

At the heart of everything we say about biblical salvation is the incarnation, that in the person of Jesus Christ we have both man and God. Without the incarnation, our salvation would be impossible. Is it any wonder that nearly every cult and non-Christian religion denies the deity of Jesus?

Christ's divinity is the linchpin of Christianity. It is the doctrine of the Trinity that sets apart our faith from every other monotheistic religion. For every biblical formulation of sin and its problems, the unique God-man alone can produce a cure. If Jesus is not fully God, then he is simply a "good man" or an "honorable teacher" and our Christian faith becomes just so many platitudes and feel good banalities. Christianity is not mental assent to esoteric, abstract propositions. It is belief in and participation with God himself through his Son.

While living in Namibia, our eldest daughter's best friend was from a Hindu family who had moved from India several years earlier. Our daughter told us that her friend had a shrine in her home for the household gods. Every morning the father rang a bell to wake up these gods. Can there be anything more pathetic than a god who needs to be awakened from his slumber? Yet, apart from Christ, the God-man, what are unbelievers honestly left with? Far too often Christians mock such beliefs, when we should be reaching out to those who are lost.

This is the Savior we trust:

> He is the image of the invisible God, the firstborn of all creation. For by him all things were created, in heaven and on earth, visible and invisible, whether thrones or dominions or rulers or authorities—all things were created through him and for him. And he is before all things, and in him all things hold together. And he is the head of the body, the church. He is the beginning, the firstborn from the dead, that in everything he might be preeminent. For in him all the fullness of God was pleased to dwell, and through him to reconcile to himself all things, whether on earth or in heaven, making peace by the blood of his cross. (Col. 1:15–20)

In our evangelism these four propositions cannot be compromised. While it might appear attractive to downplay sin and its dastardly effects— in order to make the gospel appear palatable to unbelievers—in doing so we rob the gospel of its power to save by removing the offense of the gospel. No articulation of salvation that includes sinners somehow saving themselves is the biblical portrait of a gospel of grace. We must point people to the Word of God and the God-man revealed therein. Anything else is simply slick marketing and clever gimmicks devoid of the Spirit.

We have seen thirteen distinct ways in which biblical salvation is envisioned.

1. From death to life: *Regeneration*
   Sin spiritually kills us. We must be born again by the Spirit through faith in Jesus.

2. From guilt to acquittal: *Justification*
   We stand guilty before God because of our sin. We find forgiveness exclusively in Jesus.

3. From rejection to acceptance: *Adoption*
   Because of our sin we are outside God's family. Only in Jesus are we given the right to become sons of God.

4. From bondage to liberation: *Redemption*
   In Jesus alone are we ransomed from the power of sin, death, and the devil.

5. From Satan's kingdom to God's kingdom: *Citizenship*
   Sinners are citizens of Satan's kingdom until their allegiance is changed to Christ.

6. From retribution to propitiation: *Atonement*
   Sin causes the wrath of a holy God to fall upon sinners. Only in the atoning death of Jesus is that wrath removed.

7. From enmity to friendship: *Reconciliation*
   Sinners are God's enemies until they become reconciled to God through faith in Jesus.

8. From darkness to light: *Illumination*
   Sin darkens the hearts and minds of sinners, who can be spiritually enlightened solely through the Spirit of Christ.

9. From impurity to purity: *Sanctification*
   Sinners must be refined and purified by Christ's Spirit in order to become holy and pleasing to God.

10. From barrenness to productivity: ***Fruitfulness***
    Unregenerate sinners can do nothing to please God. Only with
    a connection to the true vine, Jesus, can sinners ever hope to
    produce spiritually pleasing fruit.

11. From deformity to glorification: ***Transformation***
    Sin mars the image of God in mankind. Believers alone are
    transformed into the image of Christ.

12. From separation to union: ***Participation***
    Sin brings death. By participating in the divine nature through
    the incarnate Christ, believers overcome mortality.

13. From defeat to victory: ***Salvation***
    Eternal condemnation awaits everyone who does not have
    saving faith in Jesus Christ.

Only in the God-man revealed in Scripture can the power and
effects of sin be overcome by a gospel of grace. Apart from Jesus Christ,
we have no hope.

**Now to him who is able to keep you from stumbling and to present
you blameless before the presence of his glory with great joy, to the
only God, our Savior, through Jesus Christ our Lord, be glory, majesty,
dominion, and authority, before all time and now and forever. Amen.**

Jude 24–25

Bibliography

Primary Sources

The following three sources were the main ones used to gather background information for the original Greek terms.

Kittel, Gerhard, ed., and Geoffrey W. Bromiley, trans. *Theological Dictionary of the New Testament*. Vol. 5 edited by Gerhard Friedrich. 10 vols. Grand Rapids: Eerdmans, 1964–76. Originally started in German in the 1920s, "Kittel's" is a hallmark of scholarship on the original meaning of Greek words in the New Testament. As such, it was consulted liberally throughout the writing of this book. This ten-volume set is a highly detailed work that looks at key biblical words, exhaustively covering their usage in ancient Greek literature, their relation to Old Testament terms and concepts, and how they were employed in the New Testament books.

Danker, Frederick William, rev. and ed., *A Greek-English Lexicon of the New Testament and Other Early Christian Literature*. 3rd ed. Based on Walter Bauer's *Griechisch-deutsches Wörterbuch zu den Schriften des Neuen Testaments und der frühchristlichen Literatur*, 6th ed., ed. Kurt Aland and Barbara Aland, with Viktor Reichmann and on previous English editions by William F. Arndt, F. Wilbur Gingrich, and F. W. Danker. Chicago: University of Chicago Press, 2000. Also started in German in the mid-twentieth century, this jam-packed one-volume lexicon does similar work to Kittel, but updated for American readership and including thousands of additional citations.

Logos Bible Software 5 Standard: Starter. Version 5. Bellingham, WA: Logos Research Systems, 2014. DVD-ROM or CD-ROM or download. https://www.logos.com/. A digital library application designed specifically for electronic Bible study. Among its versatile functionality is linguistic analysis for studying the Bible both in translation and in the original languages, which were particularly helpful in my research for writing this book. Even those not familiar with biblical Greek will find Logos a helpful study tool.

Other Sources Consulted

Aulén, Gustaf. *Christus Victor: An Historical Study of the Three Main Types of the Idea of Atonement* (1930). Translated by A. G. Hebert. London: Society for Promoting Christian Knowledge, 1970. First published in English in 1931 and in French in 1949.

Barna, George. "Survey Explores Who Qualifies as an Evangelical." The Barna Group. https://www.barna.org/barna-update/article/13 culturc/111-survey-explores-who-qualifies-as-an-evangelical.

Calvin, John. *Commentary on a Harmony of the Evangelists, Matthew, Mark, and Luke* (1555). Translated by William Pringle. 3 vols. Edinburgh: Calvin Translation Society, 1845–46. Grand Rapids: Christian Classics Ethereal Library, 2005. http://www.ccel.org/ccel/calvin/commentaries.i.html.

———. *Commentary on the Prophet Isaiah* (1550). Translated by William Pringle. 4 vols. Edinburgh: Calvin Translation Society, 1850–53. Grand Rapids: Christian Classics Ethereal Library, 2005. http://www.ccel.org/ccel/calvin/commentaries.i.html.

———. *Institutes of the Christian Religion* (1559). Edited by John T. McNeill. Translated by Ford Lewis Battles. 2 vols. Philadelphia: Westminster Press, 1960.

Capon, Robert Farrar. *The Parables of Grace*. Grand Rapids: Eerdmans, 1988.

Clowney, Edmund P. *The Message of 1 Peter: The Way of the Cross*. Bible Speaks Today. Downers Grove, IL: InterVarsity Press, 1988.

Demarest, Bruce. *General Revelation: Historical Views and Contemporary Issues.* Grand Rapids: Zondervan, 1982.

Elwell, Walter A., ed. *Evangelical Dictionary of Theology*, 2nd ed. Grand Rapids: Baker Academic, 2001.

Grudem, Wayne. *Systematic Theology. An Introduction to Biblical Doctrine.* Grand Rapids: Zondervan, 2000.

Hubbard, Moyer. "Kept Safe Through Childbearing: Maternal Mortality, Justification by Faith, and the Social Setting of 1 Timothy 2:15." *Journal of the Evangelical Theological Society* 55, no. 4 (2012): 743–62.

Lewis, C. S. *God in the Dock: Essays on Theology and Ethics*. Edited by Walter Hooper. Grand Rapids: Eerdmans, 1970.

Luther, Martin. *Lectures on the Minor Prophets: Part II: Jonah, Habakkuk* (1525), edited by Hilton C. Oswald, translated from the Latin by Charles D. Froehlich and from the German by Martin H. Bertram. Vol. 19 (1974) of *Luther's Works*. American ed. Edited by Jaroslav Pelikan and Helmut T. Lehmann. 55 vols. St. Louis: Concordia / Philadelphia: Fortress, 1955–86.

Marshall, I. H., A. R. Millard, J. I. Packer, and D. J. Wiseman, eds. *New Bible Dictionary*. 3rd ed. Downers Grove, IL: InterVarsity Press, 1996.

McLaren, Brian. *A New Kind of Christianity: Ten Questions That Are Transforming the Faith*. New York: HarperOne, 2010.

Murray, John. *The Epistle to the Romans*. New International Commentary on the New Testament. Grand Rapids: Eerdmans, 1959–65. Reprint in one volume, 1968. Originally published in two volumes.

Reiser, Marius. *Jesus and Judgment: The Eschatological Proclamation in Its Jewish Context*. Minneapolis: Fortress Press, 1997.

Rogers, Cleon L., Jr., and Cleon L. Rogers III. *The New Linguistic and Exegetical Key to the Greek New Testament*. Grand Rapids: Zondervan, 1998.

Sproul, R. C., John Gerstner, and Arthur Lindsley. *Classical Apologetics: A Rational Defense of the Christian Faith and a Critique of Presuppositional Apologetics*. Grand Rapids: Zondervan, 1984.

Tozer, A. W. *The Knowledge of the Holy*. Lincoln, NE: Back to the Bible, 1961. Originally published the same year by Harper & Row.

Scripture Index

Old Testament

Genesis
1:2 217n10
1:26 191
1:26–27 191n2, 193
1:27 191
1:28 133
1:31 193
2:15 133
2:19–20 133
2:23 132
3:5 112, 151
3:8 132
3:10 132
3:12 133
3:14 133
3:15 230n7
3:16 133
3:17–19 133
3:21 119n20, 122
3:23 133
4:6 122n20
4:7 241
5:1 191n2
5:3 191n2
6:5 145n4, 241
8:21 145n4, 241
9:5 123n22
9:6 196n5
9:12 131n8
11:31 128
12:1–3 131n8
15:6 42

Exodus
3:5 156n1
4:22 64
16:23 156

19:19 204n19
20:2 86
20:18 204n19
24:8 122
25:21–22 110n3
26:33–34 156n1
34:6 117
34:29–35 204
40:9 156n1
40:35 204n19

Leviticus
11:44 166
16:14 110n3
17:11 122n20, 123
19:19 175n3
19:24 156n1
27:30 156n1

Numbers
5:17 156n1
7:89 110n3
14:18 117n13
23:19 114n10

Deuteronomy
1:31 63
14:1 63n7
22:11 175n3
32:6 63n7
32:17 102n7
32:18 63n7

Joshua
24:2–3 128

Judges
8:4–8 168n12
21:25 117

1 Samuel
15:29 114n10

2 Samuel
7:11–16 131n8
7:14 64n13
7:16 103n8

1 Kings
8:11 204n19

1 Chronicles
9:29 156n1
34:3 157n2

2 Chronicles
20:7 138n13

Nehemiah
9:17 117n13
11:1 156n1
29:3 156

Job
41:11 33

Psalms
1:4 174, 241
1:6 174
2:7 64n13
7:11 111n7
8:3–8 202
12:6 166
14:1 147
19:1 143, 203n18
32:3–5 241
35:5 241
51:1–2 169
51:10 146
86:15 117n13
103:8 117n13
105:19 167
106:36–37 102n7
119:18 151
119:105 151n6

Victor Kuligin is Academic Dean and Lecturer at Bible Institute of South Africa. Prior to this he performed the same duties at Namibia Evangelical Theological Seminary in southwestern Africa and has traveled extensively as a guest lecturer in countries such as Ethiopia, India, Sudan, and Bulgaria. Victor has also been an Adjunct Professor at Wheaton College and Trinity Christian College in the United States. He also serves as a Supervisor for doctoral candidates for South Africa Theological Seminary, and is a Facilitator in an Open Learning Centre for North-West University, South Africa. He is a graduate of the University of Stellenbosch, South Africa (D.Th., systematic theology; M.Th., church history), where he wrote his dissertation on God's judgment and the rise of "inclusivism" in today's American evangelicalism; Wheaton College Graduate School (M.A., biblical studies); DeVry University's Keller School of Management (M.B.A.); and Grove City College (B.S., chemical engineering). Victor is the author of *Ten Things I Wish Jesus Never Said* (Crossway), which has been translated into Portuguese and Korean. Victor and his wife, Rachel, have five children.